Chancers, Dancers and Romancers

by

Kevin Donnelly

To my sister Eileen who has always been there for me.

FIRST HALF

CHAPTER 1

Atholl McClackit coaxed his Aston Martin up the driveway to Castle McClackit and was struck, once again, by the complete and utter grotesqueness of the place. How his father had such an emotional attachment to this architectural monstrosity was beyond him. The mismatched windows across the front of the building made you think there was something wrong with your eyes. The extensions either side of the main building were unbalanced and probably illegal given his father's scant regard for either planners or planning legislation. It had been in the family since 1745 or at least the land had. A generous present from the grateful Duke of Cumberland to his great-great-great-great grandfather for services rendered in a couple of mopping up operations post Culloden. The Victorian gothic pile that stood before him was a present from Queen Victoria to his great grandfather for services rendered. To think that gillie John Brown copped all the flack for entertaining her majesty when old Rory McClackit had been rodgering her rotten. Outstanding work from the McClackits yet again. He tried to put the image of his great grandfather and the leader of the world's greatest ever Empire going at it hammer and tongs to one side to concentrate on the matter in hand. An urgent summons from his father meant only one thing - bad news for Atholl.

They had struggled on with a strained relationship down the years, not love and hate but more complete and utter frustration with each other for not understanding their respective points of view. The old boy had never been the same since Atholl had pointed out to him he could not simply assassinate Nelson Mandela the moment he stepped out of jail and that sometimes it's better to let things run their course. Father had not seen the logic of this viewpoint and relations had been somewhat strained over the last couple of years. However, his father had been there when needed by Atholl in the past. Atholl would definitely be there for him should any assistance be called for.

As he parked up, he noticed the flower beds and lawn were still well kept though the paint was peeling on the ground floor window frames looking out on to the lawn. Walking up to the front door he also noticed a piece of guttering hanging loose from the roof. Anything basic could be maintained easily, what might require the actions of a tradesman could clearly wait. The place reeked of decay. He rang the bell at the front door. A few minutes later he was greeted by the sight of his father's faithful retainer, Potter, as the door opened.

"Good day Master Atholl," came the usual welcome. For once Potter had managed to remove the look of distaste from his face when he addressed Atholl, which immediately put the young Master on his guard. Atholl remembered Potter being a helping hand for his father in Kenya in the 1950's as they tore around the country putting down the Mau Mau rebellion with some considerable force. He remembered his father once telling him only to visit Kenya under an assumed name as in some parts of Nairobi to this day, a person of nefarious character was still referred to as a "Emclacket". He knew Potter had been an adviser to the SAS in certain areas but it was never quite clear what his roles were. Any questions on the matter received a shrug of the shoulders or a point blank denial. As Potter picked up Atholl's bag, another sign all was not well, Atholl thought silence was the best policy and quietly followed him into the hall.

"The Laird will see you in his bedroom, Sir" announced Potter. So much for the offer of a drink or refreshments after the long drive thought Atholl.

"I take it he is alone?" inquired Atholl, silently praying his father's latest bit of stuff wouldn't be keeping him company as had happened in the past.

"Yes Sir. He's quite, quite alone but now you're here…." Potter let the sentence trail off. Atholl ignored the irony of Potter's last statement. He had never hidden his dislike of the place and was an infrequent visitor.

The smell of damp and boiled cabbage was unchanging. He noted the interior of the building was much the same as the exterior. Dots of mildew permeated every wall and the paint was flaking on the skirting boards. All light appeared to have been sucked out from the castle. If this is what it is like in June, God knows what it would be like in January he thought. He climbed the stairs to his father's bedroom averting his eyes as he walked past the family portraits of earlier chieftains of the clan McClackit.

He entered his father's bedroom without knocking, safe in the knowledge his father was on his own. When Atholl was eighteen he'd walked in to the bedroom to see him having sex, doggy style, with the wife of his father's oldest and best friend, the chieftain of the clan McChisholm. It wouldn't have been too bad, apart from the fact his father was dressed as Napoleon at the time which explained a lot of things to Atholl but didn't make the sight any more appealing.

As Atholl approached the bed, his father opened one eye and ceased his furtive hand movements under the sheets. The room was comfortably warm for his father, in other words stiflingly hot for Atholl. His father's love of Africa extended beyond long-legged Masai cattle women to the heat of the continent, a warmth he was forever trying to recreate in his bedroom.

"Ah, Atholl. Excellent to see you. Not quite who I was hoping for, but the need to speak to you, it has to be said, has surpassed certain physical needs that I may have preferred to fulfill."

Atholl had a very clear idea what those needs were and the thought of them made him even more uncomfortable. He tugged at his right ear in an effort to control his discomfort.

"I received your message father and came as soon as I could manage". This was not strictly true, as a belly dancer in a Lebanese restaurant off the Edgware Road could testify. The night before he'd planned to leave, Atholl had popped out for quick meze only to be waylaid by a pair of gyrating hips as opposed to some freshly made houmus. His large tip of twenty pounds to the waiter had gained him an audience with the dancer after she finished her set and one thing had led to another. This ended up with him getting some highly detailed and intensive private instruction in pelvic movement back at his house.

His father smiled benevolently at Atholl. "Well done, my boy. Your response is most admirable. You know I would not have summoned you had it not been a matter of great importance. Sit yourself down and I will begin a tale, which, to my great embarrassment, reflects none too well on your father." Dair McClackit attempted to push himself up into a proper sitting position but could only manage a half-hearted shrug of his shoulders. Atholl had to help him up the rest of the way.

Atholl was braced for another tale of vicious Mau Mau suppression or stories of Conservative Party funds siphoned to aid the Smith regime in Rhodesia in the 1970's but the tale was far removed from either of those murky episodes.

His father looked him in the eye, cleared his throat and began. "When I came back from Kenya in the late 50's, I was a caged lion. The army did not want me after one complaint too many from the High Commissioner in Nairobi. I asked for a transfer to the British Army of the Rhine but that was turned down flat. I was not in a mood to disagree. The thought of spending winter after winter freezing my proverbials on Lunefeld Heath did not appeal greatly. So I came back here and was looking for something to occupy my time. A new direction, a different challenge in life." Dair shook his head, a regretful look on his face.

"Sadly I went back to the old ways of wine, women and song. There were a number of clan chiefs' daughters I had but you know me, always liked a "bit of rough" for a run through the sheets every now and then to go with the, supposed, "smooth" of the daughters of the cream of Highland society. We had a number of servants in those days, unlike now when Potter is expected to do everything from cook my breakfast to repair the roof." At this point he paused, seemingly lost for a moment in another time, another place. Atholl cleared his throat and his father came back from wherever he'd been.

"One housemaid in particular caught my eye. Denise Bradley was her name. There was something about her, some hint of defiance as if she was daring you to try it on. This went on for about a month or so and then it just happened. I literally walked into her one day turning a corner as she was carrying a bundle of freshly ironed sheets. Next thing we're at it like rutting stags. One of those Highland flings I thought at the time but then I just couldn't keep my hands off her. She was just as keen, I should add." At this he paused to pick up a glass of water from his bedside table and take a sip.

"Well, we went at it like mad things for the best part of the summer of 1959. She helped sober me up and made me think about what I wanted to do with myself, Atholl. She was a great aid at a critical time in my life. I dare say you can guess what happened with all that sex. She fell pregnant. I was happy but concerned about what your grandfather would do to the both of us, so I told her it was over. She would have to leave for the safety of herself and the child." At this the clan chief's voice started to tremble but a quick cough allowed him to gather his thoughts and he continued.

"I offered to pay for an abortion but she wouldn't hear of it. She was determined to keep the child. Given the circumstances, she believed a return home to Dumfries was for the best. I have done a number of terrible things in my life, Atholl. I have killed men with my own bare hands and have gladly taken anything that a time of war and conflict could offer. How do you think this place has been so well maintained? But I have never felt the complete and utter sense of loss as I put Denise on the train at Inverness on that day in 1960. Your own birth two years later was a great consolation. I am proud of the McClackit I see in front of me today."

Atholl was taken aback by his father's words. He had expected some nonsense regarding next year's election and a plan to sabotage the Labour campaign but the conversation had gone off at a tangent. He had absolutely no idea where it would end.

"What I have to tell you now, you may have guessed already, is you have a half-brother. He was born on the 25th of June 1960 in Dumfries and his name is

Kenneth Bradley. I want you to find him and kill him." Atholl sat bolt upright. The sting in the tale had caught him unawares.

"Kill him? I did hear you right, father? You did say kill him?" asked a rather puzzled Atholl. This was not what he had been expecting. At times during the story, his father had actually appeared sentimental, not an emotion one normally associated with the old man and quite a disturbing sight if truth be told. Atholl was trying to come to terms with what he had just heard. Discovering one had a sibling after all these years was shocking enough, but to be told to kill him left him feeling somewhat numb. He had driven north expecting to listen to a rant from his father relating to the impotence of the Tory government under John Major or a request for some funding to underwrite a white coup in Zimbabwe. Most certainly not an instruction to kill a half-brother he had not known existed until five minutes earlier.

"Yes, kill him. My request is down to the fact I have been experimenting with the trial version of a drug called Ciagra. Some contacts in America managed to procure it for me. It helps to treat a diminished male libido."

Atholl raised an eyebrow.

"Yes, after all this time I have been having difficulty getting the old chap erect. The effect of the drug has been marvelous. The McClackit broadsword has been wielded to good effect of late. Sally McChisholm is coming over this afternoon as a matter of fact." And is the Napoleon outfit coming out of the wardrobe, wondered Atholl.

From his initial happiness of discussing the effects of the drug, Dair's face darkened.

"Sadly one of the side effects of the drug that they have just discovered is an excessive strain on the heart. This has led to the suspension of the drug trials and my supply is rapidly dwindling. I have been to Inverness for a check up and the prognosis is not good. It's complete rest and recuperation and they might be able to get another 12 months for me. Alternatively, I can live life to the full for another few months and take my chances. As I said, Sally is coming over so you can guess which option I have taken. Therefore Atholl, within the next year or so you will become chief of the clan McClackit. It must be a sole claim on the title and no other individual's claim must be possible. Am I making myself clear?" This last question was spoken in crisper, clearer tones than any other.

"Crystal clear, father. Absolutely crystal clear" replied Atholl. "I will need a bit of time to think this through but be assured, I will not let you down. He tugged his right ear once more.

"Are you absolutely certain he has to be killed? It is quite conceivable he has no knowledge at all of his claim the to the title."

"That is completely correct, dear boy. He might have no idea but I am fully aware of his mother's knowledge. She was no fool and I let her down very, very badly. If she saw it as a way of getting back at me and the clan, she could make him lay a claim to the title. We, or rather you, would be in a legal battle that could cost thousands. It could even prevent you from taking up your rightful inheritance."

Atholl was about to suggest it might be easier to kill the mother but he did not want to put anymore strain on his father's heart. The heat in the room had suddenly become completely unbearable for him and he stood up to try and open a window for a cooling draught. His father twitched in frustration as the temperature dropped but was powerless to prevent Atholl letting in some cool air.

At this point, Atholl sensed the meeting with his father had gone on long enough. It was a shock to the system to discover in one breath you had a half-brother, then in the next sentence, to be told by your father, the father to you both incidentally, that you should kill him. He went over to the bed and shook his father's hand.

"I see this as a mission, father. I shall not fail."

He left the bedroom and walked down the stairs in time to see Potter open the front door and let in Sally McChisholm. She must have been in her late fifties by now but was still extremely attractive. She reminded him of a Highland version of Marianne Faithful.

Sally McChisholm looked up the stairs at the sound of Atholl's footsteps.

"Atholl? I haven't seen you since you were teenager, dear boy. I expect you don't recognise me with my clothes on". At this Atholl blushed. Good God, he thought, don't these elderly types have any shame?

"I'd recognise you anywhere Mrs McChisholm" he replied.

"It's Sally to you, dear boy. Just been to see your father?"

"Yes I have."

"Is Le Petit General on good form?"

"Mais oui" replied Atholl

"Excellent" answered Sally "I hope we shall have the chance to catch up later, once I am finished with your father." She gave him a knowing look and started to walk up the stairs. He couldn't be sure, but when she was halfway up, he thought he vaguely heard an "Au revoir," waft down from above.

Atholl wandered into his father's study on the ground floor. His father's desk was positioned so that whoever sat there could look out of the large bay window onto a large garden. Atholl plonked himself down in his father's chair and twirled about for a bit, trying to come to terms with what the old boy had said. As he sat pondering his father's orders he thought he heard the strains of the 1812 Overture being played somewhere. He thought it must be drifting up from the kitchen where Potter might have the radio on. He picked up his father's ivory paper opener, yet another Kenyan souvenir he presumed, and pressed the point against the ball of his thumb. He needed to try and understand how he came to be dragged back into such a position by his father. Would he ever be free of the McClackit name and all its baggage? He suddenly realised he'd drawn blood on his thumb he'd been pressing so hard. He stood up. If he couldn't be free of the name he could certainly be free of the castle. He didn't care that he'd just arrived, he'd get back on the road and maybe stop off in Moffat or The Lakes. Another moment in this place would do nothing to improve his state of mind. He went looking for Potter. He found him in the kitchen watching a football match on TV. He seemed somewhat agitated for him and Atholl was intrigued to see this insight into a man who had remained completely cool and distant from him.

"Good game, Potter?" asked Atholl.

"Naw, complete shite if you must know" came the reply. Potter suddenly realised to whom he was talking, "Sorry Master Atholl. I was a bit caught up there. It's England v Scotland at Wembley. McAllister has just missed a penalty."

"Oh yes? Who for?" asked Atholl feigning an interest in a game he knew nothing about.

"Scotland!" came a somewhat muted reply. Potter failing completely to keep the look of bemusement at the young arsehole in front of him from his face.

They were both looking at the TV as a player in a white top lobbed a player in dark blue to score a second goal for England with a peach of a volley.

"Aw, fuck!" went Potter. Taking this as the final cue to leave, Atholl tried to re-assert his authority.

"Potter, will you inform my father, once he is, eh, free, I have decided to get on with his request straight away and as such, I am leaving immediately. I will contact him once I have accomplished what he requested"

"Ok, Master Atholl. I am sure he will look forward to hearing from you" came the reply. Potter was still staring at the TV, a disappointed look on his face.

Atholl thought he could still hear the sound of the "1812 Overture" from somewhere.

"Do you have a radio anywhere in the kitchen, Potter?" he asked

"No Sir, the only radio is in the car" said Potter a slightly amused look on his face.

"You can't hear any music then?" asked Atholl.

"No Sir, the only thing I can hear is your voice" a smile playing on his lips.

Atholl felt he'd somehow missed a joke at his expense.

"Very well. I'll say cheerio Potter and thank you for all your help"

"Anytime Master Atholl. Any time, Sir. I'll just get your bag" said Potter looking happy in the knowledge that if the football was buggered, at least Atholl was leaving the building.

Atholl reached the Dunblane roundabout just north of Stirling in good time. On the drive down he'd been thinking back to his time in the army and how his career had mirrored his father's earlier military career of the 1950's. They'd both been involved in brutally suppressing insurgent terrorists in differing areas. His father in Kenya and he in Northern Ireland. They'd both had difficulty coming to terms with civilian life but in his, Atholl's, case he'd been able to temper the disappointment of civvy street with his job. Their military background had left each of them accepting the loss of life but single minded in the realisation of what might have to be sacrificed in an attempt to achieve one's objectives. In the army, Atholl had been a one-man campaign against lawlessness in Northern Ireland until he had, even by his own admission, got a bit carried away. Had his father not got in touch with him and told him to stop, he thought he would still be terrorising the terrorists in the six counties. That phone call had made a tremendous difference to him, finally bringing him to his senses over what he was doing with his career and his life. The old boy had spoken from the heart. He'd been in the same position himself so he knew what he was talking about. Atholl had known his time in Ulster would come to an end one day and had taken similar precautions to those of his father in Kenya.

Shortly before he withdrew back to the mainland he'd discovered the IRA were brokering a cocaine deal with sympathisers in New York who had contacts with Colombians in Miami. He'd been able to intercept the couriers taking the money back to the States when they attempted to return to Knock in the south. Their cover was a religious pilgrimage from the States and they hoped no one would notice the small matter of them carrying five million dollars cash back into the USA.

Atholl had always known his nun's habit would come in handy sometime. He had followed the main man of the two into a Gents in a Little Chef, pretending to be a poorly sighted nun. The poor guy had been totally unprepared for Atholl sticking a knife in his jugular whilst protesting in high-pitched voice that they really should make the signs on the doors a lot clearer. He had dragged the body into a cubicle and knew it would only be a matter of time before the second of the two came looking. When he turned up, the end result had been pretty much the same. Atholl had left the two bodies, one sitting on top of each other, in the cubicle. He'd changed out of the habit and put it into a bag he'd hidden under the robes. Having relieved one of the bodies of their car keys, he then proceeded to drive to Dun Laoghaire for the ferry to Wales and a new life amongst the great unwashed of British civilians.

Now, as he passed the looming rock of Stirling Castle he realised the mistake his father had made and one he wasn't keen to repeat. Neither of them had come to terms with the fact they were no longer at war. Peacetime was played by different rules, yet nobody set the rules when it came to the McClackits, apart from the clan members themselves. Then again, everybody handled things differently. Atholl was determined his own actions would not be handicapped by the legacy of the history of the McClackits. At the same time, he realised he could not easily escape the responsibility of his father's command. Family duty before all else was the better choice he concluded.

Following on from this decision, Atholl attempted to rationalise the demands his father had made on him with the resources it would require to complete the job in hand. He understood the impossibility of the task as he had no information regarding his quarry. How would he find out who this person was? Where he live? Indeed if he was still alive and what type of life he was leading now? He suddenly realised this might not be quite as easy as his father thought.

17

CHAPTER 2

It was an oppressive July day in Glasgow, sultry hot with low cloud cover. The pub opposite Queen Street station had air conditioning of a sort, an open window, but this was soon closed when an OAP who had been nursing a half of lager for approximately three hours complained of a draught. The heat in the pub due to the climatic conditions was one thing but the hot air emissions from one of the drinkers was another.

"Brazilians? Don't get me stertit on those pricks. Patronisin', arrogant bastarts the lot o them. Sexy samba soccer, stick it up yer arse, like. Ah've seen those yellow-shirted tossers play in 3 World Cups and ah hate them. They're more fucken arrogant than the Germans or the French, like. Look, the ones you see at the World Cups? Where have they come fae? The slums o' Rio? Ah don't think so. They're either students studyin in Europe i.e. rich bastarts or they can afford to fly over from Brazil for the tournament i.e. even richer bastarts." The rant halted for a quick lager break.

"Ah was sittin at that game in Seville in 1982, like. We go 4-1 down when the boy behind me hits us on the shoulder, no in a friendly way either, and goes "Hey Scotland, that is how you play football". A true statement fair enough like but no one ah really wanted to hear at that moment in time. He was sittin wi a crackin burd, mind. But ye look at those scenes outside the ground in Seville, are the Brazilians samba-in wi the Tartan Army? Are they fuck! And then there's all these sad Scots pricks wearin Brazil tops wi their kilts. Exactly what do we have in common wi those cunts? They're a debt ridden third world country wi a tropical climate. We're a debt ridden third world country wi a crap climate. Ma taxes have paid for those bastarts to get to the World Cup and all ah get is fuckin' patronised. Well make no mistake pal, the next time we play those cunts ah won't be there, that's for fucken certain, like".

"So, it's fair to say you're no that keen on the boys from Brazil?" asked Kenny

"Ye could say that" replied Gus.

18

Kenny Bradley watched his pal, Gus McSween, and wondered where it all came from. He'd only got to know him that well in 1979 and seventeen years later he was still discovering new things about him. Their friendship had been forged on a trip to Oslo for the Norway v Scotland game. Scotland had won 4-0 and even more incredibly, Kenny had saved Gus' life by persuading two Marines from the US Embassy in Oslo not to tear Gus limb from limb after he had sung, non-stop for 15 minutes , to the tune of Guantanamera, "One Viet Cong, there's only one Viet Cong" in the Highlander Bar.

They had been firm friends ever since but even Kenny had not realised the bile stored up in Gus regarding Brazilians. How can five foot nothing of flabby Scotsman possess such complete and utter hatred of Brazilians, Tenby, farmers and the Wimbledon tennis tournament?

"Whit's the jackanory aboot Vienna then?" asked Gus.

"No problem, if you can actually find your way to cough up some cash for the flights and the hotel" replied Kenny.

"Aye ok, ah'll write you a cheque the now"

"A cheque?" coughed Kenny. "When the fuck did you get a chequebook? What bank manager was stupid enough to give you one?"

"Easy tiger" came the reply. "After ma gas and electricity gettin cut off ah thought ah'd better screw the nut and concentrate on gettin my fiscal matters in hand, like. So, ah've opened up a new bank account and am workin ma way towards a positive financial outlook on life. Ah've even been thinkin about investin in a PEP"

"But your gas and electricity are still cut off" pointed out Kenny

"Hey, it's central heatin or this trip to Vienna. Ye've got tae get yer priorities right, like".

"Fair enough" agreed Kenny.

Kenny and Gus stood at the bar. Kenny had just left the Glasgow Film Theatre having watched Godfather Parts 1 and 2 on a double bill. He had the videos at home but nothing compared to the big screen as far as he was concerned. He'd offered to take his friend along but Gus was rooted to the bar.

Scotland were beginning their World Cup qualifying campaign for France 98 in Austria in eight weeks time so Gus was getting in some pre-match drinking practice. As ever, despite the fact he had put away a minimum of six pints of Tennents lager in the time Kenny had been in the cinema, the wee man was not showing any signs of being the worse for wear.

"Ah think the Austrians have had a bad deal over the years, like. Why should the actions of one person who just happened to be born on their soil, damn them to the end of eternity?" said Gus, a philosophical tone entering his voice, now his rant was finished.

"You mean Hitler?" asked Kenny wanting to see how far a stupid question would push his little fat friend.

"No, Baron Von Trapp ya muppet!" exploded Gus. "Of course ah mean Hitler. What other Austrian's been responsible for the death of millions and a world war?"

"Forgive me if I am missing something here but how did we get from Austria to your anti-Brazilian rant?" enquired Kenny

"The Odessa File! Ye said ye'd been watchin it on TV the other night, Jon Voight and that dark haired bird wi the big jugs that also appeared in the Likely Lads film," replied Gus.

"Ah yes, and I'd made the mistake of saying how I never understood how so many Nazis actually made it to Brazil. Of course, how forgetful of me," mused Kenny as he tried to work out how such an innocent question could provoke such unbridled fury. The opening bars of Wonderwall sung by Oasis began to waft across the bar. Gus perked up at the sound of the song.

"Too right, today is goin to be the day, ma man. Got an appointment with the financial adviser later on like. You may have noticed ah'm a bit smarter dressed than normal, like. Dress to impress, if you get my drift," said Gus with a certain note of pride in his voice.

"Please don't tell me it's a woman," said Kenny giving Gus a once over to see what exactly he had done to improve on his dress sense. Working in a white-collar job as a union rep in the finance industry, Gus had better than average taste in clothes. He was normally a fastidious, if conservative, dresser. His clothes were clean and his shirts always ironed but one or two personal quirks tended to lessen the overall sartorial effect. In this case, his buckled, Cuban-heeled cowboy boots which were cut off at the ankles.

"How many times have I told you not to wear those bloody awful boots? And with chinos! People with a complex about their height wear those. Oh sorry, I've just realised I am talking to a five foot tall Scotsman, so I apologise for stating the truth so bluntly. For fuck's sake, she's going to take one look at those and think they're cut off boots for a cut off guy."

Gus squirmed uncomfortably in the corner. He had gone for the boots as a last resort. He'd only spoken to the girl, what was her name, Fiona or Maria, after the teller in the bank suggested he might want to meet a financial adviser to ensure his long term financial goals were attainable. He hadn't been keen and when he told the teller his short term financial goals were getting his gas and electricity re-connected, the wee laddie had looked a bit abashed to put it mildly. When the kid had pointed out she'd only take half an hour of his time, Gus had perked up. A she. This was better than Dateline, it was free and she had to talk to you. Ya beauty. He'd been having a few drinks to give him a wee confidence boost but nothing too over the top.

"Ok, maybe they werenae the right choice but ah don't know how tall she is, like. Ah don't want to feel she's dominating me into takin out a pension or an endowment mortgage. Anyway, forget aboot that the now. What's the Hampden roar about this double header then? Riga and Tallinn! Does it get any better?" said Gus trying to regain some control of the situation.

"You havenae heard the price of the flights yet" Kenny replied, an element of frustration creeping into his voice. "I've been looking at a domino ticket. I don't know why they call it that but we can fly with SAS from Edinburgh to Copenhagen then from Copenhagen to Riga and on the way back Tallinn to Copenhagen and Copenhagen to Edinburgh. We've only got to make our own way from Riga to Tallinn but I am sure we can get a bus or a train or something. I'm definitely up for it but what about you?" replied Kenny who was wondering just what the wee man was going to do for funds to pay for the double-header trip. It sounded a belter. A few folk might be put off by the expense, especially after it came so soon after the Austria away game but a trip to the Baltics was unmissable.

Gus looked thoughtful. "There are some things in life that are not to be missed so ah'll get the money together somehow. The fanny in Tallinn is worth the cost of any flight, like," was his reply.

"So given that this financial adviser is hardly going to be swayed by the state of your finances, what do you expect to come of this meeting?" he asked Gus.

"I don't know, to be honest but if ah can get her to come out on a date it will be a cheap one for me, that's for certain," Gus replied, a gleeful smile playing on his lips.

"Are there any other kind for you?" replied Kenny, a mischievous look on his face.

"Ha fuckin ha. Once she's seen my personal books she'll know ah'm right in the financial clag, so to speak, like. So, if we go out for a meal, she's goin to have to cough for her share, like, as she'll know ah've no got the cash. Then again she can get a full dividend from ma bounteous loins later on if it all goes to plan. She'll maybe take a deposit from my sperm bank, if ye catch my drift. Ah'll definitely be giving her a special rate of interest, like." Gus rubbed his hands together in anticipation.

"So how are you going to explain the hair transplant loan?" asked Kenny.

"Shut the fuck up about that. People might hear ye," pleaded Gus, a hurt look on his face.

"Fuck off! People with impaired vision can see that bit of turf has been stitched on to your scalp. It wouldnae be so bad but it is also ginger. Whatever possessed you?"

This had been an ongoing argument for the last three months since Gus, in a fit of depression due to the ending of another relationship, had become convinced women didn't respect him due to his baldness.

In his eyes, his complete disinterest in a woman once he'd had sexual intercourse with her was not an issue. Nor was his continual lateness should they go out for an evening. Nor his complete and utter disinterest in any part of that woman's life. His lack of interest in joint holidays had also been a handicap in his attempts to forge strong relationships with numerous girlfriends. The last nail in his relationship coffin, the fact they were barred from his away trips supporting the Scotland football team, hardly enamoured him to a few either.

One previous girlfriend had made the mistake of giving him an ultimatum after they'd just had sex. Standing over Gus as she was hooking her bra on she started on him, "It's a trip to Yugoslavia to see that useless shower of bastards called Scotland or it's me. You've had my last words on the subject"

Gus hardly helped matters by then asking her if she could iron a couple of shirts for him while he looked for his passport. Another one bit the dust.

Gus had regretted the transplant, but it was too late. He'd been influenced by the freak of nature that was his goatee beard. Trying to look trendy, he had grown a goatee only to find it had come out ginger in direct contrast to the remaining hair on his head which was dark brown. He hadn't fancied the ginger effect until he thought one girl in a nightclub told him he looked like Frank MacAvennie, a footballer whose reputation as a Casanova knew no limits. Gus had taken this as a compliment even though the girl had actually said "rank fanny" as opposed to, "Frank MacAvennie". Gus had forgotten all about MacAvennie's ginger pubes reputation and had gone on to get the hair transplant done in bright ginger. Some cruel soul once said his scalp now looked like Rannoch Moor in autumn except more windswept.

"Look, ah know it's not perfect but get off ma back. Ah'm carryin an injury as well, like." he replied.

"Injury? Just how the fuck are you injured?"

"Ah've got a bit of a cold, like." At this Gus sniffed, just to complete the effect.

"But it's July. How the fuck do you get a cold in July, ignoring the fact we are in the middle of a typical Scottish summer?" Kenny was getting bit worked up by now as was often the case when he spent more than 30 minutes in one to one contact with Gus.

"The duvet cover was a bit damp when ah put it back on, like. Ah think I've got a chill," muttered Gus in a low tone.

"Am I right in thinking from you saying this you only have one set of bed linen?" said Kenny in an equally low voice.

"Aye, that's right. How did ye guess? How many sets o' bed linen do you have, like?"

"Three" replied Kenny

"What's the point in havin three, ya daft twat?" This reply was accompanied by a big smirk from Gus.

"Because then I don't get a cold through being forced to put my one set of damp bedding back on the fucking bed, you thick muppet" shouted Kenny. "No wonder you can't maintain a relationship. What a chat up line "Would like to come back to my place and roll about in some damp sheets?" Fuck me, it would be like shagging Fungus the Bogeyman. When are you ever going to get a grip on reality?"

Gus was not amused by Kenny having a go. He was trying to get in a good mood for meeting this financial adviser and here he was winding him up like a cheap watch.

"Look here, pal. We dinnae all have bed linen comin out of our ears or time to worry about how tae iron a fitted sheet." In a moment of drunken madness Kenny had once complained to Gus about the difficulty in getting a good iron on fitted bedsheets, how the elasticated edgings were a nightmare to get straight on the ironing board. He had regretted it ever since.

"Most of the time you sit on yer arse trying to avoid pickin up customers in that taxi of yours," moaned Gus who was rapidly losing the plot through a combination of drink and nerves at the blind date or rather, financial consultation, coming up in twenty minutes.

"Hey lads, let's keep it down a bit". Kenny and Gus turned to the bar where Alex the barman was holding out his hands, palm downwards in a placatory gesture.

"Oops, sorry about that Alex" said Kenny, "Got a bit carried away with the ginger ninja here".

"Ach, shut it, you" replied Gus. "No problem Alex. Ah'm just off to meet my date anyway. Ah'll speak to you later," he said to Kenny, wagging a finger in his face.

Gus was halfway to the door when Alex shouted to him "Wait minute Gus, there's a question I've got for you"

Gus turned and walked back to the bar.

"What is it, big man? Glad you've asked somebody with a bit o' intelligence, unlike some o' yer customers here" At this he shot a venomous glance in the direction of Kenny.

"Ah've always wondered," said Alex "How *did* so many Germans end up in Brazil at the end of the war?"

CHAPTER 3

Atholl was surprised how swiftly the meeting with the private detective was concluded. He hadn't expected the detective to be a female or quite so businesslike. He had thought of asking if she'd like to see his private dick but thought better of it when she'd let it drop into the conversation, ever so casually, she was a black belt at judo. She viewed his request for all the personal details of Kenneth Bradley with barely concealed contempt, promising him a complete report in a week. When he'd asked if it would include photographs, she replied that photos would delay the report arriving for another week and would cost an extra 150 pounds. This had given him a chance to flex his financial muscle, "Make it £250 but they must arrive before the end of the week". This had appeared to impress the young lady but not enough for her to accept his offer of a drink in the Atlantic Bar. Oh well, she was a bit on the tall side anyway, so no real loss.

As he thought about his father, he wondered if Kenneth Bradley was the only half-brother or sister he had. There had been rumours in the family that when it came to sex, his father had been in the same mould as Rory the Rodgerer. If he'd screwed so many women, was it possible there were only two children sired? As ever, Atholl took the objective approach and realised there was no point in worrying about something he could neither qualify nor quantify. The main issue at the moment was, who was Kenneth Bradley and how much of a threat, if any, he posed to the clan McClackit? As he gazed out his office window at the Thames, he realised that stiff action might be called for. He'd done it before, he could do it again. When the report arrived at the end of the week, Atholl had expected a bit more for his money. He had been used to military files in the past where every scrap of information, however useless, had been included. The private detective's report seemed to be very basic, giving one little or no sense of feel about the man himself.

Atholl had scanned the skimpy personal details and decided to concentrate on the photos. So my half-brother is a Glasgow taxi driver, he thought as he looked at the photo of a man climbing into the driving seat of a black cab. Initial appearances were of an average looking guy in his mid 30s with a full head of dark hair, greying at the sides. Smartly dressed for a taxi driver and relatively slim for his age with the beginnings of a paunch. Married with no children, wife's name is Alison and he is normally known as Kenny. Degree in Film and Media Studies from Stirling University but living in a flat in a part of Glasgow called Hyndland. Atholl had always believed that the home and where it was said a lot about the individual. It was not *always* true, as he had met some Belfast drug barons worth a mint, who had lived in an immaculately decorated house in the middle of a council estate, but those were extreme cases. He picked up his phone and spoke to his PA.

"Carol, speak to the property department would you please. Ask them to get me a valuation on a two bedroom flat in Hyndland, Glasgow. Could I have it as soon as? Thanks."

Five minutes later his phone rang and Carol duly informed Atholl that a two bedroom flat in Hyndland would be worth somewhere in the region of 100,000 pounds but selected areas could be £150,000 plus. This made Atholl think. The black cab work in Glasgow couldn't be as lucrative as it was in London. What did his wife do? Part time accounts work for a souvenir company on the south side of the city said the file. I suppose if you put both salaries together, it might work out, given they had no kids. But something didn't seem quite right.

No kids, eh? They were both in their mid thirties. The clock was ticking for her, so where were the rugrats? The way things were going there would be no heirs to the McClackit title from either of them. Atholl had been married once, a lovely girl called Fiona. He had sometimes wondered where it had all gone wrong but the answer to that was simple. Coming home to find your wife in bed with two members of the New Zealand women's netball team was where it had all gone a little sour. Fiona had thought the issue could be solved by asking him to join the three of them for a little fun and games. But it was too little, too late. They'd both been open minded with regards to their relationship but this was a step too far, especially as he had been coming home early to discuss with her the production of a little McClackit of their own.

Had he been hasty? He would never know but it was all water under the bridge now. Fiona had left their marital home shortly after the episode with the Kiwis and he believed she was now in Baja California, helping an old friend run a boutique hotel that catered to the special needs of Hollywood stars. He had a very clear idea of what those requirements were as he had visited the hotel once with Fiona. One night the pair of them had ended up in a hot tub orgy, the most famous participant being an extremely coked out River Phoenix. Special needs indeed.

Getting back to the matter in hand, Atholl felt he had been short changed by the detective agency. In terms of general information there was little or nothing. No details of personal interests, friendships or the casual dross which is part and parcel of a normal life. He needed background info if he was going to get to know his target and this was just not good enough. Atholl picked up the phone to call the lady he'd met a week earlier and this time he would be asking for a little more than Kenny Bradley's name and bloody address.

*****

Kenny sat in his cab outside Central Station. He'd been up since the crack of dawn trying to work up some funds for the trip to Vienna. Morning was not his best time of the day. His mood had hardly been helped the night before when Alison had burst out laughing as he told her what he was planning to do.

"You're meant to be supportive," he'd pointed out to her once she'd regained a bit of composure. "I thought it says in all those women's mags that a relationship is a mutually supportive organism, each individual helps the other to achieve their goals in life for the mutual benefit of the relationship as a whole".

"Aye, but where does it say your lazy arsehole of a husband is going to get out of bed at 6am for the first time in his life in an effort to drum up the fare to Vienna?

28

If Craig Brown knew you were doing this you'd be in the squad. I've told you, if you need the spends I'll give you some cash. It's not an issue." She reached for her handbag, prepared to pull out her purse. "In fact why don't you wake up early and stay in bed to give me a nice wee early wake up call, eh? It'll be a real treat going into work with a smile on my face for once."

Although tempted, Kenny had been feeling more guilty than normal recently with regards to living off his wife. Gus' crack about the ironing had needled him more than he had let on, so he had told Alison he was going to try and do something for himself for once. He appreciated her offer but work was work. He wasn't going to let the chance of a fly midweek shag get in his way.

It was 7.30 am and he was first in line outside the station, anticipating a nice wee trip to Parkhead industrial estate or even Bishopbriggs. The back door opened and the voice said, "STV studios at Cowcaddens Kenny and don't spare the horses".

Kenny turned round at the directions to face long time friend and Scotland fan, Cammy Douglas.

"Cammy, you bastard. I've been waiting for a fare for fifteen minutes and now you just want to go up the road."

"Sorry, but is the customer not always right? You've got to accept the fare or I'll be reporting you to the city authorities. Now my good man, less of your proletarian lip or there will be no tip".

"Lazy poof" quipped Kenny. "I thought you would have been interested in a bit of walking to keep the weight down."

"Poof yes. Lazy no. I got more than enough exercise last night I can tell you. That's why I am, literally, too shagged out to walk up to the studios. Well, that and a need to meet up with the rest of the mincing queers in that place and sort their lives out. For fuck's sake, how do they expect homos to get on in life if a broken finger nail results in a cab ride to A+E accompanied by all and sundry? It's hard being a man's man in a gay man's world."

"Still supporting the Gers?" asked Kenny.

"I am that. That's what's done me for Scotland games, Kenny. Used to be, in Europe you had a couple of away trips before you got knocked out by Christmas, the rest of the season you could concentrate on Scotland, but the fucker who came up with this Champion's League group qualifying stage wasnae a big club and country fan."

"Not a problem I am ever likely to suffer with," said Kenny.

"Aye, the only Queens in Europe are, to quote Joan Armatrading, me, myself, I. You been to Palmerston lately?"

"No, only when I go down to see my mum. You must get some good trips though?"

"You can only take Derry's Walls being screamed at some peasant girl in the middle of the steppes so many times, man. The meatheads that crawl out from under those stones in Belfast leave a bit to be desired, though there's some quality shagging to be done on these trips"

"No way," said Kenny. "You always boast you're the only gay Rangers fan in the world."

"I never said fellow "Sons of William" were getting in on the act. It's the rugged manly types in these far off places that just can't get enough or give enough. Many a good night to be had in the depths of the Athens' gay scene, I can tell you," replied Cammy.

"So how is it going with the 38 club?" asked Kenny, a big smile on his face.

"If that question refers to my attempt to have sex with a male supporter of every football team in Scotland, it's going not too bad. Just as well I did an Aberdeen fan in the early days as it is pure hatred with the sheep shaggers nowadays. Put a Raith Rovers notch on the bedpost last Saturday after a wee trip to Starks Park. The Gents at Kirkcaldy bus station at six o'clock on a Saturday night would put a San Francisco sauna to shame. I've still to crack it with a Queen of the South fan, though Kenny. Funny how men can love Queens but not be homos, eh? Any time you get sick of the lovely Alison, you've got my number."

"There's no chance of that. Can you just imagine Harold's reaction if she went and told him I've left her for a poof?"

Kenny looked in the rear view mirror just in time to see Cammy grimace.

"Point taken. I don't think your father-in-law would approach the matter in calm and rational manner. Most likely he'd come at it with a blow torch in one hand and chisel in the other."

Kenny turned the taxi into the entrance of the STV studios at Cowcaddens.

"Got change of a 50 pound note?" asked Cammy.

"You have got to be joking" said Kenny.

"Ach, keep your pubic hair on. Just a wee wind up. There's a tenner for taking you from your spot. You can buy me a drink wi the change the next time I see you. You going to Vienna?

"Aye, why do you think I'm up at this time? I'm looking for all the big tippers".

"Well, have a good time and if you ever meet a gay Queens fan, point them in my direction as I've only three clubs to go"

"Does that include Celtic?" asked Kenny.

"Yes, I still can't find it in my heart of hearts to shag a Tim. Bit of a moral dilemma and that's a first for me. If it's male and got a pulse it's in with a chance. But squinty-eyed fenians are another story. Enjoy Austria."

Cammy shut the cab door and trotted up the stairs at the front of the studios. Kenny watched him disappear through the doors and wondered about the chances the mad bastard was taking, going to Europe with Rangers and then looking to pull guys. Oh well, each to their own. As he was wondering what to do for his next fare, his mobile phone went off. He was amazed it was actually ringing. He rarely used it and very few people actually knew the number. One reason for this was Kenny wasn't actually sure of the number himself so was unable to inform anyone who might want to call him. The phone had been a

Christmas present from Alison and, but for that, Kenny would have binned it months ago. He picked the phone up but was struggling to remember how to answer the call. He finally pressed the button with the little green phone on it and spoke, very slowly, into the phone. "He-llo, Ke-nny he-er."

The voice of his father-in-law came ringing through the earpiece, "Never mind the phone's batteries, are your batteries runnin down or somethin, ya daft prick! Why don't ye speak up, ah can hardly hear ye."

Kenny was frozen in his seat. A number of questions ran through his head. Why does Harold MacMillan want to speak to me? How did he get my number? What could be so urgent that he's called me on the mobile? Is Alison ok? The last question seemed the most reasonable to begin with so he remembered to speed up and blurted out "IsAlisonalright?"

"Aye, calm down for fuck's sake. She was awright two minutes ago when she handed me yer number, if that's what ye want tae know."

"Oh thank God for that!" exclaimed Kenny. His palpitations had subsided but then picked up again when he realised Harold was still on the line. Kenny had good reason to be scared. He had unknowingly married into the MacMillan criminal dynasty who ruled the south side of Glasgow with an iron fist in an armour-plated glove. He loved his wife dearly but a little bit of warning regarding what he was getting into wouldn't have gone unnoticed. How could a sweet wee Glasgow girl whose main interests in life were accountancy, sex and interior design, normally in that order, have sprung from the loins of such a fruit and nut case?

"Where are ye?" came the question in a quieter tone.

"Just outside the STV studios," said Kenny, regaining control of his voice.

"Well, put a fare on the meter tae Pollok Golf Club. Come tae the front entrance and ask fur me. They'll show you intae the member's bar where ah'll be waitin." Harold cut the call and the phone went dead.

Kenny wondered what the problem was. Sorry, should that be "opportunity"? He'd read somewhere about a management style, somewhere in the States, where there were no problems, only opportunities. Aye but I bet they were never on the wrong side of Michael "Harold" MacMillan which could involve a fucking feast of "opportunities".

Harold's physical similarity to the Conservative Prime Minister of the 1950's was purely coincidental in that they both had grey hair and a bushy moustache. Admittedly, the ministerial Harold MacMillan never looked like some 1970's porn star, unlike his father-in-law, nobody ever being brave enough to tell him that a feather cut and a Zapata moustache went out with the Raleigh Chopper. Alison once told him her dad had a head of pure jet-black hair until he was hit by an arrow from a crossbow. The arrow shot had resulted in a glancing blow causing him to lose his eye. His hair went grey virtually overnight. Well, losing an eye was one thing but Kenny had never thought or dared to ask about the fate of the archer who had fired the arrow. The southside of Glasgow was not the merrie olde England of Robin Hood but he could imagine a suitably medieval fate had awaited him.

Kenny put the cab in gear and headed off in the direction of Pollok Golf Club. He'd never planned on being a taxi driver and definitely not in Glasgow. He'd grown up in Dumfries with no fixed plans or interests apart from football, football and more football. It might have helped if he'd been any good at the game but being a competent amateur right back was never going to see him parading his skills at the San Siro.

Kenny had actually become a taxi driver due to Harold MacMillan. He'd been unemployed when he'd got married. A situation that had not caused him or his wife any problems but it had not reflected well on Harold. After the ceremony, Harold had called him and Alison into a little ante room in the hotel where the reception was being held. He told them he was very happy for them both and wanted to give them their present. He'd handed Kenny an envelope which had a substantial object in it. Kenny had opened the envelope to discover a Glasgow taxi drivers badge.

"What does this mean?" Kenny had asked.

"It's yer passport tae a new career, Kenny. Nae son-in-law o' mine is goin tae be unemployed," said Harold. "Looks like ye've just got yersel a job which allows ye to be really good at what ye do best, sit on yer arse all day."

"But Harold, I can't drive" had been the reply.

"Whit? Ah've spent ten grand on a taxi licence for ye and ye cannae fucken drive" Harold erupted.

"Calm down Dad. It's just his idea of a joke. He can drive. He's just to lazy too do it normally. Thanks, it's a great present" Alison interceded.

Harold calmed down. At one stage Kenny thought his false eye was going to pop out but Kenny's brand new wife had saved his bacon.

"Fuckin magic. Ah've just let a wind up merchant marry ma daughter. It just gets better and better. Ah'm away for a drink" Harold had walked out of the room and into the reception area.

Kenny pulled into the car park at Pollok Golf Club. As he passed the main sign on his way in some wag had sprayed over the first o in Pollok with a vertical line topped off with a dot. This summed up Kenny's attitude to golfers, a right bunch of pilloks. He'd tried it a couple of times in his younger days at the Royal Dumfries but his fellow junior golfers had been less than welcoming and the less said about the seniors the better. A good walk spoiled indeed.

As he parked the cab and walked up to the entrance he suddenly remembered the story of Harold's trick on the first tee when he was wanting to put his opponent off. Harold would tee up his ball and then step back. He would ask his opponent if he knew why Harold was such a good golfer. If the other player said he didn't know, Harold would take his glass eye out and roll it up to where his ball was teed up. "It's cos ah always keep mah eye on the ball." This normally did the trick in putting the opposition right off their game but Harold had been forced to

34

put an end to it one day. He had not realised the greenkeepers had given the tees a light sprinkling of fertiliser first thing. He'd put his eye back in following the trick, only to have to make a hasty withdrawal to the local A+E to get treatment for inflamation of the optical nerve after double bogeying the third hole. As he was led into an ambulance, he was heard to utter the immortal words "This isnae a fucking forfeit by the way. Ah'll be back as soon as they've washed ma eye oot." He mentioned Harold's name to the old boy at the door and was ushered into a huge clubroom. There were three large bay windows looking out onto the 18th green. A large bar stretched down the opposite side of the room, backed by a gantry which appeared to house just about every whisky in the world from what Kenny could make out. Harold sat in a leather armchair in one of the bay windows talking to a guy who looked in his late 50's, roughly the same age as Harold but with both eyes fully functional no doubt.

"Hello Kenny," said Harold as Kenny approached the table. The other man turned round and stood up with his hand outstretched. They shook hands and he introduced himself.

"Hello Kenny Brian MacDowall. I was just leaving, so apologies at disappearing so quickly. Ok, Harold, I'll be in touch about the matter we were discussing."

Kenny immediately realised this was a man to reckon with, as Harold didn't normally allow people use his nickname in public unless they were particularly close to him. Kenny used it as he knew it got on Harold's nerves but this was the first time he'd heard someone use it who wasn't a known member of Harold's inner circle.

"Sit doon Kenny. Ah'd offer ye a drink but ah know yer drivin," said Harold with a smile on his face.

"They don't serve non-alcoholic drinks here then?" asked Kenny with a mock disappointed look on his face.

"Alright smart bastart. D'ye want a coffee?" grunted Harold.

"No, it's ok. I'm fine" came the reply. Kenny sat down just across from Harold. "What did you want to see me about?" asked Kenny, hoping the note of fear in his voice didn't come out too strongly.

"These two games comin up in October wi Scotland. They're playin Estonia and somebody else, Latvia is it?"

"Aye, Latvia first in Riga and then Estonia in Tallinn. What about them? You know as much about football as I do about golf i.e. hee haw" Kenny was extremely puzzled by Harold's question and did not anticipate his next comment.

"Very good! Ah'm goin tae them"

"You're what?" Kenny sat bolt upright. "You cannot be serious, Harold! You hate football."

Harold looked at Kenny for a moment, a smile playing on his lips, and then said "Ye're right but there's somethin else. Ah've made a business contact in Tallinn and ah'm goin to pay him a wee visit. Thought ah'd hook up wi you and ye can show me the ropes, Tartan Army style."

"Where did you meet a business contact in Tallinn?" asked Kenny whose mind was racing with a number of scenarios, none of which were particularly appealing.

"Ye know ah went tae Jamaica last May? Lovely place. First time ah've ever experienced an all inclusive holiday. Ye pay a big wedge up front bit after that fuck all, as yer food and bevvy is included. Went to this place called Sans Souci, without a care ah think it means, near Ocho Rios. The complete and utter dugs baws. On the second week ah went tae play a round o' golf and the steward at the club asks if ah would mind pairin up with this boy called Leo who was over fae Estonia. Leo was sufferin ah can tell you. Couldnae handle the heat. Ah wasnae much better but ah had a hat on and had been stayin off the bevvy. He'd just done a big lunch wi wine and beer so was right oot the game. We get to the fourth hole and he fucken collapses. Ah thought it was a heart attack but it was just wee bit of sunstroke."

36

"Anyway, ah get him back to the clubhouse on the golf cart. Ah was drivin like Jackie Stewart ah could tell ye. So he gets taken off to hospital but the next day comes roond the hotel looking brand new. He's brought me a bottle of champagne as a thank you and we get intae a wee bit of a chat. Turns oot he's in the same line as me"

"What, he makes tartan tat Scotland souvenirs?" asked Kenny in an innocent tone. Harold's legitimate front was a souvenir company, run in the main by Alison, Kenny's wife.

"No, ya daft bastart. Crime wi a capital C. Ah never realised there was so much goin on in these old commy countries. So he's invited me over for a look see to see if we can work somethin oot the gither. This Scotland trip sounds like ideal cover so it's up tae you tae get me sorted. Ah think ah'd look good in a "c u Jimmy hat"?" Harold laughed but Kenny didn't join in. This was his worst nightmare come true. Short of England winning the World Cup again, chaperoning Harold MacMillan on a Scotland trip won hands down. No way. No fucking way. How would he break this to Gus?

"Are you sure you're really going to need me, Harold? You're a well travelled man, what can I help you with?" Kenny realised a completely pathetic tone had crept into his voice but going anywhere with Harold had to be avoided at all costs.

"Ye know how tae make me look like a real fan. How am ah goin tae get tickets for the game? Ah want this to be as official as possible fur me and the boys."

"The boys are coming as well? Oh for fuck's sake" said Kenny. It was a blustery day outside but the shiver Kenny felt had nothing to do with the weather. He should have realised from the start Harold would not be flying solo to somewhere like Tallinn. The boys, as he casually referred to them were his minders. The sort of people that ate lightly poached lightbulbs for breakfast, washed down with a couple of mugs of brake fluid.

"Of course they are, ya thick bastart. Ah'm no gaun over there withoot some back up. They'll be travellin as fans as well. Ah was thinking about buyin a kilt as well, to help blend in."

Fucking Mel Gibson, that Aussie bastard thought Kenny. He had noticed since the release of Braveheart the year before the number of guys wearing kilts had shot up. Gus witheringly referred to them as the "Braveheart boys" who now couldn't go to a game without painting half their face blue and wearing a kilt. He knew one boy from Canada, of all places, who'd gone the whole hog with the Braveheart gear and did look really good, but for the rest there was no hope. He'd seen a guy at Villa Park for the Holland game with just his eyes and the side of his forehead covered in blue facepaint. He hadn't been too pleased when Gus had told him "Never mind Braveheart son, you look like the Tartan Lone Ranger"

"I think a kilt might be a wee bit over the top, Harold just for a couple of games. Then again, you could wear it to weddings and other sorts of functions," said Kenny. "If you want tickets, you'll have to join the supporters travel club. I can organise that for you but I'll need three passport photos, one for each of you. I'll get the forms and we can take it from there. You're really sure about this?"

Kenny had visions of his father-in-law ending up in a gulag somewhere in Siberia and Alison nipping his head all the time about how he'd got her father into trouble. He'd got her father into trouble? Aye right.

"Sure? Sure ah'm sure. It will be a wee family holiday. Just me, you and the boys"

"But I normally travel with Gus," Kenny felt he had to make a stand somewhere and this was the easiest way of doing it.

"What? The poisoned dwarf will be there as well? Magic, he's always good value the wee man. Tell him ah look forward to meetin up wi him again."

Kenny suddenly remembered Harold setting up Gus with a ladyboy on Kenny's stag trip in Amsterdam. They'd found a bar staffed entirely by gorgeous Thai transsexuals, then Harold had bribed one of them to do the business. Harold had warned Kenny but nobody told Gus. One of the boys organised a raffle for a blow-job and had fixed it so Gus won. They had been sitting downstairs in the hotel bar when Gus returned from his winning assignation somewhat pale faced. He'd refused to tell them what had happened but Kenny had later prised it out of him. "She was getting into it good style, man, and ah got bit carried away. Put my hand up her skirt and got a bit more than ah expected like. Her baws was like two fuckin hard boiled eggs in a hanky, ah'm tellin ye. Ah just shot ma load and got the fuck out of there. Did you know it was a bloke before ah went in?" Kenny had lied, saying he thought it was a woman but he knew Gus still suspected him.

Kenny's thoughts drifted back to the present. "Ok, well that'll be 75 quid to sort out the membership of the supporters club," said Kenny trying to focus on what needed to be done.

"That's a bit pricey just for joinin a supporters club. Is it honestly 25 notes a head?" said Harold who was looking a bit stunned at the news of this expense. Kenny stood up and had a big smile on his face "No, it's only a tenner each membership but you owe me 45 quid for the fare here. You did say to put it on the meter"

*****

Atholl lay back in his sofa and tried to collect his thoughts. He'd had a busy time at work setting up some bodyguards for UN officials in Rwanda. The feedback from the first few personnel he'd sent out had been so bad they'd had trouble getting new people. On top of that, there was his father's request that he kill a complete stranger who, apparently, was his half-brother. The detective agency had finally come up with the goods regarding Kenneth or "Kenny", as he was known, Bradley. He'd read the file twice making notes as he went and felt he was finally getting an understanding of his quarry. He'd been inclined, yet again, to question the amount of detail but there was a covering letter from the agency saying they could do no more without attracting unwanted attention.

Atholl had noted that he travelled abroad a lot, both with his wife and on his own. Kenny appeared to be a keen follower of the Scotland football team but these trips he makes without the wife. He'd searched his memory for some image of a Scottish player or the national team but Atholl had spent his formative years outside Scotland at Eton and Oxford so had no great interest in the national teams of any sport. People expected him to be interested in rugby, given his background, and he had been down to Richmond to see London Scottish a couple of times but just didn't really feel comfortable. He'd always been a bit of a loner and the one area of his schooling he'd found difficult was forced participation in team sports.

As he read about Kenny's travels, Atholl formulated a plan. He'd heard of the trouble caused abroad by England fans and he could remember some match from the mid 80's when a large number of people had died in Rotterdam or Brussels or somewhere. Atholl had been up to his neck in death and brutality himself at the time so had paid it little heed. If he, Atholl, went abroad with lots of other fans, the chances of him getting noticed would be lessened. He couldn't go as a fan as he simply knew nothing about the game. What he needed was cover, a role to play but as whom? He tried to think of a reason why he would want to talk to people and appear genuinely interested. He could say he was on business but that would appear suspicious if he kept on turning up at games. Maybe a journalist? Yes, a freelance journalist, someone working on commission from a foreign magazine trying to identify different types of football fans. He thought about changing his name but he had been working under the alias of Andy Muir since leaving the army so had no real problem over his identity. He didn't plan to make himself that well known. But back to the assignment, were all football fans animals? Why do they go abroad to drink and fight? He wondered when the next away game was. He would get his personal assistant to find out the next day.

He got up from the settee and wandered through his open French windows out on to the patio. It was a warm day and summer looked like it had finally appeared

40

in London. The only trouble was it was the first week of August but better late than never he supposed. He paced up and down the patio for another couple of minutes and then realising he had just about managed to totally confuse himself he went back inside. He tried to create a plan of action in his mind but it was no good. He much preferred to sit down and write it out. He pulled an A4 pad out of a bureau drawer and took it over to the coffee table by the settee. He started sketching out his plan of operations.

If he went to an away game, he could try to meet up with the fans in the city. There couldn't be that many fans going to an away match could there? He could seek out Kenny Bradley in the crowd. Hopefully, having met him and established a rapport, Kenny's guard would be down and he could start and finish the job in double quick time. The job must be completed to both his and his father's satisfaction. Thinking about killing his half-brother had initially disturbed Atholl. He wondered if getting to know him would deter him from his task but he felt it could be achieved in a straightforward, single-minded manner. He knew Kenny Bradley's life from the file and felt he wouldn't be missed. His wife might grieve for a bit but life goes on he thought and he, Atholl Forbes Lothian Farquharson McClackit, must become the sole claimant to the title, Clan Chief of the Clan McClackit.

As he pondered his destiny, Atholl realised he had better get his old kit out. He did laugh when he saw these American films where the assassin has every gadget under the sun. James Bond was a joke to most people who'd served in the forces but it never ceased to amaze him the American fixation with hardware. He preferred to travel light, knowing just how much havoc could be wreaked with a couple of simple tools and a creative imagination. Time to disturb the fishes he thought. In a corner of the lounge Atholl kept a reasonable sized fish tank. His friends had teased him about it, asking him when he was going to get his own private bar installed next to it like some Doncaster builder. Atholl had laughed but he'd never seen the humour in those private bars. He's seen quite a few in

Loyalist households in Ulster where he'd received superb hospitality and knew that when you dare not go out of an evening for fear of being shot, they could be a big consolation. The fish tank served a couple of purposes for Atholl. It had surprised him what a turn on it had been for a number of women, especially the little beauty from Japan who thought he was keeping the fish as a source of food. She had even offered to make him some fresh seafood sushi with the contents of the tank. His main aim when buying the tank had been to provide cover for a couple of pieces of equipment he didn't really want lying about the house. One was a Smith and Wesson pistol he had removed from the hand of a dead terrorist in Northern Ireland. The other was his little box of tricks which he didn't think the police would appreciate a civilian being in the possession of.

He removed the lid of the tank and picked up a large rock from one of the corners. In the opposite corner a similar sized rock contained his pistol. Atholl laid the rock on a towel he'd put down on the carpet. Once he'd dried it off, he turned it so the base was facing him and unscrewed a couple of large plastic screws. The base came away to reveal a black rubber zipped case about the size of a filofax. Atholl removed it and unzipped the case to reveal, what had previously been, the tools of his trade. Now that he considered the contents, he wondered how he'd achieved so much with so little. He hadn't had the case out for a few months, the last time was to do a bit of maintenance on the equipment to keep it in good nick. He was struggling to remember the last time he'd used any of the gear in anger. Then it came back to him. The French family next door and that dog of theirs. A very noisy Alsatian which would bark loudly for hours, day or night, at the slightest provocation. Atholl had always loved animals, especially dogs, but the last straw had come on the 13th of July the previous year. Having fully celebrated the glorious 12th of July with an old army colleague who shared his love of the Protestant cause, Atholl had been awoken from his alcohol induced slumber by the dog next door. His hangover had maintained its consistency for the rest of the day, in much the same way as the dog had continued to bark.

When the French family left for a Bastille Day celebration at the French Embassy on the 14th, Atholl had decided enough was enough and the dog had to go. Looking back, he was shocked how much it had upset him when he had killed the dog by driving a whelk removing implement into the dog's ear. Well, at least the tool was French, he supposed, as he'd stolen it from a seafood restaurant in Saint Malo. He struggled to come to terms with his unhappiness at first, especially when he'd done much worse to numerous members of the public in Northern Ireland. He'd knocked the dog out by throwing a fillet steak stuffed with three sleeping tablets to it over the fence separating the two courtyards. The beauty of the whelk tool was that it left minimal external damage whilst skewering the brain.

He looked down at it now, nestling between his rubber-coated pliers, a tube of electrical jelly and the three industrial strength bangers. On the other side of the holder were his knife, some pipe cleaners, a military issue cigarette lighter and a small bottle of a clear liquid, the contents of which were both highly flammable and highly poisonous. Atholl tested each part of the kit where he could. Everything seemed in good working order, unaffected by the time spent in the fish tank. He zipped up the case and put it back in the hollow rock.

Screwing the base back on, he felt a small thrill at getting back to what he knew best, getting back in the saddle, so to speak. Thinking of that, didn't he have the number of that little Japanese filly somewhere? Sushi might not be on the menu but he definitely felt like something Japanese.

CHAPTER 4

It had been an innocuous enough comment on what good shops at airports there were these days but it had been enough to set Gus off, "Economic apartheid, that's what this is, like. The haves versus the have nots. Rich versus poor. The financially franchised against the economically disenfranchised. Are you listenin to me?"

Gus took a mouthful of lager and gave Kenny a pitying look.

"Ah thought we were all part o' Europe now. One big happy EE fuckin C but no. Every time we want tae go tae somewhere in Europe, we're forced tae come through London like. Boost their bloody economy whilst deludin ourselves this is the golden age o' travel and we should be happy they're actually lettin us use this shitehole o' an airport to get out of the UK. We're just economic units to these people like. Customers not passengers. Mere units to be counted and discounted as the years progress. Bought and sold for English gold right enough."

Gus paused for another mouthful of Carling. "You can hardly find a seat, like, they've opened up so many shops. Why don't they close down fucken Harrods and put in a bar? Eh? That would keep the punters happy. But here we aw are, crammed into some mock fucken olde English pub shoebox that looks like it was nicked from the original set of Emmerdale fucken Farm. Heathrow man, you can fucken keep it."

"So on your list of hatreds Gus, where would Heathrow come? Above or below Tenby?" asked Donny.

"Lower down than farmers?" asked Kenny.

"Aye don't worry, those rural bastards are still number one. Ah admit tae be being pretty much a son of the soil myself, coming from Dumfries, like, but ah've yet to see a poor farmer. And they all moan like fuck. The dairy ones are the worst, goin on about havin to work 365 days of the year because the cows won't milk themselves. Then goin on to say the farm has been in their family for four generations. Well hello, let's wake up and smell the Bovril, pal. If you grew up on

44

a farm where you could see your old grandad and then your dad working 365 days of the year, did the penny not drop a career as a lion tamer even might be a little less demandin? Don't get me started." said Gus. His mouth opened again but this time for lager. A quick swallow later he continued.

"To go back to your original point on Heathrow's place in ma league o' hate it's probably equal with Tenby in terms of pure dislike. Slightly ahead on goal difference ah suppose as ah have to pass through it so often. The funny thing is ah don't hate England or the English. Had many a good night in Blackpool like, then again maybe that's only because ah was wi a load of Scots but there's a good time to be had in London town by the way. Then again preferably when it's no' a Wembley weekend and every muppet and his brother from north of Gretna become Scotland fans. Last summer was alright but ye cannae win. No wanks from Scotland with their Bay City Roller gear on but loads of English casuals looking to kick fuck out of ye if you've got the slightest bit of tartan. Fuckin Gary McAllister. Right who wants another? What's that cloudy stuff your drinking Kenny? It looks like somethin you'd find at the bottom of a barrel, for fuck's sake."

"Its called Hoegaarden. It's a wheat beer and it's a magic drink. I'll have another pint. You should try it."

"What's Tenby ever done to you by the way?"

"A long story, best kept for another day" said Gus with a rather guilty look on his face.

There were five of them sitting in a transit lounge at Heathrow Terminal 2. Kenny and Gus had met Donny, another regular traveller on the flight down. A couple of new guys making their first trip were also in their company. They had flown down from Glasgow earlier that morning to get a connecting flight to Vienna for the Austria v Scotland game on the Saturday. Kenny had heard about this Belgian beer that was being released on to the UK market so thought he would give it a try. It had been tasty enough and he was feeling pleasantly mellow. Not normally a feeling he associated with a Scotland trip, but then again, they hadn't been to the game yet so no doubt a maelstrom of unpleasant emotions lay in store for him.

"Aye, maybe ah will. Always up for a new experience, alcohol wise," said Gus with a wide grin on his face.

"You going to buy this out of your winnings from yesterday?" asked Kenny with a big grin.

"Oh no, Gus," said Donny in a tone of surprise, "you've never been back on the gee gees. William Hill must be laughing all the way to the bank"

"Ha, fucken ha. Ah was a wee bit unlucky wi ma four selections like" snorted Gus. Kenny exploded with laughter. "A wee bit unlucky? Three came last and one died"

The group burst out laughing leaving Gus picking his way through the chairs muttering, "Miserable bastarts, the lot o' yous"

Gus headed off to the bar and Kenny turned to his mates, "Wait until he gets the price of the round off the barman. This stuff is £3.20 a pint"

"No way," said Donny. "There'll be a riot."

"No, the barman is safe but I'll get it big time. When he comes down here Gus likes to pretend he's the last of the big spenders and nothing fazes him. I reckon he'll have gone up the bar with a tenner, expecting it to cover five drinks and he's going to be donald ducked when he gets the final sum. Pity about the horses."

They all turned to look at the bar where Gus was speaking to another customer as he was waiting for the drinks to be poured. The barman put the last two pints of Hoegarden in front of Gus and entered all the prices on the till. He looked up and mouthed a figure at Gus. All they could see was the sight of Gus' shoulders tense involuntarily. He appeared to say something to the barman who repeated the figure. Another tense of the shoulders was cancelled by him reaching for his wallet in his sporran.

At this point, the other customer at the bar leant across and gave the barman a note, indicating for him to keep the change. Gus turned to face the other customer and said something. He then nodded in the direction of the rest of the party. They picked up the drinks between the two of them and came back to the group.

"Alright boys, this is Andy Muir but watch what ye say, he's a fucken journo. That's the down side. The good side is he's on expenses and has just got this round in. As for you Bradley, ya chancing bastart. £3.20 for a pint of Belgian bottom of the barrel. You must be off yer heid. Ah telt ye Andy, he's a wind up merchant"

Andy sat down, trying not to look too concerned over Gus' introduction.

"This is extraordinarily fortunate for me. To meet you guys here is really excellent news. I've just been commissioned to write an article on the Scotland fans who support the football team. Some might say you were a Tartan Army". These words were spoken in the rounded tones of a classically educated English actor. The guys were pretty taken aback by the accent but the last comment left them looking awkwardly at their feet.

"Eh, you could say that, Andy " said Kenny "A tartan army indeed".

"Of course, I immediately feel part of it as I am Scottish myself."

"Aye right", said Gus "You can cut out the wind up now Andy. You sound more like Laurence Olivier than Kenny Dalglish."

"Well, be that as it may, I am a Glasgow man myself" said Andy, a confident smile beaming across his face.

Loud guffaws echoed round the company.

"A Glasgow man. Who's your team in Glasgow then?" asked Kenny, who was thinking we've got a right one here.

"I'm not really a follower of one team but if you push me, I am a bit of a Clyde fan" replied Andy.

This just gets better and better" said Kenny. "I can see you going down a storm at a Bully Wee social night"

"I am sorry, "a Bully Wee social night?"" asked Andy with a bewildered look on his face. The others looked at each other and decided the guy was either a care in the community case or having a wind up.

"The Bully Wee is Clyde's nickname, Andy for fuck's sake. Keep up pal.. It doesnae matter." said Gus, trying not to look too guilty for bringing a complete dickhead into the company. To cover his embarrassment, he proceeded to neck most of his Hoegaarden in one go.

"No a bad drop Kenny, even if it is a mortgage job for a round. Right, who wants another?" asked Gus.

"They've just called the flight Gus, I think we'd better get to the gate" said Donny.

"What's yer rush? Andy here'll see us alright for a round of halves, a wee freshener before the stewardess comes round wi the trolley. What d'ye say, Andy?"

"Well, I.... "Andy had taken one sip from his pint of Guinness

"Good man, come on and gie's a hand to carry the drinks back"

Gus had dragged Andy back up the bar whilst the rest of them started to get their bags together.

"What do you make of him then, Kenny?" asked Donny.

"I don't know but he's the poshest speaking Clyde fan I've ever met" replied Kenny.

They had all stood up by the time Gus and Andy returned from the bar. Gus had gone for a large gin and tonic but had bought, or rather had Andy buy, vodka and cokes for the rest of them. These were duly despatched and they made their way to the flight.

By this stage, the three large Bloody Marys in Glasgow airport, the three pints of lager plus the Hoegaarden and a large gin and tonic were starting to have an effect on Gus. He was all over poor Andy like a rash, gibbering on about the kilt being the greatest aphrodisiac in the world, the women he'd shagged because of it, how everyone in the Tartan Army was equal and it was the only army in the world with no officers.

Kenny remembered Gus was normally a bit of a media tart, if any photographer turned up with a camera before a game, Gus would be girning away in front of the camera trying to get his photo in the paper. Sadly, the only time he'd made the front page was when he'd passed out on a car bonnet in Paris and his kilt had ridden up to show the tattoo of an octopus on his left buttock. A few people had started calling him Captain Nemo after that incident until Gus pointed out it wasn't in fact a tattoo of an octopus, it wasn't a tattoo at all but the remnants of a follow through from when he thought he was about to fart and it had turned into something a bit more substantial.

As they were queuing to get on the plane, Kenny realised something wasn't right. A minor twitch in his bowel regions had grown into a spasm and he suddenly began to regret drinking the Hoegaarden. And to think he'd just been laughing at Gus' gut problems. He'd suffered from irritable bowel syndrome in the past, the only humorous side to it being when he told Gus who had proceeded to ask him, in all seriousness, if he planned to go and see a speech therapist. Kenny realised the cloudy effect in the Belgian beer may have been through added wheat. All of a sudden he became very concerned but then realised he should make it to the loos on board in plenty of time. He calmed down on realising this but as he relaxed, he let off a silent fart. Oops he thought and immediately looked around for someone to blame for the smell, so casting suspicion onto some other poor passenger. The first person to his left was Andy. There's something no right about you pal, he thought, so you might as well cop for this one.

"Jeezo, was that you Andy? That's minging." Kenny pulled a face which didn't take too much effort as it was a totally gross fart combining an essence of the yeast of the Hoegaarden, the beans from cooked breakfast he'd had at Glasgow airport and a touch of the Guinness he'd been drinking last night.

"Holy fuck, Andy" cried Gus. "There's women and children present here for fuck's sake. That could stunt the wee yins growth"

Andy looked bemused at this until the smell hit him full on up both nostrils. "Dear God! What is that smell?"

"Calm down Andy" said Gus "Ah think ye've attracted enough attention to yirsel by other means, like. Don't want to over egg the pudding old boy as you've clearly over egged something already judging by that fart ye've just dropped"

"You don't think that was me, do you?" Andy looked around him to be met by reproachful stares by a number of passengers plus a steward who'd been alerted to the smell by another passenger.

As they approached the door the steward looked down at Andy and asked if everything was alright.

"Yes, fine thank you" was the reply.

"Well, if you are in need of any assistance Sir, we are always on hand to help but I hope you can appreciate how awkward it can be for other travellers if passengers have difficulty controlling themselves" commented the steward.

"You tell him pal, that was Charles Laughton so it was, like. Andy, if you're going hang around wi us pal, no more of the human stink bombs. The only person ah know that does it worse than you is that bastart, Bradley. Hey, wait a minute, Kenny, have you just papped the blame onto Andy here?

Gus was trying to progress down the aisle while shouting at Kenny, "It's not on big man, it's just not on."

Andy struggled into his window seat and sat down. Kenny had gone too far down the plane and on his return arrived at the correct row at the same time as Gus.

"Don't worry Kenny, ah'll just sit next to Andy to give him the lowdown on the TA. He'll get no decent info from a borin bastart like you."

"That is actually my seat," replied Kenny in a somewhat pissed off tone, as Gus sat down next to Andy in the middle seat.

"Ah know, but it's only a wee flight. We'll be there in no time. You just take mine on the aisle while ah talk to Andy." Gus had a pleading look on his face as he was saying this, barely masking his desperation to get his name in the magazine.

"Ok, have it your way" said Kenny and sat down in the aisle seat.

As soon as they took off, Gus passed out and slumped on Andy's shoulder.

By this time Kenny had had enough. Like a lot of football fans he was barely tolerant of people who had no idea about the game but felt they could talk endless pish on the subject. Most of them betrayed a lack of knowledge of the game but also, and more importantly to Kenny, a lack of feeling for the game. The way things were going Andy was going to get a gold medal for knowing sweet FA about football. The beautiful game? He wouldn't know a football if it bounced off his head. Kenny's antennae were twitching after Andy's question about the Bully Wee, which any self respecting football fan knew was the nickname of Clyde.

Just after the aeroplane had taken off, Andy had shrugged Gus off for a moment and asked Kenny if he thought Scotland would win. Kenny had replied they could well get a result as they had won the friendly the last time they played in Vienna. Andy had then made the cardinal error of asking who they'd played in the friendly. Kenny had initially thought he was taking the piss then realised it was a serious question.

"They beat Austria 2-1" was his reply

"Oh, it was Austria they were playing was it?" asked Andy, aware that he'd said something wrong but not quite sure what it was.

"Aye, who else would Scotland be playing in Vienna?" came the reply from Kenny in a tone of voice Andy felt bordered on the hostile.

That clinched it for Kenny. This prick didn't even realise Scotland would be playing Austria in Austria. Kenny needed a drink. Fortunately, the stewardess was just approaching with the drinks trolley. He ordered a large Bloody Mary and tried to relax. In doing so, he ignored Andy's efforts at restarting the conversation by asking where they planned to go out tonight.

Gus and Kenny had heard of an area called the Bermuda Triangle which was the nightlife centre of Vienna. That was where they were headed but hopefully it would be a journo free zone, thought Kenny. Then again, if Andy was still on expenses, Gus would be sticking to him like glue. Gus and free drink? It didn't bear thinking about.

Another issue was the U21 game tomorrow. Where the fuck was Amsteten? It sounded like a nice wee day trip out of Vienna, have a few beers, mix with the locals and hopefully get a result before heading back into Vienna for a good night out. The bulk of the travelling support would be arriving on the Friday so there would be a big crowd of Scots out on the town at night.

Just as Kenny started to think who else would be travelling, Gus woke up. He attempted to straighten up and stretch in the limited space of his seat but his neck had cramped up, as his head had been lying at an angle of ninety degrees when he passed out on Andy.

"Ooh, ya bastard," he cried out as he attempted to move his head. "Christ, could ye no have done somethin for me, Andy? Neck's fucken killin me, like. Might have to get it massaged when we get to Vienna or maybe even get one o these stewardesses to do the necessary. Might even get asked if ah want extras, like?" He turned to Kenny with a grinning leer on his face, "What's wrong wi your greetin face Bradley? Did ye no get me a drink when the burd came round with the trolley? It's all about you ya bastard. Ye don't think of your travellin buddies in the slightest. It's all me, me, me with you pal."

"I thought you'd had enough, given the Sleeping Beauty act" said Kenny "Andy's worried you were ignoring him".

"That right, Andy? It was the early morning call that did for me then. Some guys get a hard on when a plane takes off, I just fall asleep. Never been able to work out why, like"

"Nothing to do with the copious amounts of alcohol you consume before you set foot on a flight?" asked Kenny.

"Ah, shut it, you. Ye ken ah'm a nervous flyer and the drink's jist to calm my nerves. Anyway Andy, ah'll no be ignorin you the night. You're wi us an we're goin to show you a night in Vienna ye'll never forget."

"Really, can't wait" said Andy in a less than enthusiastic tone.

"Me neither" said Kenny in an equally subdued tone. He realised this was going to be a night to remember, probably for all the wrong reasons if Andy was coming along.

CHAPTER 5

Tadger Currie sat at the back of Molly O'Driscoll's, Vienna's finest Irish bar, nursing the last of his lager and lime. The pub sound system was playing a song that seemed to be called "Macarena". He thought it must be some kind of advert but every time it came on these burds started doing a weird dance. He wasn't happy to be drinking this lager and lime pish but this was one of the occasional pitfalls of minesweeping for drinks. "What sad prick drinks this stuff?" he thought to himself before realising he was that sad prick. Ok then, what sad prick pays money to drink this pish was a thought that went down better than the lager and lime.

He'd picked it up from a table near the Gents so had marked the area off in his mental quadrant. He'd once seen a TV programme where it showed the police at a crime scene marking off the area in squares. He thought he would apply that to his minesweeping technique. It had paid off brilliantly, apart from a couple of times when the drink had caused him to forget he'd already passed one square of the grid and the drinkers were only too aware of what he was up to. He was sure he'd had a mouthful of piss in that Mexican bar in Moscow last year but again, it was a small price to pay when the commie bastards were charging a fiver a pint for lager. Well, ex commie bastards, he supposed.

The lime had left a bad taste in his mouth and he needed something to take the taste away. The bar had warmed up nicely, as he knew it would. Scotland fans and Irish pubs were made for one another when you travelled abroad. A large number of fans only drank dark beer at home and were prepared to pay for Guinness rather than drink lager all the time on foreign trips. A white wine spritzer would be nice but then he remembered Austrian wine-making was famed for its liberal use of anti freeze in its winemaking process. Fuck that, he thought I want to cleanse my palate no strip it bare.

He was about to head off to a new square on the grid when he saw a couple of faces enter the bar that were as welcome to Tadger as a kick in the puss. Kenny bloody Bradley and the wee nyaff Gus McSween. They'd sussed him a long time ago for his drink hoovering antics and he owed them. In fact, thinking back, they were standing very close to that table in Moscow last year when he'd picked up the glass of lager or rather what he thought was lager but turned out to be home brew from McSween's kidneys in all probability. It wasn't beyond that wee bastard McSween to pull that sort of stunt.

Then there was that round they'd conned him into buying in Sweden last year. Told him the wee sister of one of the burds they were with was right into him and it would greatly help his cause if he bought a drink for her. He's gone up to get one in for the lassie as it was a good deal. She'd only wanted a Sprite, but then she came up to the bar and said she didn't have any money so could he possibly get a drink for her sister and their two friends? Apparently, they had been very good to her by taking her out for a meal the night before. Put him right on the spot it did but he's seen the bigger picture and knew the possibilities of what lay ahead wi this hot Scandinavian babe, especially as he liked them young.

Twenty five quid for four fucking drinks never mind the Sprite. Bradley and McSween both had nips with a bottle of coke as a mixer for each of them and the burds were drinking wine. Seven pound each for a glass of wine a fly couldnae do a breast-stroke in! The final insult came when he asked the wee lassie why she wasnae drinking. She said she had to leave soon to get home to do her homework. Homework indeed! The very mention of the word made him remember how they'd stitched him up. Not only that, they'd then left to go to a nightclub with the burds having drunk their round and bought him fuck all. As he thought of this, Tadger got more and more angry, thinking payback time is here for Tadger Currie and it's Messrs Bradley and McSween that will be footing the bill. He could make out a third person with them who was just going up to the bar. Another wee guy but his face wasn't familiar. Ah well, it looked like he was getting the round in so it would only be a matter of time before it was a target-rich environment.

Atholl struggled to the bar. He was sweating heavily but that was more to do with the crush than what he was about to attempt. He had tried to remain cool and collected but McSween had got on his nerves to such an extent he thought he might as well try and remove him from the picture. Not permanently, as with Bradley, but just teach him a lesson, a couple of nights in hospital, say, ensuring he would miss the match. Fortunately, they'd both asked for vodka and lemonades so it wouldn't take much poison to do the job. They'd both headed off to the Gents so he made his way to a column with a little shelf, allowing Atholl to easily hide the drinks from view. People were too busy having a good time to pay much attention to what he was doing and Atholl realised he was having a good time himself. Back in the old routine or what? The larger dose of the drug was swiftly poured into Bradley's drink and a second, much smaller amount, went into McSween's. Andy had never used this stuff before on a job but it came highly recommended from one of his company's employees who swore by the stuff for an effective, but clean removal of an enemy. There was a slight aftertaste but by the time the drinker had realised, they were halfway dead.

He was awaiting their return when he realised someone was standing next him, staring intently at him. The somewhat miserable looking and shabbily dressed man, even for a Scotland fan, then motioned to him with his head.

As Andy moved towards him the man said to him "Ye're in there, pal"

"What?"

"Ah said, ye're in there pal. Rat blonde in ra corner"

"What are you talking about?"

"Rat blonde is hotter ran the Sahara for ye, pal. Jist hae a look"

Atholl realised what the man meant and turned round to look at the blonde but it was like a Hitler youth rally in the pub. How many blonde Austrians could you expect in a Viennese bar? He looked in vain for a blonde who was giving him the eye but the only person giving him the eye was McSween, beckoning him to come over with the drinks.

"I don't think she's looking at me" he said and turned to an empty space. The guy had vanished.

Better get to the others thought Atholl and reached for the vodka and lemonades. They were gone. A couple of wet glass stains on the shelf were all that remained of his poisoned chalices.

Oh shit, thought Atholl. Somebody's nicked the drinks. He looked around to see if anyone had clearly picked up a vodka and lemonade by mistake but it was all sweaty beer stained guys in kilts holding pints of lager or Guinness. A couple gave him a funny look when they found him staring at their drinks but he was too worried about other matters to let that concern him. He felt an urgent tugging at his sleeve and turned round to see McSween's contorted face looking at him.

"Did ye get a round in?"

"Yes, but"

"Yes but what, Andy? You've been away so long, ah thought you were distillin the vodka. Where's the drinks?"

"They've been taken. There's been a terrible mistake"

"Whit? The only mistake you've made is takin yer eye off the ball man. Ye should know what these guys are like if anybody leaves a drink unattended. Come on, lets get back tae the bar. We've got three real honeys lined up over there, like. As ah said before, the kilt is the greatest aphrodisiac known to man. Ye'll be knocking them dead in five minutes, Andy"

Tadger Currie stood close to the entrance of the bar, ready for a quick getaway should he be spotted. He didn't plan to savour the drinks as he would need to polish them off quickly and find another bar. The first one tasted a bit off when it went down. Must be using cheap vodka, the tight bastards. He thought about cutting his losses and leaving the other but then thought, fuck it! and necked the second in a oner. Rough as fuck man Wait a minute, really rough.............

Kenny was thinking times just get better and better. He was in deep with a gorgeous Austrian who reminded him of Michelle Pfeiffer, always a bit of a fave.

Her brother was on the door, so it was also looking good for a lock-in, should they not already be installed in the hotel before closing. Might need to have a word with the wee man to ensure that if he pulled, he was going back to the burds as opposed to the hotel. He was wondering how to break it to the wee man when Else came back from the ladies

"You crazy Scots guys drink too much, you know?"

"Aye well, if you'd grown up in Dumfries in the 1970's you might have a drink problem. Has some cun, er has somebody been hassling you?"

"No, my brother has to lie a guy on a table. He has fallen. He is helpless."

"He'll be alright. Must have been drinking some of that wine of yours with the anti-freeze in it."

All of a sudden Kenny felt a chill in the air. "That is not funny, you know. Many wine producers add chemicals to help the wine mature"

"Aye, fair enough - but anti freeze?"

"Well nobody asks you to drink it, you know" she replied

"Speaking of drinks, can I get you another?"

"No, I have a headache and I think I must now go home" was the cool reply. Else picked up her bag and walked towards the exit. Kenny finished his beer and stared at the empty glass in his hand.

Kenny was pissed off but determined not to show it. "Ok then, catch you later" he murmured. Pissed off right enough but not with the Austrian girl, with himself. How many times had he got into a good position with a foreign lassie then blown it?

Just at that moment Gus bounced up with a large smile on his face.

"Ah'm looking favourite for a leg over tonight, old boy. Want to make it a foursome?"

"No, I'm just going to stay here and catch up with a few guys" said Kenny.

"Ha ha, don't tell me bigmouth strikes again, you sad twat. What did ye say to her? Ye'll be getting banned fae farms again wi that foot in mouth disease."

"We agreed to disagree on the benefits to Austrian wine of adding anti freeze to the end product."

"Adding anti-freeze to wine? Ye'd have been better off pourin it down the front o' her knickers. Right, well ah cannae carry any passengers as there's shaggin to be done, like. Don't wait up, big boy, see you in the mornin."

Kenny wondered what the fuck he was doing with his life at that particular moment in time. Scotland had better get a result tomorrow night or that was it with the Tartan Army. It had been a dark, desperate night coming out of Villa Park after the Switzerland game earlier on that year and he didn't know how much more he could take. Hopefully this game would get them on track for France '98. Just when he thought things couldn't get any worse Andy appeared. Oh Christ, thought Kenny, Gus doesn't want to carry any passengers but I've got to put up with this prick.

"Where have you been?" asked Kenny. "I thought you were with some Austrian burd?"

"I was, but made a total mess of chatting her up. Probably asking if all Austrians really wanted to be Germans wasn't the smartest of moves and she's gone. What about you?"

"A similar fucking story. Maybe we've got more in common than I thought" Kenny replied.

"I dare say," said Andy who had a slightly bemused smile on his face.

An almighty scream pierced the bar. Kenny looked over to the door to see a bouncer with his arms wrapped round a young blonde who was clearly having some kind of panic attack. A space had been cleared round a table where a body lay comatose. Kenny thought the figure looked vaguely familiar and then realised it was Tadger Currie.

"What the fuck has he gone and done now?" said Kenny to no one in particular.

"Do you know him?" asked Andy

"Know him? Suffered him more like. Tadger Currie the sweatiest boil on the sweatiest arse of the Tartan Army. A complete loser who comes on trips, mooches off other fans who don't know him and when your back's turned, he'll hoover up all your bevvy. Gus got him a good one last year in Moscow when he got an empty pint glass and pee'd in it till it looked like half a pint of flat lager. Better go and see what's up with him."

"Well, if you know him on you go. I'll wait here"

"Suit yourself" said Kenny.

Atholl thought the body on the table may have been the guy who had distracted him earlier on and taken the drinks. From what Kenny had just said it seemed highly likely. Better not hang around the scene of crime he thought and headed off to the side exit. He consoled himself with the thought there would be plenty more opportunities and that he was just getting his eye in. Opportunities were all over the shop in this scrum of humanity.

As he approached the table, Kenny could see that the mood had changed. The woman had been led away and two bouncers plus a guy Kenny presumed was the manager judging by his suit and tie, stood by the table.

"Is he ok?" asked Kenny

"Nein" said the manager. "He is, how you say in English, dead as a doodoo."

"Dead drunk, I think you mean?"

"Kaput," said one of the bouncers who looked like he'd just found out steroids made you impotent.

"But how?" asked Kenny.

The manager said something in German and in response to Kenny's quizical look, one of the bouncers motioned with his cupped hand approaching his lips.

"Bevvy? No way. That prick would only expire through drink if he had to buy a round." Kenny looked round for Gus for some moral support but then remembered he was off on manoeuvres. He wondered if Andy would have any idea what to do but he had vanished.

"Fuckin' brilliant, last man standing again."

"What's goin on, Kenny?" said a voice behind him.

"Alright, Wullie." The man asking the questions was Wullie Fraser, a long time fellow traveller in the Tartan Army. "These guys seem think to think Tadger Currie's pegged it. I think he's just passed out wi the drink but I don't speak German and their English is about as good as mine. Any ideas?"

"Wait a minute, one of our lads was in the works in Munich. If I can get him away from this blonde, I'll see if he can get a translation going."

"I wouldnae rush if I was you Wullie. I think they might just have a point, the Austrian boys. Look at that"

Tadger's sporran had fallen to the side when they had laid him on the table. Initially Kenny had returned it to its proper place but it had moved once more. This had nothing to do with the movement of the crowd around him or the table but the fact that Tadger had a tent pole of a hard on. Where the sporran had previously been, it was once more dislodged and now replaced by a tartan teepee.

"Fuck me," said Wullie "It's Tadger's last stand."

CHAPTER 6

The flight back to Glasgow from Heathrow was relatively smooth. They'd only had a 30-minute wait between planes but it had still been enough to prompt a rant from Gus regarding the cheapness of duty free vodka at Heathrow compared to Glasgow airport. Kenny couldn't see the difference but didn't want to provoke a full scale outburst from the wee man so bit his tongue.

They'd spent the Sunday wandering round Vienna and Kenny had even managed to get Gus and a couple of others out to the Schonbrunn Palace outside the city where they had visited the Gloriette, which Kenny believed was a tribute to Empress Marie Theresien. This had provoked the comment from Gus that she must have been some ride if the boy saw fit to build something that big as a tribute to her. The only tribute he'd given to any of his conquests was to moo like a cow when he came but only if she was somebody really special.

Kenny had thought it best to keep them out of bars after Gus had earlier embarrassed everybody by finishing an Austrian bloke's lunch in an Irish bar. The guy had entered Molly Malone's and ordered haddock and chips plus a pint of Guinness. He'd drunk his pint but had taken only one bite of his fish and hardly any chips. All this had been keenly observed by Gus who had been appalled earlier at the prices charged for food and drink. The Austrian was barely out the door before Gus had swooped on his plate. His only comment was "Well, if he's no wantin it"

The game had been a pretty dull 0-0 draw but it was a reasonable start to the campaign as they would have settled for any kind of positive result pre match. Compared to the U21s the day before it was a real achievement. They'd gone down 4-0 in a match best described as a gubbing going on complete annihilation. The three of them sat in a row on the shuttle to Glasgow. Donny, Kenny and Gus. They had received some funny looks from the air crew as they got on, given that Gus was still wearing his kilt and flip flops with a pair of white running socks. Any fears about getting removed from the flight had evaporated when a stewardess with a broad Glasgow accent had come up to them and asked them if they were getting back from Vienna.

When they said they were she replied, "No a bad point but we'll need tae dae better in the double header comin up. You'll be going to that ah take it?"

When they nodded that they were, she continued "Well, yous had better get ready for aw that fanny in Tallinn. Ah wiz there fur a hen weekend last month. Talk aboot takin sandwiches tae a banquet, we felt right stupit cows. Nane o us got a lumber the whole weekend. Ah well, ah'll be round wi the drinks trolley in a few minutes so just let me know what yous are wantin."

"Aye, ye can take the girl out of Glasgow......" said Donny.

"Still cannae get over that Gents man" said Gus. "That one with the self cleanin seat, like. The number of places ah've had a shite in that could do wi somethin like that doesnae bear thinkin about."

"Another thing that doesn't bear thinking about is the state of you after smokin one joint. What the fuck possessed you to try it again? You know what it does to you," said Kenny.

"Aye, it's a fair cop guv. Ah can only hold ma hands up and accept full responsibility for ma actions, like"

"More like inactions" piped up Donny "You were comatose outside the ticket gate. If Kenny hadnae come out to get you at half time you could have been lifted."

"Aye, ok, don't go on. Ah was a complete mess and ah know it. Must have been strong stuff, by the way, to leave me in that state, like."

"Fuck off. "Strong stuff"!!!! You eat a poppy seed muffin and you're in la la land. A Lemsip gives you hallucinations."

"Ok, ok, ah admit ah'm a wee bitty susceptible to foreign substances and ah admit ah was in the wrong. Can we just file it under f for forget all the fuck about it?" pleaded Gus.

"End my drug hell cries Angus McSween, 34 of Anniesland. I am addicted to Lemsips, Beechams Cold remedies, Tennents lager and the Scotland football team. His mercy cry echoes round Great Western Road as he struggles from day to day desperate for an Anadin extra or news of the latest Scotland squad"

"Aye awright, everyone's a fucken comedian," muttered Gus

"You lads awright for drinks?" asked the cheery air stewardess.

"This your first day?" asked Donny

"No, why di ye ask?" she replied

"You seem remarkably cheery for an air hostess. I thought they'd have ground it out of you by now" said a very perplexed Donny.

"Maybe ah'm just like you three"

Gus snorted derisively "How are you like us three?" he asked.

"Just naturally high on life, ya mug. Enjoy the rest of your flight" At this she turned and walked towards the rear of the plane.

"Ah could be in love" said Gus as he screwed his head round to get one last glimpse of the stewardess. "Ah wonder if that English boy on the flight fae Vienna to London has worked out what ye were talkin about, Kenny.

"Fuck him" came the reply. "I know you don't have to be an arsehole to be English but in his case it definitely helped. What a prick. Speaking to strangers on planes is always dangerous but all I'll say is, he started it."

"What are you on about? " asked Donny.

"It must have been when you nodded off. This guy was a Geordie who loved jazz and just couldn't shut up about some Vienna jazz festival that was on at the weekend. When I told him I thought it was a lot of tuneless nonsense, he told me I just didn't understand the pain of jazz. I told him I perfectly understood the pain of jazz as my ears bled everytime I had to listen to that Coltrane pish. At that time I hadn't realised he was wearing two tone shoes, obviously from when he was stompin at the Savoy. But his bowtie, braces and armbands should have alerted me to the fact he was an old jazzer. To appease him I said "Wasn't there a jazz blues film set in the north east?"

"Yes" he said

"Tommy Lee Jones played a villain"

"Yes" he replied.

"It was directed by Mike Figgis?"

"Yes"

"Sting was in it along with that blonde American actress Melanie Griffiths"

"Yes" he enthused, "Have you ever seen it?"

"No" I said.

He gave me this queer look then gave up on me. He'd pissed me right off when he asked me not to crush his trilby in the overhead locker when we got on. Fuck knows the state of that as I made sure my duty free landed right on it. More of a flat cap than a trilby now, I think."

The pilot's voice came over the aircraft speakers asking them to fasten their seatbelts and that it would be ten minutes to landing.

"Whatever happened about Tadger Currie?" asked Donny.

"I don't know. I saw a bloke's Daily Record at Heathrow and there was a few lines at the bottom of page 10 about his death. Just the usual, mystery of Scots fan's death in Vienna, blah, blah, blah."

"More than the miserable bastard ever deserved" said Gus

"How can you be so callous about the death of another human being?" asked Donny in mocking tones.

"Agh, shut it you. Folk are dying everywhere every second of every day, like. Tadger Currie wouldn't have pissed on any o us if we'd been on fire so no loss to me."

"Did it say anything about a cause of death?" asked Donny

"Suspected heart attack with an added complication of wallet failure. Nah, the heart attack was the most likely. It was lucky I didn't get roped into staying to identify the body. I gave the cops a complete statement as did Wullie so they accepted that. I think they were just relieved it wasn't related to any agro" said Kenny.

Gus looked lost in thought but Kenny didn't think this was out of respect for Tadger.

Gus looked up, "Ah've just remembered, what happened to that journo called Andy?"

"I don't know" said Kenny "He vanished from that bar where Tadger died like snow off a dyke. Speaking of dykes, Gus, how did you get on last night with that burd that looked like a lesbian?"

Gus thought back to last night and a resigned look passed across his face.

"Aye, it was a bad call by McSween on that one ah'm afraid. Nice enough lassie, like, but neither me nor the rest of the male population of the western world was going to get anywhere wi her. Pity about that boy Andy. I thought he might have been on the same flight back as us. Could have ponced more drink off him at Vienna airport"

"Ah the new Tadger Currie is born" said Donny.

"Hey, less of that you cheeky bastard. Ah stand my round and you know that. Anyway Bradley, is there any money left in the kitty?"

"You mean, is there any money left after you did your best to spend it all on roses last night cause you thought the bird selling them wanted to get into your pants, as opposed to just getting into our kitty?" asked Kenny.

"That girl was gaggin for it man. Ye think ah was just buyin those roses to get her interested but you didnae see ma master scheme at work, if ah didnae get lucky wi her there's always Plan B."

Kenny sighed heavily, "And this scheme was what? Buy loads of roses and if the seller gives you the bum's rush, you can then find another burd to try and woo her with all the flowers."

"Fuck's sake, was it that obvious? Ah must be losin my touch if a torn faced bastard like you can see the game plan and where it's leadin."

"It was going nowhere. How pished were you to buy all those roses when you know you get hayfever eating a salad! You must have sneezed twenty times in five minutes after she thrust that bunch in your face. She'll be wearin a surgical mask the next time she goes out sellin after all the germs you sprayed in her face. Now that I think of it, you don't think that would help you with women?"

Gus looked up, "What, buyin them roses?"

"No, you wearing a surgical mask. It would hide half your face which could only be a good thing," said Kenny

"Aye but what half would he wear it on though? The top or the bottom?" chipped in Donny.

"Ha fucking ha. The day ah need to take advice from the likes o' you with regard to the fairer sex is the day ah take a vow of celibacy, like. Right, where we going fur a drink when we land then?"

Kenny suddenly remembered he had agreed to meet Cammy in the Horseshoe at 6.30 that evening. The relationship between Cammy and Gus was one which had not taken off quite as well as Kenny had hoped. Gus' extreme homophobia couldn't see past the fact that, apart from being gay, he and Cammy had the same interest. Drinking, football and having as much gratuitous sex as possible. Gus was always polite in his company but Kenny knew he had a real issue with Cammy's sexuality but there was nothing he could do about it.

"I'm meeting Cammy at 6.30 in the Horseshoe if you fancy it," murmured Kenny.

"Fan fucking tastic" replied Gus. "How is Govan's answer to Quentin Crisp these days? Has he moved to Queen's Park yet? That must be nap to be his spiritual home, like."

"Look, he likes you. I don't know why you have to be so antagonistic towards him."

"That's jist the problem, ya tube. Ah don't want him to like me. Ah want him to fucken hate me, like. Wan step up from likin is fancyin and there is no way he's gettin anywhere near my arse like, no wi ma piles, that's for certain"

"I honestly don't think you have anything to worry about on that score. He likes them young and slim. No middle aged wi a bum like a deflating airship. Come on let's get off this plane and get a bus into town."

As they entered the Horseshoe there was a muted air about the place. Only a few hardy souls had come out on the Monday night and others seemed intent on putting off the journey home for as long as possible. They walked round the bar till they found Cammy sitting at a table at the back. He was reading the report of the game in that night's "Evening Times".

As they approached he looked up and finished the last of his lager.

"As ever, Gus, perfect timing. I'll have a pint of Tennents my good man and if it's service with a smile, you even get a wee tip." Cammy had long been aware of Gus' dislike for him and took sincere pleasure out of winding him up.

"For fuck's sake, ah've jist walked into the pub and ah'm being financially raped. Still better than being raped in another way by the likes o you. Ok, what do you two want?"

Gus got the order and headed off to the bar.

"Alright, Cammy? How's it going?" said Donny.

"No too bad. No too bad at all." He pointed to the paper, "Broon keeps this up, ah might have to look in my little black book for my contacts at PSG for France '98. Shite game but a good result from what I can make out. Watched it on the telly and nearly fell asleep it was so crap. A good trip nonetheless, I take it?"

"Aye, it was ok. Vienna's no the most mental of places but hopefully the next two venues will liven things up a bit"

"Oh aye," said Cammy "Riga and Tallinn, the wild east. A good time should be had by one and all"

"You up for it, Cammy?" asked Donny.

"I'm always up for it Donny," said Cammy with a wicked leer, "You should know that. No, I'll be giving these two a miss as I am somewhat financially challenged at this moment in time. Anyway, speaking of being up for it, here's somebody who always raises something in me"

Gus had returned to the table with the pints and had just missed Cammy's last remark. He was looking in a happier state than when he'd left.

"What's wrong wi' you?" asked Kenny. "You look like your coupon's just come up"

"Might well have done. Ye remember that burd ah had the interview wi about ma finances? Ah jist bumped into her at the bar. Gave her a bit o' chat and ah'm jist heading back up there, like. Her tongue's got unfinished business wi ma cock."

"Aw Gus, leaving so soon? I was hoping we might get a chance to know each other a little better," said Cammy a disappointed pout on his lips. "You know my tongue is available for you any time, whatever business you may wish to complete."

"Aye well, when ah decide to go that way, they can dig me up and ye can open ma coffin for first dibs Cammy. This lassie could be the one, ye ken"

"Good luck. But I thought you said she had the sexual prowess of a panda?" said Kenny " Oh well, I hope everything works out for you and it's the real deal for a nuclear family McSween"

"Thanks very much Kenny. Ah didnae see you being so positive aboot me and ma love life, like."

Cammy burst out laughing "Gus, you don't see the bigger picture my wee tartan love terrorist. If you get married and settled down, Kenny here doesnae have the burden of you trailing round Europe with him. Talk about a win-win situation.´

At this last comment Gus turned and walked off muttering as he passed the drinkers at the bar.

Kenny turned to Cammy. "Speaking of family matters, how's your sister getting on Cammy?"

"Don't ask Kenny. It's a living nightmare" came the reply. "When Hughie finds out he'll kill the guy first and God knows what he'll do to my sister"

"Have I missed something?" said Donny

"Put it like this" said Cammy, "This live football will be the death of someone, namely the stupid wee tim who is shagging my sister."

"I still don't get it" said Donny.

"Ok, I'll paint you picture. A guy comes round to my sister's house to put in cable TV. Within twenty minutes it's mad passionate how's your father on the kitchen table like Jack Nicholson and Jessica Lange in "The Postman Always Rings Twice". The only problem is he has the names of all the Lisbon Lions tattooed down his right arm. I'll never eat another meal at that table without thinking about Jinky Johnstone, I can tell ye. The amount of twisting and turning that must have gone on between that pair."

"Oh dear" said Donny.

"Oh dear, oh dear, oh dear says I when I find out. This is my own flesh and blood married to one of my closest mates and she's shagging a Celtic fan!"

"But what's all this got to do with live football on the telly?" said Donny.

"Well, before live football" said Cammy "you could set your watch by when a game would be played. Saturday afternoon at 3pm, one game at home one week and the following week an away match. Now wi' all this live pish screwing up the football calendar ma sister don't know when a shagging slot is going to become available. She's getting more and more worked up cos she's no getting her legover regular, like. To make matters worse, Hughie is getting a wee bit suspicious of the phone ringing and nobody answering it when he picks it up."

"So is Hughie no doing the necessary between the sheets?" asked Kenny.

"Well, he says he is but I'm no sure. Ma sister says he's having a bit of a problem down below and it's the last straw as far she's concerned. This Celtic Casanova has pushed her to the brink and she's even talking about leaving Hughie. I don't know how many services that engineer boy provides but he's definitely been laying more than cables. She cannae stop talkin' about him. Ah'm usually right up for someone telling me about their sexual experiences with a man but only when it's a man telling me. It's disgusting some of the stuff you heteros get up tae" Cammy tried to take away the distaste of his sister on the job by swallowing a large mouthful of lager. The bar had filled up quite considerably for some reason and the trio fell silent as they considered Cammy's predicament.

"It's no an easy one and that's for sure" said Kenny trying to buy some time while thinking how to get out of the conversation and back home to Alison.

"Don't you worry about it, Kenny. I'll sort something out with the pair o' them," said Cammy "Though what pair I don't know. Maybe I'll send Hughie on a TA trip wi Gus and he can fall for some sexy foreign babe to take his mind off things. Then again if he can't get it up, he's no use to no cunt. Literally."

*****

Atholl sat back in his chair and pondered his next move. The light was fading in his lounge and he got up to switch on a lamp. The light illuminated a portrait his father had given him of Castle McClackit. It had actually been painted by Atholl's mother who, like Atholl, had maintained a profound dislike for the place all her life. It made him wonder if what he was doing was really necessary. Was it that important that he become the next chief of the McClackits? Living in the castle had driven his mother to suicide. Well that and his father's continual cheating. Could he really risk everything he had built up just to lay sole claim to that hideous pile? He'd called home on his return to speak to his father. Potter had answered the phone and informed him the Laird was entertaining at this moment in time and he could not be interrupted. Atholl took that as a good sign, as there was clearly a lot of life left in the old fellow yet.

Despite his failure to eliminate Kenny Bradley in Vienna, Atholl was convinced it was a minor setback. He'd been out of the game for a few years so all it was going to take was another opportunity. Atholl was sure these trips abroad were the best way of ensuring he accomplished his task. If what he had seen in Vienna was anything to go by, the chaos of these football matches allowed a person to get away with anything, including murder. And yet. Atholl put from his mind any doubts over his actions. He had been brought up with a clear sense of duty throughout his life. His duty to the army had been exemplary, after a fashion, and he wished the same to be said with regard to his attitude to his family name and the McClackit heritage.

The next morning he asked his secretary to get a full list of fixtures from the football association of Scotland. As he looked at the next couple of games he saw they were back-to-back away games in Latvia and Estonia. He sat up at this as he had recently been discussing with the MD the possibility of moving into the Baltics with their security service operations. Various tales of Russian Mafia kidnapping and robberies had gripped the imagination of the British press and he thought there might be some business opportunities available.

He asked his secretary to get Bryce, his managing director, on the phone.

"Bryce, it's Atholl. How's things? Get down to Quins at the weekend?"

"Hi Atholl, yes I did get down but it was grim. Bloody Bath, will those west country bumpkins ever get any worse. It's just not on. What can I do you for?"

"I've just been reviewing the conversation we had about the Baltics last month and was looking to take a trip out in October, have a scout around a couple of places, Riga, Tallinn. I was thinking of posing as a UK businessman looking to invest but worried about protection. I can get a few quotes on the competition and see how they match up with the services we offer. Really dipping a toe in the water sort of thing."

"Sounds good. Draw up an itinerary with a couple of objectives, just to make it look official, and I'll sign it off. Any other ideas just let me know as we're looking to get out of Africa as much as possible. These places are virtually round the corner compared to the likes of Angola and Nigeria. You up for a game of squash Thursday lunchtime?"

"Sounds good. Just one small point. You will be going as Andy Muir? Don't want anything to go wrong when Atholl McClackit flashes up on the immigration screen, do we?"

"Fair point. See you on court at 12.30"

At the sound of the tone, Atholl realised why Bryce had been so good in the SAS. He was prepared to think differently and was always looking for a new way of doing things. Riga here I come he thought.

CHAPTER 7

Dominic Fraser appeared in Paddy Whelan's, Riga's finest Irish bar, a bulky carrier bag under his right arm. The bar was full of Scotland fans taking advantage of the cheap Latvian prices. There was a wee bit of a bottleneck at the front but when you pressed on into the bar it opened out. The pub had clearly been bought in a pub supermarket, definitely in the Irish shop/bar section. He saw Kenny Bradley and Gus McSween in a booth and wandered over. Dominic was the editor of the Scotland fanzine, Sporran Legion, and a long time acquaintance of Kenny and Gus'. The Spice Girls "Wannabe" was blaring out of the pub sound system but still couldn't totally drown the hubbub of noise coming from the fans.

"Alright lads?" said Dominic.

"No, no really" said Kenny "Just had a wee bit of aggro wi' some locals"

"What? That's no like you"

"All, ah'll say is we didnae start it. Just had to calm Rambo down a bit before he started World War III" said Gus who was clearly enjoying taking the moral high ground for once.

"They burnt ma hat, they fucking set fire to my hat and burnt it," said Kenny, an anguished tone creeping into his voice.

His attempt to get taken seriously wasn't helped by the fact that he was wearing a tartan baseball cap which had a piece of plastic stuck on its front, the bit of plastic having "Think Scottish" printed on it.

"Who did this? They honestly set fire to his hat?" Dominic asked Gus.

"Aye, unfortunately he wisnae wearin it at the time, like. It was the hat he bought in Red Square last year. This old boy from Stonehaven came over and told us a couple o locals were upset at Kenny wearing a Russian hat. He suggested Kenny take his baseball cap and he'd look after the cossack bunnet. We went to see Frances Fairweather at her hotel to say hello and came back 30 minutes later to find out these two Latvian boys had started usin the hat as an ashtray, then taken

74

it outside and gone the whole fuckin' hog, like, makin' a wee bonfire out of numbnuts hat. He's no a happy camper by the way, so go easy on the poor wee soul."

"Ach, shut it you. If this isn't bad enough on its own, I've to listen to you getting on your high horse and telling me I was in the wrong. I accept that and all I will say in my defence is after I called him a fucking Latvian homosexual bastard, I did offer to buy him a drink. Once I had cooled down." Kenny felt he had gone a bit over the top towards the end especially when he realised the size of the locals involved.

"Sure it wasne once your hat had cooled down?" said Gus, an evil grin on his face. "Ah've always had you down as a bit of a hothead, like".

"So did they have a drink wi you?" asked Dominic who was bemused by the whole story but concerned to see Kenny so worked up.

"Well one did but his mate was less than chuffed over the homosexual remark. I think he still wants to kill me judging by the stares he's given me." At this last remark, Kenny nodded towards a large blond youth sitting at the bar who was giving him the evil eye.

"Christ, Kenny, you know how to pick them. He looks like Dolph Lundgren's big brother."

"Aye well Dominic, if bigmouth strikes again he knows he can always count on us for back up. We'll no leave you stranded Kenny whatever the cost to our personal well bein, like" said Gus.

"Magic, that's me well protected then"

"You could always call Harold for a bit of back up if things get really nasty" suggested Dominic in a less than convincing tone of voice.

"Christ, this just gets better and better. First, my hat gets burnt then you two come up with ideas like calling up Harold and the boys. Get fuckin' real. Anyway, forget about man-mountain over there and concentrate on the night. How's sales Dominic?"

"No bad, bordering on complete shite."

You still floggin that comic?" asked Gus.

"No, essentially I am just carrying around seventy five copies around Riga and allowing Scotland fans to tell me to fuck off when I ask them if they want to buy a copy"

"That good?" asked Kenny.

"Aye, that fucken good. You'd think I was askin' them to cut off their right arm as opposed to coughin up a pound."

"Just as well we're subscribers, like" said Gus

"You? A fucking subscriber? Don't make me laugh. Kenny subscribes and you read his copy, you tight wee sod. That barmaid in Amsterdam couldnae have been as tight as you."

"Hey! Where you'd hear about her?"

"Hey! Never reveal your sources" said Dominic "But from what I heard you got more than you bargained for"

"What the fuck do you mean by that?" exploded Gus worried his secret was out.

"Does the word "ladyboy" mean anything do you?"

"Get tae fuck man. No way. No fucking way Pedro"

"Aye well, don't let the truth get in the way o' a good story," replied Dominic.

"What yous up to tonight?"

"Well I believe there's a gallery opening tonight in the old town so we may well take that in before going to admire some outdooor sculptures in a forest whilst the sun sets to the sounds of a live classical string quartet." said Kenny.

"Just getting gassed then?" replied Dominic.

"Too fucken right" said Gus. "Ah've heard enough pish about art the day to do me a lifetime."

"What the fuck are you on about? You're about as artistic as my last fart" said Dominic.

"Funny you should say that as it reminds me of a conversation earlier today regarding art and wind," said Kenny . "Gus here is the man for the beauty and pain of classical art, aren't you my fat little friend."

"Hey, ah wisnae tae know ah was sittin next to the world's most intelligent burd."

"This sounds good" says Dominic.

"Good? This is better than good. Our friend here, as is his want, decided to impress the female passenger next to him on the plane over. Give's it the usual chat, "You travelling on business or on holiday?", "Where you from?", Thought I recognised the accent", "How long you staying?" and then the best bit comes right at the end when he asks her what she does. "Actually I'm a curator for the Guggenheim museum in Venice and I'm on my way to pick up piece of art by the Latvian artist Laartu" she replies.

To which fannybaws here goes, "Oh really, I'm a bit of art fan myself but mainly the classical stuff, I don't know a lot but ah know what ah like."

"No way" said Dominic. "I don't know a lot but ah know what ah like. Classic."

"To this she goes "Fantastic, who is your favourite artist?" So here it comes, the piece de fucking resistance "My favourite artist is Mistral, though mainly the early period" comes the reply.

"Mistral?" she goes, "Isn't that the wind?"

"So Gus goes, "No, no. Ah know where you're coming from but this guy was a real classical painter, like. They did a TV programme about him when ah was younger. It was a dramaticisation of his life, and he was played by that American boy that did the time for a wee bit of Charlie, as they say. What the fu... what was his name again? Peach, no Keach, Stacey Keach. He was such a good actor cos he always got his lines straight"

"So I'm sitting there thinking he's got this wrong," says Kenny. "I couldn't fucking place it but then it clicked. He's thinking of "Mistrals Daughter", a mini series from the 80's based on somebody like Matisse or some other French painter. I try to point this out but he's not having it. Talk about when you're in a hole stop digging, so he goes on trying to tell this American bird he's always admired Mistral and his fucking early period but can never seem to find any of his works in the museums he's visited."

"When the fuck were you last in a museum?" said Dominic

"Last year in Moscow for the Russia game, you cheeky bastard"

"What? To use the Gents for free?"

"And what if ah was? 30p for a shite in one o they tardis things in the street. Get that tae fuck man."

"A point well put, young Gus." Kenny looked down the bar just in time to see Andy Muir's had bobbing up and down around the bar. "Aye, aye, here's our journo pal from Vienna. Must still be doing research on the wonders of the Tartan Army. You should have a word with him Dominic, he might be able to plug the comic."

"Not a bad idea Kenny. Who does he write for?"

"He's freelance. Says he's going to try and get a piece in the New Yorker or Harpers and Queen, an upmarket look at down market guys."

"Hey, there's nothing downmarket about me ya tube. It's only top quality burds that are after me, like" said Gus

"Just like the one on the plane I suppose" said Kenny.

At this Andy Muir approached, shaking himself free from the scrum at the bar.

"All right chaps, who wants a drink? Expenses are still looking good, so the milky bars are on me."

"No problem Andy," said Gus "Good to see you again, especially when you're buyin. Come on I'll gie you a hand at the bar, my good man. Lagers all round or whatever the local pish is?" Getting a quick nod from the remaining two Andy and Gus headed off to the bar of Paddy Whelan's.

"That bloke's a journo?" asked Dominic.

"Says he is," said Kenny "Why do you ask?".

"It's just that all the ones I've met have been tighter than a duck's arse. The idea of them spending any more of their expenses than they have to is fucking odd. If he's spending it on fans that's even more incredible".

"It's funny you should say that as a couple of things don't quite add up about him. He hasn't got a card with his contact details and has always stayed clear of the tartan hack pack despite me offering to introduce him to the ones I know. Still, he's no doing anyone any harm but something's no quite right. Maybe it's just because he's a posh Scot" Kenny finished his lager.

"A posh Scot!" Dominic exploded. "Those wanks get right on my nerves. Ok, I'll catch you later, I'm going to see if anybody else in this bar doesn't want a fanzine". Dominic walked off to the far end of the bar to another table of fans just as Gus and Andy came back with the drinks.

"What happened to him?" said Gus. "John Menzies gie him a call for another ten copies?"

"He's just away to try and punt some more copies. He'll be back in a minute," Kenny replied. The sound system was now pumping out "Firestarter" by the Prodigy and the place was definitely warming up.

Gus had a big smile on his face. "Hear that Kenny? Special request from yours truly."

"Very fucking funny," said Kenny who proceeded to explain to Andy what had happened earlier on.

"Ok chaps, now we've broken the ice with the locals, what's the plan for tonight?" asked Andy.

"A bit quieter than the last time Andy. Got the father-in-law with me" said Kenny.

"Where is he now?" said Andy

"He's, eh, looking into a possible business opportunity" came an unconvincing answer from Kenny, who had managed to forget all about Harold and his Baltic enterprises.

"Your father-in-law a big Scotland fan?" asked Andy.

79

"No, he hates football. More of a golfer actually. It's the usual Scottish story in that you could be a bit of a nutter, play off scratch and everybody would think you were slightly misunderstood. As it happens, my father-in-law is a crazed lunatic and does play off scratch but I wouldn't advise you to call him misunderstood, should you be unfortunate enough to meet him"

"Calm down Kenny," said Gus "Walls have ears." The alcohol was having more of an effect on Kenny than Gus, who knew it wasn't wise to mouth off about Harold on an away trip.

"Fair point," said Kenny.

Kenny looked around Paddy Whelan's trying to put any thoughts of Harold MacMillan out of his head. Harold had spoken to him briefly at the airport when they arrived in Riga. He'd told Kenny he'd speak to him at more length in Tallinn. After that he had disappeared into a long black Mercedes which was waiting for him outside the terminal building and sped off into the night. Kenny had not heard from him since and presumed he would be making his own way to Estonia. Turning his mind back to the present, he looked around him. The bar was pretty mobbed with Scots and he could see a couple of guys already making inroads with the local females.

"Anything caught your eye?" he asked Andy.

"Well, I was at the Independence Monument earlier on today watching the changing of the guard and did you know those two large buildings further along the river were actually Zeppelin hangars but are now cheese and meat markets" said Andy.

Gus snorted, "Funnily enough ah don't really make much of an effort to get to cheese markets when ah'm on tour," he said.

"Aye but you've been to enough meat markets" said Kenny, a grin on his face.

"Shut it you!"

"That kind of sight wasn't exactly what I was talking about Andy" said Kenny.

"No?"

"Fuck's sake Andy man, get a grip," Gus went on "He's talkin about Hugh McIlvanney! Talent. Burds. And as it happens in this place ah'm right in ma element, like. And ah can see a vision of loveliness even as ah speak."

"Tell me it's not that big dark headed thing sitting at the bar. Talk about quantity not quality." said Kenny.

"Hey, she's a love machine pal" replied Gus in a gleeful tone.

"Love machine? It looks like she's just come out of one of those Zeppelin hangars Andy was talking about"

"Leave it to me, my man," said Gus getting up from the table and running his hands through his hair transplant, trying to get it under control. The music now playing was Fast Love by George Michael. "You'd better get a move on wee man, now they're playing your tune," said Kenny.

"What if she doesn't speak English?" asked Andy astonished at what he was seeing.

"It doesn't matter I'm fluent in the language of love, and romance is my middle name. Angus Romance McSween. Don't wait up."

Andy watched amazed as Gus casually strolled up to a woman who was a foot taller than him and at least twice his weight. He had listened intently to Kenny's tale of the hat burning. He was slightly concerned about the local youth's attitude and considered what he might have to do if it turned nasty. Was he going to have to protect someone he was trying to kill?

"How does he do it?" he asked Kenny.

"It's a percentage game. Ask enough Robbie Fowlers and one of them is bound to say yes. You should get all the gory details off him tomorrow. You might get an article for Penthouse out of it, "My Night of Passion with Liga from Riga" or "My Latvian Lover Loved Me and Left". Maybe that's got too many L's. Anyway, you're the journalist, I am sure you can come up with something a bit snappier"

"Yes, if you say so. Where are you staying in Riga?" asked Andy, trying to get the conversation back on semi normal lines.

"We're staying at a half-renovated hotel called the Victoria or Victorija. The renovated half is very nice but unfortunately they have still to work their way down to ours on the first floor. The plumbing is bad as we don't have an en-suite so you've got to walk down the corridor for a pee and as for the electrics, don't get me started."

At this Andy's ears pricked up. "Is it the same the UK where if you're on the first floor your room number begins with a one? I had heard say there was going to be some old baboushka type on each floor who would only present you with your room key after you had shown your passport."

"No, it's no that bad. There's a reception but when I've asked for the key they've just ended up giving it to you without asking for ID. Where are you staying, by the way?" replied Kenny.

"Eh, the SAS Radisson across the river." said Atholl

"Nice one. Those expenses must just be rolling in to cover you for that. Is that not where the squad is staying?"

"Yes, I believe so" confirmed Andy. That explained why those small thin chaps with Scotland tracksuits in the Radisson coffee shop had taken exception to him asking them if they supported the team at every match. They were the team.

He had to think quickly to try and get Kenny's room number. "Funnily enough I asked for a room on the first floor at my hotel 18 is my lucky number you see so I was hoping that they could see their way to giving me it but everything goes from 100 up. What number have you got in the Victorija?"

"Close but no cigar. We're in room 11."

"Excellent" thought Andy. Just as he'd worked out where this left him, a large presence loomed over the table. The hat burning youth from earlier on had finally drunk enough to tip him over the edge and into confrontational mood.

"You" he said pointing an unsteady finger at Kenny. "You Scottish fucking Scottish homo" At this he took a step forward and Andy managed to stick his leg out in time to trip up the guy. The Latvian put his arms out to stop his fall but Andy managed to grab one arm and pull him down whilst trying to make it look like he was helping him. Blood spurted across the table as the youth's nose hit the edge. "Oops, somebody had one beer too many" said Andy as the bar staff came over to sort out the mess. The Latvian was dragged to his feet whilst a barman clutched a towel across his face to try and stem the blood flow. The manager asked if everyone was ok. When he received a favourable response he removed a couple of glasses and cleaned up the table.

"Shall we move?" suggested Andy.

"Anything you say" said Kenny who was a bit stunned by what he had just witnessed.

"Actually, I'm sorry but maybe I had better leave. I am going to cruise a few more bars and try and get some more background stuff for the comic. Will probably see you at the game tomorrow" said Andy who didn't really want to draw anymore attention to himself.

"Aye, no problem, Andy. We'll be in this bar or around here somewhere. The stadium's no that far out so we'll probably just jump in a taxi. Catch you later" Kenny was relieved he'd gone. There was something not right about Andy Muir but he just couldn't put his finger on it.

Atholl left Paddy Whelan's and turned right down Grecinieku Street. He had seen a taxi rank at the bottom of the street and wanted to move quickly to get the job done. He felt on a bit of a high after the scene in the bar, the old skills not completely forgotten. Atholl walked on down the street which was extremely dark. It appeared only twenty five percent of the streetlights were actually functioning. It was so dark he walked into a couple of elderly guys in kilts who were deep in negotiation with a couple of hookers. He apologised but as he was walking on heard one of the men remark, "Come on Doll. Why don't Jock and I take you and your pal for a wee drink and get to know each other better?" Life in the old dog yet thought Atholl. He could see the cab rank at the end of the street so picked up his pace. The door of the first cab in the rank was slightly ajar and he pulled it open and jumped in saying "Hotel Victorija, please".

*****

Kenny had had enough. It had been half an hour since Andy left and there was only so much shite you could talk about the Scotland team. The earlier incident was preying on his mind as well. The team was picking itself these days and they were hoping to build on the result in Vienna, even with Darren Jackson in the squad. A couple of guys suggested a brothel which featured in the alternative Riga guidebook but having seen a guy's arse smoking a cigar earlier on Kenny knew he had seen it all.

Some wee squat barrel of a guy had passed out in what could loosely be termed Paddy Whelan's beer garden. After the Tadger Currie incident Kenny had made sure the guy was alive but he just wanted a kip by the sound of his mutterings so Kenny left him face down on a picnic table contraption. It was then that some comedian had lifted his kilt and put a Castella sized cigar between the cheeks of his arse. He had lit the cigar and then used the guys bum cheeks like a bellows to get a light going. It was all going really well and a crowd had developed to see the arse smoke a cigar. Sadly, all had not ended well when the cigar fell out of his crack and set light to his anal hair. A kindly volunteer had thrown the remnants of his pint over the inferno before it got out of hand and set fire to his kilt but sleeping beauty was less than impressed when he pointedly remarked, "Just trying to get a wee kip and some cunt sets fire tae ma pubes. It's not on. It's just not on."

"Aw right, am for the off," said Kenny.

"Ye taking Casanova wi ye?" asked Dominic who had returned on Andy's departure.

Kenny turned and looked up the bar to see Gus and his new girlfriend snogging the face off each other whilst sitting at the bar.

"Good God. Is he still at it? I spoke to him in the Gents and he said he's going back to her place. The worrying thing is she has said she's up for anything and if any of you boys want a shot, please feel free."

"You're kidding? You'd need to roll her in flour to find the wet spot" said Dominic.

"Sadly, I am not joking. I think he's spread the word around and they've found another couple of desperadoes for their posse. I'm off to my kip and to prepare myself for tomorrow."

"What you've got a big day ahead?" asked Dominic.

"No to prepare myself for his tales of sexual depravity. I'm away to see if he can take his tongue out of her mouth for long enough to say cheerio."

After he left Paddy Whelan's, Kenny wandered down Avenue Kaka towards the Victorija. He'd thought about getting a taxi but was desperate for a slash once the cold night air hit him so he'd gone up a close to relieve himself. On coming out of the alley he'd nearly bumped into a group of Shetlanders he knew and considered it a close escape. Those guys were truly mental once they got on the bevvy. He remembered the story of one of them who'd shagged his hotel cleaner for forty dollars the year before in Moscow. Unreal. Riga had to be one of the most poorly lit cities he'd ever been to. The smell of cheap diesel filled his nostrils as he kept walking at a steady pace. He tripped a couple of times on broken paving slabs. Anyone watching this must think I'm totally blootered he thought. He wondered if a taxi would have been a better option but the streets were as quiet as they were dark. Bizarrely, as he walked past a taxi, which had stopped at the traffic lights, he thought he saw Andy Muir sitting in the back. It had taken him a few seconds to accustom his eyes to the gloom but by that time the lights had changed and the taxi was gone. Funny thing was, it was heading back into town. Andy said he was going to cruise a few more bars but didn't say anything about going out of the city centre. Maybe he'd been tipped off about somewhere out of town and it was closed.

Kenny was just walking up to the hotel when a taxi pulled up outside. The passengers were two elderly gentlemen in kilts plus two twenty something bottle blondes with tight red tops, black mini skirts and those spangly tights favoured by Eastern European hookers. As one of the men turned round he saw Kenny and shouted out "Kenny bloody Bradley! How you doin?"

"Not nearly as well as you Jock Paisley, you ugly old git." Jock Paisley was another old time pal of Kenny's. Jock went way back to the nightmare trip that was Brussels in 1962 when the greatest Scotland team never to play in a World Cup had blown a play off with Czechoslovakia. He'd been a regular through the good times and the bad times, including Argentina. Kenny never knew where he got the stamina from and sometimes wondered if this would be him in 30 years.

"Hey son, come on. They're practically givin it away and at these prices it would be rude not to. I need a word actually. Well more than a word. Harry here has got first rights on our room. Is there any chance you could give me your room for an hour. Go to the bar, have a nightcap and put it on our tab. I'll come and have a drink with you when I'm done. What do you say?"

"Jock, come on. I just want my kip but...well as it's you. It's room 11. I'll go and get the key. It's a twin room so take the bed closest to the window as that's Gus'. He won't be using it tonight, that's for certain. Come on, I'll get the key."

The receptionist gave Kenny a funny look when he asked for the key but handed it over. Kenny passed it to Jock saying "Ok, one hour. The meter's running and I'll see you in the bar."

Kenny went up to the hotel bar on the first floor. Whoever took the photos of these places for hotel brochures must be a genius with a camera, he thought. What had appeared in the promotional pamphlet as a wide homely bar with a large selection of drinks now looked like something you would see in the bar of a Highland caravan park. The furnishings looked like they'd been liberated from a Victorian sauna. The solitary poster of Riga featured the Zeppelin hangars reminding Kenny of Gus and his night of passion ahead. I knew he liked team sports, thought Kenny, but that was going too far.

Continuing to scan round the bar, he saw one lager pump, three bottles of vodka and one dodgy Latvian whisky. The night porter looked extremely hacked off at having to serve Kenny a beer so Kenny consoled himself with the thought that this boy had seen nothing yet. It was two am but the night was young for most of the Tartan Army. He would he would be getting more, not less, custom as the night wore on and the troops drifted back.

Kenny had taken a couple of sips of the lager he'd ordered and was thinking more about Jock Paisley and the remarkable stamina of the guy. All of a sudden there was a flickering of the lights in the bar followed by a loud scream. The night porter stuck his head round the door of his restroom. He looked enquiringly at Kenny, clearly waiting for a response that would mean he could go back to sleep and pretend nothing was wrong.

"Sorry pal, but I think I just heard someone scream," said Kenny in apologetic tone. Suddenly footsteps came crashing down the staircase and Kenny saw a blur of gold, black and red flash past the door to the bar. He thought it might be one of the girls who had been with Jock and his mate but which one? His room was closer to reception than Jock's which was on the fourth floor so it must be Jock's girl who was doing a runner. But why?

Kenny ran up the stairs to the first floor and looked down the corridor to his room. The prone figure of Jock Paisley lay half in and half out of the room. There was a smell of burnt flesh, which grew stronger the closer he got to Jock. He reached down but he could see it was too late.

The night porter had finally appeared and looked down at Jock then up at Kenny. "Ambulance?" he asked.

"Nope, I don't know what Latvian is for undertaker but that's what you're going to need. So no, no ambulance"

*****

87

Atholl sat in the bar of the SAS Radisson Riga drinking a brandy. It had turned a bit nippy out so he felt in need of warmth and comfort. Might even run an eye over the hookers later, he thought. After all, he was on expenses. He laughed at his own joke. Those guys were two of thickest individuals he had ever met. All you had to do was tell them you were from a paper or a mag and they would just roll over for you. He'd tried it on another couple of fans with exactly the same results. Outstanding. He'd had no difficulty getting access to room 11 in the Victorija from the receptionist who had hardly taken her eyes from a Latvian soap on TV whilst she had given him the key. He had known what he wanted to do as soon as Kenny Bradley mentioned poor electrics in the hotel. He'd unscrewed the main light switch in room 11. To make matters better it was a double switch, one switch for the bathroom and one switch for the bedroom. He then connected the live wires to the switch itself. He'd held the wire in place with a small piece of matchstick. Once the light was switched on, the switch itself would become live but the wire would come free after the small bit of wood had been burnt off and it would look like genuinely loose faulty wiring. A small bit of accelerant on the switch added to the overall effect.

It had worked once before in Northern Ireland when an informant had been getting a bit mouthy and asking for more money than he was worth. No prizes for originality, but never mind. He hadn't wanted to stay on in Latvia but thought it might look a bit odd if he disappeared. The thought of another night in Riga did little for him but there were certain comforts available to make life a little more bearable. Hell, he might even go to the game. He was Scottish after all. Ha ha, Christ two jokes in one night. He was on fire and speaking of hot, who was this vision approaching. "Is there anything I can get for you, Sir?" she asked in heavily accented English.

"Yes, I dare say there is," replied Atholl reaching for his room key

*****

Atholl had felt he was losing control for the first time in his life. The following morning he had gone for walk round Riga. It was matchday and he was planning to stay away from the main drag, especially Paddy Whelan's pub where he expected most of the fans to be gathering. He couldn't go back to the Victorija hotel in case he was recognised but he needed to get verification on whether or not his job was done.

He was walking across the main bridge over the Daugava into the old town when he recognised a Scotland fan coming towards him. He couldn't be sure but he thought it was someone he might have seen the previous night with Kenny and Gus. The guy seemed to be doing his best to ignore him but he had to get confirmation he had been successful in removing Kenny Bradley.

"Hello" he said cheerily as the chap approached. "It's Dominic isn't it?"

"Aye, hello, how ye doin?" came an unenthusiastic reply.

"Out getting some air before the game. Trying to blow the cobwebs away. You?" replied Atholl.

"I'm just going to see Frances Fairweather at the team hotel," said Dominic

"Oh yes. Who's he?"

"It's not a he. She's a she." said Dominic in an exasperated tone. "She runs the supporters club, I've got a bit of bad news for her about a fan."

Atholl thought at last, he's gone. "Nothing serious I trust?" said Atholl.

"No, it is serious all right. Fucken terminal to be honest. One of the fans was killed last night in an accident in the hotel. Bit of faulty wiring on a light switch and he was electrocuted. No that big a shock but given his age it was enough to prove fatal. Or so they think. I'm no expert" came the reply from Dominic.

"What do you mean given his age?" demanded Atholl. This didn't sound like what he was expecting to hear.

"It was an old guy called Jock Paisley. He was in his 60's, was a heavy smoker, had a wee heart attack last year so was susceptible to something pushing him over the edge. Worst thing was, it wasnae even his room. He'd borrowed the room key off Kenny as he had a hooker wi' him. Kenny and Gus are pretty shook up."

"You are telling me Kenny Bradley is still alive?" said Atholl in a quiet voice.

"Aye and it's thanks to amazing Grace" replied Dominic.

"What are you talking about?" said Atholl, the sudden understanding of another failed mission coming down hard.

"Well, that was the name of the hooker Jock had met Grace. If it hadn't been for her it would have been Kenny that walked in and turned the light on. I've got to crack on as we tried to phone Frances but I think she's in a security meeting so she needs to be told in person. She might be able to get in touch with his family back home. Catch you later if you're still around."

The bridge was broad and open to the elements. As a chill wind blew down the Daugava River Atholl realised he had to get a grip. Losing control at this stage would not help him or the McClackit clan. He had to identify where he had gone wrong and clarify his new objective. He started walking towards the old town. As he crossed the road at the end of the bridge he saw a coffee house, He went in and ordered a brandy and an espresso. Sitting at the window gazing out at the river he began to put together his earlier strategies and see where they had failed him. One of his strengths in Northern Ireland was that he had never become overly confident. That was helped to a large extent by the fact the amount of time he spent in the Six Counties was minimal. He often wondered if the IRA and UDA would have been amused to find he spent most of his time in the Republic posing as a gay antique dealer, only nipping across the border as required. He reviewed what he had attempted to do in Vienna and Riga, realising the flaw in both cases. Lack of control at the point of completion. The deed had not been done by his own hands but if that was what it took then so be it. It had been a few years since he'd got his hands dirty at the sharp end of the business but needs must.

*****

90

The train had been moving for about four hours after leaving Riga station. Atholl sat back on the carriage seat and looked out at the bleak Latvian countryside. After the brandy and coffee earlier on, he'd returned to his hotel managing to avoid any more Scotland fans. He'd checked out and made enquiries as to how one might get to Tallinn. The air prices were prohibitive, even on company expenses, but the train sounded a more reasonable method of travel despite it taking seven hours. He'd thought a quick escape from Riga might be in his best interests in case the hotel receptionist at the Victorija gave a description of him to the police. He'd managed to get a seat on the lunchtime train and was surprised how quiet it was, even though it was a Saturday.

The view from the windows was unchanging. A low flat plain interspersed with forests dominated the landscape as far as the eye could see. There was no livestock in the fields. The whole vista denuded of life. At points the grey sky appeared to merge with the fields offering a panoramic scene of grey. He'd dozed off it was so boring only to be shaken awake by a border guard demanding to see his passport. He was obviously back on good form as he'd bent the guard's wrist backwards before he realised he wasn't being attacked. The guard was a spotty teenager whose shock at such treatment left him too scared to go and complain to a senior officer.

Once his passport was stamped, the guard using his other hand to complete the job, Atholl tried to calm down with some breathing exercises his ex-wife had taught him. They were going well until he remembered they were part of her warm up exercises for tantric sex. As he was faced with another three hours on the train Atholl stopped the breathing exercises. He didn't think it was pragmatic to spend a railway journey in a foreign country with an erection that might last the best part of ninety minutes.

To take his mind off all matters of a sexual nature he thought about the Scotland fans he had met so far on his travels. He was part of them but they appeared to come from another Scotland to the one he knew but then again, how well did he know Scotland? His view of the country was dominated by family and clan gatherings, summer balls on the big estates, loch side barbecues with freshly caught fish and regimental dances. All this, plus the odd shooting weekend in autumn, hardly exposed him to the country and its people as a whole. To most of the fans he met, the idea of barbecued meat revolved around a well-done kebab once the pubs had closed.

His thoughts moved on to his father and Castle McClackit. He had no real attachment to the place but found it hard to think of actually letting it go. No doubt the few remaining McClackits would emerge from under their stones in Virginia and Tasmania to protest against anything he did. Distant cousin Lionel in Richmond, Virginia would be the biggest problem given his complete devotion to the clan and all things McClackit. Atholl realised how far from grace the clan had fallen when its biggest supporter was a southern bigot chiropodist who believed George Washington, Henry Ford, Marilyn Monroe and Elvis Presley were all clan McClackit descendants.

Thinking about it in these terms, Atholl had no desire to live in Scotland and be hounded by these distant clan members. The quicker he got rid of the castle once his father pegged it, the better. This thought reminded him to contact an Aberdeen estate agent with regards to getting it valued. He would make sure Potter and the other estate workers were looked after but that would be it. Protecting the family name by killing Bradley would be one thing, living in Scotland would be another.

The train pulled into Tallinn station at 7pm. Atholl walked out of the station and jumped in a cab. He suddenly realised he didn't have a clue where he wanted to go. So much for planning ahead he thought. Clearly he'd got too confident, believing he would complete the job in Riga.

"Hotel?" asked the taxi driver.

"You know hotel?" asked Atholl

"Hotel Viru, good hotel" came the reply.

"Hotel Viru it is then" said Atholl and the taxi drove off in the gathering gloom.

CHAPTER 8

"Fuck's sake man, more fuckin trees. This journey is never endin and the scenery is complete shite, like." Gus burped.

"The brochure never said it would be like this, like. Pass me another lager Dominic. It's only bevvy that's goin to get me through this. Hey, did ye see the match programme the other night? The printing was rotten man, it was semi fuckin legible."

"Should be all right for you Gus" said Dominic

"How's that then?"

"You're semi fuckin literate," said Dominic passing a can of lager to the seat in front of him.

"Well done smart arse! You been sittin there thinkin these side splitters all the way up from Riga?" came a less than impressed reply.

Gus, Kenny and Dominic were sitting at the window on a 52-seater coach travelling up to Tallinn from the Estonian-Latvian border. They had been on the bus for six hours but that included a three-hour stop at the border where a supposed computer malfunction had halted their journey.

"Ah told ye that guy Drew should have offered the border guard bastard a bribe" said Gus after he'd opened the can of lager and taken a slug.

"I think it was the offer of a bribe that caused the problem" replied Kenny.

"Naw, it wisnae. It was the size of the bribe. Ye've got to think like these Baltic types think. If you bale up in a 52-seater and only offer a bribe suitable for a four door saloon Tatu the border guard is goin to think we're taking the piss. And he'd be right. If ah was runnin this bus we'd be sittin in the Hell Hunt having a pint of Guinness and a shepherd's pie"

"If you'd been running this bus we'd still be in Riga," said Dominic. "Given the fact you had to be physically carried onto the bus you were so out of it. What the fuck could you have organised?"

"Alright, smart bastard, ah take yer point" said Gus. "Ah was drinkin to Jock Paisley, like. That Jagermeister's fuckin rocket fuel by the way. And to think ah only had the three."

"Aye, three pints" was the reply from Dominic. "You've got a point about this scenery though man. What a dull country this is. Flat bit of barren land then trees, another flat bit of land then more fucking trees, God knows what it is like in the depths of winter. Mind you if it looks dull outside, the view of the inside of this bus is positively frightening. Maybe they were calling for reinforcements at the border and that's what the hold up was."

They were on the bus courtesy of a conversation in the Hotel Victorija Kenny had held with another Scotland fan called Drew who came from a mining village just outside Nottingham. The guy had told him there was a group of sixteen from his village who had booked up. They were all miners from Fife who had moved down after the last pits closed in Scotland. The bus that picked them up at the airport in Riga was a fifty-two seater when they had been expecting a mini bus. He had asked the driver if it was the same bus that would take them to Tallinn and he had said yes. Drew told Kenny he didn't see any problem in them hopping on board as the trip was paid for and all they would have to do is give the driver a few bob to keep him happy. As they were all staying in the same hotel this had been the dream ticket, until Gus, on the back of his Jagermeister frenzy, had invited every Scotland fan in the hotel on the bus trip north to Tallinn.

Their party of sixteen plus Kenny, Gus and Dominic had now swelled to approximately 46. Drew the bus organiser had taken it remarkably well and commented, "The more the merrier, plus it will be less for you boys to chip in to keep the driver sweet"

A carry out of ten cases of lager, ten bottles of vodka and a box of Hooch for the women had been loaded on board and they were off. When he finally awoke, Gus had perked up considerably when he discovered there were women on board.

The fact there were only three and they were all with boyfriends hardly registered.

"Had many a good time with burds on busses down to Blackpool and back on the September weekend. Oh yes, ah'm a maestro at the mobile shaggin like. Ah was always one to enjoy a good bus ride if you get my drift. Even better on the trains mind. Well, it used to be. Since they've introduced those airplane type carriages it's no sae good. When you're on a train it's no got quite the same cachet to ask a burd if she'd like to join the five feet high club."

"Did you just use the word cachet?" asked an incredulous Dominic Fraser.

"Aye ah did fannybaws. Think you're the only Guardian reading twat with an education on this bus? Get tae fuck. As ah was saying those six seater carriages with the sliding doors were the best, like. Let the train take the strain indeed. Ah remember that time we got the overnight train to Cardiff in 1979, eh Kenny? Ah met this runaway from an orphanage in Northern Ireland. Ah wis only 17 at the time, she must have been 16 going on 46. She was up for anythin, like. After half an hour o' my silver tongue, she had her silver tongue wrapped round a certain part o' my anatomy and ah'm no talking about ma big toe. Those older guys we were wi were spewin as they thought they should have had first go like, age giving them seniority, but she wasnae interested in them. She wanted the youth squad, no the coaching staff wi old heads on old shoulders."

"So you're telling me that within half an hour of meeting this girl, she'd blown you?" said an astonished Dominic.

"Aye, as God or Kenny Bradley is my witness."

"Talk about sad but true!" Kenny said "What made it worse was just before she got off in Birmingham she told me she'd really fancied me but as I hadn't made a move, she'd taken second best. I thought the day couldn't get any worse then we got gubbed 3-0 by a fuckin John Toshack hat-trick. Got back to Dumfries at 5 am on the Sunday morning. A complete nightmare! No sleep for two nights and young Lochinvar here telling everybody he met he was in love with a runaway who had runaway with his heart. She'd given him her phone number you see and he tried it when he got back. You know who answered it?

"No, go on?"

"The office receptionist at Belfast Dogs Home."

"Ha fucking ha. You two are well suited, like. Losers in love the pair of you. The last time either of you cunts had a ride there was a Labour government in power and Abba were number 1. Where the fuck are we now? Is he stoppin? Wait a minute, is that the sea?" said Gus in an excited tone.

The driver had pulled over for what was described by Drew as a quick piss stop. The bus emptied quickly but not nearly as quickly as the bladders that had been storing cheap Latvian lager for the past hour. Above the smell of piss, Kenny could smell the sea and decided to have a look. After walking through a small wooded area found himself on a long, desolate beach. A biting wind blew sand in his face and he was about to turn back when he saw Gus sitting on the sand, taking off his socks and shoes.

"Are you about to do what I think you are?"

"Too right man. Cannae come to the beach and no have a paddle, like" replied Gus.

He's off his fucking head thought Kenny as it is baltic by the Baltic. He'd heard somewhere about the Baltic Riviera and presumed it was a wind up but this was a beautiful stretch of coast. He was thinking of joining Gus for a laugh but then Drew shouted at them from the edge of the trees.

"Come on, we've wasted enough time at that fucking border if we're to get there before the pubs shut. For fuck's sake don't go for a paddle Gus, we're out o here."

"Logic like that ye cannae argue wi" Gus replied. "Pubs closing versus freezin my nuts off in the Baltic is a no brainer. Come on you, get back on the bus pronto."

Kenny spent the rest of the journey trying to sleep. It had been a nightmare bus journey and he couldn't wait to get to his bed. He'd been in Tallinn once before in

1994. He'd missed the Scotland game there in 1993 to go to Portugal instead. Talk about making a wrong choice. They'd been totally gubbed 5-0 in Lisbon. The game had often been referred to by some as the night a team died. Then Scotland had played in Tallinn in May and apparently it had been the trip of a lifetime. A town totally unused to westerners, cheap bevvy, loads of gorgeous women, a truly magical place with a Disneyesque old town. He'd even heard they didn't have sellotape. Shop-girls wrapped all the purchases in brown paper and tied them up with string. The only plus was that Gus had missed it as well. They had, however made a trip in 1994. Estonia were playing Croatia on the Sunday before Finland v Scotland on the Wednesday. They'd got the ferry over from Helsinki. Kenny never realised the two places were so close. They booked into the Hotel Viru, a complete monstrosity of a hotel which had been built by the Russians as their Intourist show hotel.

It had been a good game in a dilapidated stadium. Croatia had had several superstars playing for them and the fans had been granted free licence to roam everywhere. After the match somebody had complained that Prosinecki of Real Madrid was an ignorant bastard as he'd been sitting picking his nose as fans were wandering through the dressing room post match. The day was also memorable for Gus discovering cans of Estonian gin and bitter lemon. He had thought it would be like the old-fashioned lager and lime he got when he was a kid, approximately 0.2%. He hadn't realised it was the real deal with approximately four nips of gin a can.

After Gus had demolished three of the said cans in the second half, he'd disappeared until the following morning when he had pitched up at the Viru to collect his gear. He had briefly mentioned a sauna, another two Scots guys, changing lots of money at 3am, three hookers, something about paying for it but not getting it and waking up fully clothed in the Hotel Suzi, five miles out of town. Kenny knew the full story would come out eventually and looked forward to that day with great interest funnily enough.

At the time he'd thought Tallinn was akin to a frontier town in the Wild West but after the events of Riga, it would be like an eventide rest home. As he thought back, Jock Paisley's death still gnawed away at him. Hopefully, they'd be able to keep it out of the newspapers back home that he was with a hooker when it happened. Poor lassie. Knowing Jock, Kenny realised he wouldn't have paid until the services had been rendered, so there may well have been a financial dimension to her state of distress.

He'd been pretty surprised at how quickly the police had appeared then disappeared. They wrote it off straight away as dodgy electrics. They were confused as to why Jock was going into Kenny's room but they accepted his explanation with minimal fuss and had zoomed off as soon as.

The guy from the British Embassy was a different matter. The prick wouldn't have known a football if it had bounced off his head. When he looked at Jock Paisley he must just have seen pile of paperwork, no doubt to be completed in triplicate. To him they weren't British citizens. They were a temporary problem to be endured for as short a time as possible. If we could lose just a couple of passports, it would be a hindrance but no more than expected. If we decided not to decimate the city, even better. The repatriation of a body was another matter and it had got him out of his kip at 2 am on a Saturday morning. He was not a happy camper. Fortunately for Kenny, he had been able to summon an undertaker and get the body removed pretty quickly. Kenny wasn't sure if this was going down as "death by suspicious circumstances" or some such nonsense but death was fucking death so they had better get on with it.

Kenny gave a statement to the diplomat containing the best of his knowledge of what had happened but was inclined to leave the rest to Harry, Jock's pal who had been with the other hooker. It had not been a pleasant sight going up to Jock and Harry's room earlier on. The other old boy must have been keen to get on with it as he had left the door ajar. Kenny pushed it open and was greeted with the sight of a naked pneumatic Latvian blonde bouncing up and down on the face of a pensioner from Leith. From the contents of the glass on the bedside table at least he'd had the good grace to take his falsers out. No chance of pubes in the teeth there then.

To make matters worse, when the girl had eventually climbed off, her thighs had caused a vacuum in the old boy's ears and he couldn't hear a word until Kenny had encouraged him to swallow a couple of times. Kenny couldn't resist the temptation of giving him the glass of water to help him rinse his mouth out. The teeth went back in the mouth from the glass, but not quite in the manner Harry had hoped for, much to Kenny's amusement. He realised he had better screw the nut otherwise there would be a second corpse that night through choking on falsers.

When Harry got his teeth in the right way he was less than amused with Kenny and it had nothing to do with almost swallowing his false teeth.

"What the fuck are you up to ya daft bastard? I've only had twenty minutes worth and you come in here fucken ruinin it for me?"

"Harry calm down. I've got some bad news" said Kenny.

"Bad news? You're the fucken bad news. It's taken me twenty minutes to get this fucken hard and now you've fucken ruined it!"

Kenny now realised how distracted he had been by the hooker's activities and he looked down at an elderly but impressive hard on which did not exactly appear to be in the first stages of collapsing.

"It's Jock. I'm sorry Harry but there's been an accident and he's been electrocuted to death." Kenny was trying to find a bit of gravitas from somewhere. It was bad enough telling somebody their friend of forty years was dead but saying it to a pensioner who was standing in front of him, completely naked, with a stiffy you could balance a pint on was not exactly how he had imagined breaking the news.

"Get tae fuck! Are you on the wind up ya mad bastard?" shouted Harry.

"No, there's no wind up. Go down to room 11. There's a few people that want to speak to you. You'll need to formally identify the body."

Every part of Harry had crumpled at the seriousness in Kenny's tone. In this case every part really meant every part and Kenny had been relieved to be no longer staring down the barrel of an angry Scottish cock. What a bloody night.

The bus continued on through the Estonian plains. More flat, empty fields, stretching out to a bleak grey horizon. In the depths of such boredom, it was hard to remember there actually had been a game in Riga. A fantastic 2-0 victory in which a couple of remarkable things had happened. Firstly, Scotland scored from what looked like a rehearsed free kick routine. Usually, it looked as if they had practised the free kicks with some circus clowns the element of slapstick was so high. The second remarkable thing was Darren Jackson scoring. Not only had he scored, but it was a tasty goal involving a decent run into the area, before putting it past the keeper with no little skill.

The gaining of three points had been somewhat soured by the state of the stadium. The only Gents was a passable copy of a trench at the Somme with a two inch coating of lime. It would appear that the Latvian idea of toilet cleaning was to cover everything in lime, which left you gagging for fresh air once you were out. Some guys had just gone behind the stand and had been having a quiet pee when the Riga police had appeared. Immediately, they began fining people on the spot. No paperwork involved, so he guessed all the fines had gone straight in the back pocket. One guy had been done for 20 lats, which equated to 20 quid. Kenny had been done for a fiver himself but the biggest laugh had been Gus maintaining he had no money on him. The cries of "Ah'm fucking skint man. Your dodgy hookers have taken it off me. Go and arrest that tall blonde in Ronnie Whelan's. She's got all my dosh. Ah'm brassic lint. This is police harassment. 10 lats for a piss? How much would ye be wanting for a shite?" had echoed round the stadium just as the teams were coming out for the second half. Gus had missed Darren Jackson scoring the second goal but felt it was a small price to pay compared to, as he'd put it, "20 pound for a slash. Get that tae fuck man." Bizarrely, the floodlights were the strongest Kenny had ever seen for a stadium that size. It was like something from the film Close Encounters of the Third Kind if you looked directly at them.

They'd gone back up for the Under 21 game the next day. The stadium looked even worse in bright sunshine. They could see the covered terracing they had stood in the night before was a death trap with crumbling steps and poorly maintained crush barriers. On the opposite side of the ground, the windows of the "executive boxes" had all been put in. Some journos were sitting at a table in one box, staring out at the U21 match through an open space. "Wouldnae mind the Everest franchise for this place" had been Gus' only comment. He'd taken the news of Jock Paisley's death badly as he was a good friend from way back.

This had detracted from Gus' earlier activities on the night of Jock Paisley's death. Gus had left the pub with Greta, as the girl was called, and a couple of other guys. They had gone back to a room in some hotel and proceeded to have what Gus described as the best group sex experience of his life. Kenny thought it was probably the only group sex experience he'd had in his life but didn't like to point that out. The night had threatened to go horribly wrong at one stage when, in a fit of extremely unbridled passion, Gus had moved round to kiss the girl on the lips, and had instead kissed big Hughie's cock as he was putting it into Greta's mouth. A nasty scene had been avoided only by Greta insisting it was a night for love not war and they were all friends. Hughie had taken a few minutes to recover his composure and another five minutes to recover his erection. Gus had washed his mouth out with vanilla vodka, muttering about not knowing where people had been putting certain parts of their anatomy. For once Gus had taken his camera out with him and promised to show Kenny all the gory details once they got to Tallinn and he could get the film developed.

"Ah'm tellin ye man, the karma fucken sutra's got nothing on these photos. These are quantruple X never mind triple X. Yes, indeed, what a fuckin night, like. And to think people keep saying to me "Why are you wastin your time followin Scotland abroad?" How little they know man, how little they know. The third time ah came you couldnae have filled a teaspoon wi it, like but was ah complainin? Not on your nelly. One of the boys was keen on getting her to come up to Tallin wi us but she had to stay behind to wait for her boyfriend coming back. He's a long distance lorry driver. Bet he's never gone long distance wi his burd the way we did. Put a few miles on the cock that night did, that's for sure." This scenery just didn't get any better. More bloody trees. There was little or no traffic on the road. Another flat bit of land then more bloody trees. Any advertising hoarding was either boringly familiar, in that it was western, or it was totally unintelligible as it was written in Estonian. To be honest, there was more going on inside the bus than outside due to the characters on board. Kenny had had to ask one of the original Nottingham sixteen to sit down and stop singing. He was well into some song about his "rag a bag, shag a bag mother-in-law" when one of the girls had objected. Fair play to her but the miner had looked most put out. Gus had seen an opportunity and had gone up to offer her his support, saying there was no need for that kind of language from the guy and if he hadn't shut up he'd have gladly the decked the cunt for her. She thanked him kindly and then went back to the arms of her boyfriend who was doing a very good impression, at that point in time, of a man trying to make himself invisible. How long would this bloody bus take? The price of flights direct to Tallinn had been crazy but they were now looking cheap at half the price. 20/20 hindsight strikes again thought Kenny.

"Anybody see the bright lights of Tallinn?" asked Dominic.

"Don't worry, you'll smell this place before you see it," said Kenny.

"That bad?"

"No as bad as Riga really but once you're in the Baltics and the smell of dill and cheap diesel hits your nostrils, you cannae get rid of it until you've been back in

Scotland for three weeks. Ask sleeping beauty about dill, he just cannae get enough of the stuff"

Having had his advances spurned, Gus had crashed out. Dominic knew better than when to push it but did see the chance for a good photo opportunity. "You still got that banana from breakfast" he asked Kenny.

"Aye, it's around here somewhere. Don't tell me you're hungry?"

"No, have you seen the way the wee man is sleeping?" Dominic pointed across the aisle to where Gus was draped across a double seat fast asleep. His head was leaning slightly over the seat edge onto the aisle and his mouth was wide open. Dominic told Kenny to get the banana out, unzip his fly and then place the piece of fruit in his jeans so that it looked like his dick was hanging out. He then told him to stand with the piece of fruit dangling over Gus' mouth. Kenny achieved this with a little bit of difficulty as he didn't want to wake up Gus. Dominic had his camera ready and was waiting for the flash to come on. The rest of the bus had become aware of what was going on and Kenny was being encouraged to see how far he could put his fruit into Gus' mouth without the wee man waking up. He'd got it a good two inches in when the bus hit a pothole and Kenny's groin was thrust into Gus' face.

"Wharefaaak" came the muffled shout from Gus. The rest of the bus howled with laughter as Gus tried to remove Kenny from his face whilst not choking on the banana. He had bitten right through the yellow fruit with the shock of what happened. He finally managed to sit up and spat out two inches of banana.

"You bastart" he cried. "What the fuck did ye think ye were up tae? Ah've already had the misfortune to kiss one cock this trip and now ye're trying tae choke me tae death wi' a banana."

Kenny had hit his head on the luggage rack when the bus hit the pothole so was slightly dazed.

"What about my banana, wee man. I was going to have that for my tea! Did you get it?" he asked Dominic.

"I definitely got the point of entry so congratulations, Gus. With your eyes closed wee man it looked like you were in a euphoric state, just about to lovingly take Kenny's top banana in your warm and moist mouth. Ever ready to caress it to death with your strong darting tongue"

"Darting tongue, ah'll give you a darting boot up the arse Fraser. Ah knew a miserable fuck like you would be behind such a cruel stunt. Wait a minute! Who the fuck was that? Was that you Bradley or have we just driven past a pig farm? Talk about silent but violent."

Kenny Bradley owned up to dropping a fart that smelt like something created in the depths of Porton Down chemical weapon research centre. Even Dominic Fraser was affected by it.

"Jeezo Kenny. That's caught right at the back of ma throat. What you been eating to bring that on?"

"Nothing really, it's just this gassy Baltic lager that makes me fart."

"Gassy lager? Anything makes you drop minging farts so for fuck's sake don't blame it on the bevvy" erupted Gus.

By this stage the last remnants of the fart were affecting the others seated around them. Kenny normally managed to absolve himself from blame by farting then immediately blaming some innocent party close at hand. This time the amusement of seeing Gus choke on a banana had clearly thrown him.

At this point everyone on the bus perked up as they realised they were finally coming into Tallinn. The street lighting was not the best but it was like the Blackpool illuminations compared to Riga. The city looked very quiet with a little traffic but few people on the streets. Drew came up to Kenny and told him they would be dropping off centrally first and then the bus would take Kenny, Gus and Dominic out to the Hotel Sport.

"What's the plans for tonight Drew?" asked Gus.

"Well it's Tallinn so anything could happen but I guess we'll be looking for that bar owned by the Scots guy. Is it the Nimita?"

"What kind of name is that for a bar?" asked Gus. "Be better off with no name than that crap."

CHAPTER 9

Kenny and Gus signed in at the Hotel Sport. It was a bit out of Tallinn but it was on the seafront. It had been built for the Moscow Olympics in 1980 to accommodate the sailing teams. The small matter of Moscow being 19 hours away by train hadn't seemed to bother the IOC funnily enough, and for the Scotland fans it was a good hotel at a good price. One of the biggest plusses was that it was not the Viru. When Kenny signed in, there was a brief confab between the receptionists. One of them eventually approached him and said "There is message for you." Kenny took the piece of hotel stationery and realised the holiday was over. The writing said "Scandic Palace Hotel, 9am." He didn't understand but he recognised the handwriting. Michael "Harold" MacMillan, his father-in-law was in town and requested his attendance. He knew he had to face the music with regard to Harold sometime but about what he had no idea. He had thought of phoning Alison to find out if she knew what was going on but then realised the less she knew the better.

"Oh well, there goes the party" he said to Gus.

"What do you mean? We've only just arrived. The party starts now. As Russ Abbott used to say "I love a little party atmosphere" and this town is party town," said Gus who had brightened up considerably since the incident with the banana.

"Aye well, maybe for you but I'm off to my bed. I've been summonsed to a meeting with Harold tomorrow at 9 am so I had better have my wits about me. Anyway I'm shagged out after that bus trip. Who would think sitting on your arse all day could be so tiring? It must be like working for a finance industry union."

At the mention of Michael MacMillan's nickname, Gus had started on his Albert Steptoe impression shouting "Harolld!!! Harolld!!" at the top of his voice. He'd once been caught doing this by one of Harold's boys and was informed that if he didn't shut up, he would become a rag and bone man, as that was all that would be left of him, rags and bones. He had pulled up at the mention of the union and looked a little put out.

"There's no need for that. We work relentlessly for our members and no sacrifice is too great."

"What like leaving the pub on a Friday afternoon to do some work?"

"Ye're a bitter man Bradley. A very bitter man to bring up work at this stage in the holiday," said Gus, a peeved tone to his voice.

"Aye well, you go on and enjoy yourself wee man. I am going to try and work out what the main man wants. And please, no dodgy hookers at 3 am, eh?"

Kenny went up to the room with the bags. He was pleasantly surprised by the quality of the room and immediately did what any self respecting football fan does, checked to see what channel the porn was on. Things definitely seemed to be changing in Tallinn. Even on tonight's brief drive into the city centre, he got the impression a lot had changed in the two years since he was last here. Some wag on the bus had been going on about the Baltic tiger economy. He'd said the place was ripe for development and all the Baltic nations wanted to forge stronger links with the west. He even reckoned the three states, Estonia, Latvia and Lithuania would be in the EEC in the next decade. They might even try to get into NATO. Gus who had been sleeping up until the last bit of conversation blew the guys arguments to bits by asking if NATO was a nightclub in Tallinn.

Kenny unpacked and decided to have a shower before going to bed. The warm water acted as a reviver, so much so that he was tempted to jump in a taxi and head into town. He then put such thoughts to the back of his mind and tried to concentrate on what Harold could want with him. As he towelled himself off he gave up as he realised Sigmund Freud couldn't work out the goings on in Harold's mind, never mind a Glasgow cabbie. Looks like it will just have to wait until the morning, thought Kenny as he climbed between the sheets.

*****

As Kenny was getting into bed, across town Atholl had just woken up. Since he'd arrived on the Saturday his time had passed in a blur of prostitutes, alcohol and cocaine. After checking in, he had gone down to the bar in the Hotel Viru and two

108

hours later found himself in a "menage a trios" with two leggy Estonian blondes in the sauna of the Hotel Suzi. The hotel was set in a large Russian built housing estate on the outskirts of Tallinn and had been highly recommended by the barman in the Hotel Viru bar. The past couple of days had been a self indulgent sexual blur, but he had calmed things down and was getting up to go hunting not shagging. Atholl had realised with the bulk of the fans not coming up until the Monday he could afford to pass his time in some hedonistic pursuits as all he could do was wait for Kenny to come to him, once the games in Riga were passed. He showered and got dressed, then headed down to reception.

A group of fans were just checking in but he didn't recognise any of them and they paid him no attention as they were trying, with little success, to get an old communist era receptionist to check them in as quickly as possible. Atholl felt a twinge of sympathy for their plight. When he'd turned up without a reservation the two old biddies behind reception had gone into virtual meltdown over his simple request for a room for five nights. He left the hotel and crossed the road, heading up to the old town gate. He was going to stroll up to the town square and take it from there. He'd asked around his various female companions over the last couple of days and they had told him there were many Scotland fans who were spending their money heavily on them. They had reeled off a list of bars and he thought he would trawl the bars until he found someone who might know where Kenny Bradley was staying. He didn't have long to wait.

He pushed open the door of the Hell Hunt and walked into Gus McSween who was carrying three pints of Guinness in his hands. " For fuck's sake man, watch where you're, Andy Muir! How's it gaun? Gus' face lit up like the Riga floodlights when he realised it could be a night's drinking on somebody else's tab. "Eh, fine. Yourself?" asked Andy.

"Aye, no too bad as it happens. Flying solo like but it shouldnae be a problem. Kenny's a great guy but he can be a fifteen stone handicap when yir chasin fanny, like.

"Really, where is he then?"

"Tucked up in bed at the Hotel Sport if you're askin. He's got an important meeting the morn's morning, like."

"Who can he have an important meeting with in Tallinn?" thought Andy. He was just about to enquire further when he was bumped from behind. "C'mon Andy, this place is mobbed and there's too many Braveheart boys in kilts. We've nae chance here. We need to git in somewhere quieter wi local talent"

Gus was pressed into Andy's face breathing Guinness and vodka fumes directly up his nose.

"Where are ye staying Andy?" enquired Gus as they squirmed into a bit of space and Gus handed out the pints to the two guys he was with, one of whom was a bemused looking Dominic Fraser.

"I'm in the Viru" replied Andy.

"Oh for fuck's sake man, that monstrosity of an Eastern European tart's boudoir? What possessed ye to go there?"

"Eh, girl in the office booked it," muttered Andy, "You know how it is. Some young sloaney type with her head up her arse books the first thing in the guidebook"

"Oh aye. Ah have the same problem aw the time wi ma job travellin round Fife. Ye jist can't get the staff," said Gus, a wry smile on his lips. He finished his Guinness in a long swallow, wiped his mouth with the back of his hand, burped and turned to Andy.

"C'mon, lets find some fanny."

*****

The following morning Kenny sat in the taxi en-route to the Scandic Palace. What passed for a morning rush hour in Tallinn consisted of numerous Coca Cola lorries clogging up a main road. "So things don't go better with Coke after all," thought Kenny. He'd had a good night's sleep, considering how Gus' arrival at 4 am had woken him up. Fortunately for Kenny, as requested, Gus had returned on his

110

own. He'd been gibbering on about a beauty contest in a nightclub that was won by a Finnish girl whipping off her T-shirt in the final decider to reveal a pair of tits you could land a helicopter on. She'd won a weekend trip for two people to Edinburgh. What tickled Gus was that he knew that her boyfriend was Scottish. The laugh was that they actually lived in Edinburgh so there was fuck all point in them getting a holiday. "Some pair, mind you" were his last words before falling into the land of nod and Kenny didn't think he was talking boyfriend/girlfriend.

The taxi took him past a well-known Tallinn landmark, the Kik in de Kok. Excellent, Kenny thought to himself, the Kik in the Kok en-route to a kick in the balls. Just what the fuck did Harold want with him?

As the taxi drew up he could see Harold looking out from a window in the coffee lounge next to the hotel reception. He looked alone but Kenny had no doubt his minders wouldn't be far away. Harold's personal assistants were in more straightforward terms scary, brutal, malicious, evil, large bodyguard bastards. Kenny walked through reception to the table where Harold was sitting looking at a local paper.

"Didn't realise you were fluent in Estonian, Harold" said Kenny sitting down in a chair opposite and wondering where the twins were as Harold looked completely alone.

Harold looked up and his face cracked a tight smile.

"There's a lot ye don't know about me Kenny but it's probably fur the best. Fur you that is. How's the trip so far? How many years ye taken off yer liver this time?"

He put down his paper and appeared to be preparing himself for something.

"You know I just drink to be sociable, Harold. Lets cut to the chase. What do you want to see me about?" Kenny had decided he was going to take the initiative in this meeting. What was it the Americans called it, "playing hard ball". That was it. He would be driving this conversation the way he drove his taxi.

Harold sighed and stroked his moustache.

"Ah appreciate yer candour Kenny. Ah know ye're a busy man. The pubs'll be open in half an hour so ah'll keep it brief. Ye're a bright boy but a waster. Ye know ah don't like ye and but for the fact ah would never deny Alison anythin, the two of ye would never have got the gither let alone get married. However, once in a while ah get soft hearted and she knows right when to take advantage. A bit like her mother, God rest her soul."

This was not what Kenny had expected. A wee crack appeared in his hard balls. The caring sharing side to Harold MacMillan was even worse than the dark side. It would bring tears to a glass eye, even Harold's, if he continued at this rate.

"But ah digress. Ah want to tell ye a story as Max Bygraves used to say. Ye remember Brian MacDowall don't ye? Ye met him briefly at Pollok Golf Club a few months ago."

"Oh aye, the bloke in the golf club bar" replied Kenny, not quite sure where this conversation was going and wondering how he was going to drive the conversation like his cab when he didn't know the direction it was taking, never mind the final destination.

Kenny thought hard and remembered a fleeting introduction to the guy in the clubhouse. He also remembered him calling his father-in-law by his nickname. A significant moment he remembered.

"Brian used to be a DS wi the Strathclyde Polis but somebody, who, ah should add, is no longer wi us, saw fit to grass up Brian for takin consultancy fees, as ye might call them, from ma company. Now Brian had been smart, nae flash car, nae exotic holidays or anything else drawin attention to his extra curricular income and he had done me a good turn or two. When the force found oot about oor, how shall ah put it, business relationship, he was offered the chance to resign or face the consequences. As ah said, Brian wasnae daft so he came to me and offered me a share in a private detective agency he was planning tae set up. Nice idea and a chance for me to make sure he didnae get humpty and go back to his old employers wi tales o where the bodies were buried, if ye catch my drift. The agency did well and it soon became part of a national network throughout the UK. Amazing' the number of bent coppers that decide tae continue in private law enforcement once their public service days are done or, tae be more accurate, they've been caught wi their hands in the till"

"What the fuck does this all have to do with me?" asked Kenny.

"Patience, Kenny, patience," replied Harold a frustrated look on his face.

He resumed his story. "So one day Brian gets this call fae London. A background job fur a client doon there. The usual stuff, personal history and some photos of said individual's current coupon. The name rings a very large bell with Brian. It turns into fire alarm style ringin when the individual's details get revealed tae me. Want tae know the name o' the surveillance target?"

"I'm like a genetically modified mouse," said Kenny.

"Whit?" said a bemused looking Harold.

"All ears"

"Ok, smart bastard, listen to this. The name o' the individual was Kenneth Francis Bradley."

"No way." A slight chill played around Kenny's ears. It felt like someone had just opened a window behind him but he didn't turn round as he knew what was causing the sensation.

"Sorry but *it's* you. Brian came tae me straight away and explained what the situation was. In fact, we were talking about it that day at the golf club. He'd tried to stall them initially, givin' oot a minimal amount o' detail. Sadly the client wanted mair personal background so he had to tell him more about ye. Ah have tae admit ah was interested. No, that's no the word, intrigued aboot why anybody in the smoke would want tae know about you of all people? Brian was able to find out a couple of bits of info about the client so, out of pure curiousity, ah had this guy followed, did a bit of diggin and got a few souvenir photos, just for a wee keepsake. Ah have them wi me now but before ah show them to ye Kenny, all ah want from ye is the truth. Ah need to know the reason why ye think anybody would be hirin people to follow ye and look intae yer background. Ah knew it wasnae the polis as they wouldnae need to do this privately. The next thing ah'm thinkin o' is a jealous husband but that doesnae wash as who do you know in London? No cunt. All the time ah'm gettin curiouser and curiouser. It's probably one of the reasons ah'm here today. Rubbish disposal is a lot easier in these ex-commie countries than it is at home. Or so ah'm told."

Kenny tugged his right ear. He was amazed to find out he was being investigated. As if that wasn't bad enough, he knew if he didn't come up with a reasonable version of events in the next 10 seconds he would be swimming in the Baltic with concrete flippers.

"Harold, I don't know what to say." He managed to speak through lips which had gone curiously dry, his hard balls being shattered to dust a long time ago.

"Good, that's what ah wanted to hear because ah've even more to tell you," was the reply. Harold was smiling. Harold smiling was not good. Harold smiled rarely and only when he knew he was in a position to make someone suffer. This was not good, most definitely not good. On a not good scale of 1 to 10 it was a 39. Harold reached under the table and pulled an A4 envelope out of his travel bag. He pulled three black and white photos out of the envelope and slid them across the table.

"Hae a look. Recognise the guy?"

"Aye, it is Andy Muir, a posh Scot journo. He's appeared on the scene at the last couple of away trips." said Kenny.

He was looking down at a black and white photo of Andy Muir getting out of a very expensive looking sports car. It was parked in front of what looked like an office block. The second photo showed him emerging from what he'd sometimes heard referred to as a mews terrace house. The final photo showed him sitting in a crowd of Scotland fans in what appeared to be an airport lounge. Gus was there and Donny and then Kenny saw the image of himself, sitting just to the right of Gus.

114

"What the fuck is all this about?" said Kenny, an angry tone coming into his voice. "Ah'm not certain Kenny but a wee bit o' diggin has uncovered some rather unpleasant facts about our mystery man. Sorry, ex mystery man, Andy Muir. Ye've triggered the interest o a nasty wee piece of shite there Kenny. His real name is Atholl McClackit. He's a posh Scot like you say. Eton, Oxford and then quite interestingly, military intelligence. One o' Brian's guys is ex army and went back tae a couple o' his ex colleagues to see what they could tell him about the bold Atholl. The mention of his name resulted in a dead tone comin from the earpiece of the phone and funnily enough, they're still no returnin his calls. Now where in the last 25 years has military intelligence been workin its proverbial nuts aff?"

"Luxemburg? Greenland? Northern Ireland?" Kenny was trying to buy a bit of time by cracking a few jokes. The direction the conversation had taken had his mind racing and his sphincter twitching.

"Well done, Kenny. More to ye than just good looks. Ah had to dig a bit harder for the next information and it didn't come cheap but by this time ah was hooked. The Monarch of the Glen after my son-in-law? What's the silly prick done to deserve this?" Harold realigned himself in the chair. Kenny could see he was beginning to enjoy this wee chat.

"Anyway, after a wee bit stronger prying with the military it would appear Atholl was the brightest star for the army in the six counties for a good few years." Harold continued "He had a nice wee network of informants from both sides helpin the army land a couple o' big munition hauls and allowin them to keep the tin lid on things in areas where the natives were getting restless."

Harold stopped talking to take a sip of his coffee.

"Funnily enough, his father had done exactly the same in Kenya and other parts of the British Empire in the 1950s. Well, that was until Atholl's star burnt out. His boss received an unusual request one day. A request for a meetin signed by the joint chiefs of staff of the IRA and the executive council of the UDA. Amazingly, they had a complaint. And dae ye know what the complaint was?

"Go on" murmured Kenny who was starting to lose his grip on reality.

"Atholl was costin them too much in terms of manpower and money."

"What?"

"Aye, ye can have too much o' a good thing. Wee Atholl was judge, jury and executioner in certain parts of Ulster. Catholic or Protestant, IRA, UDA, UVF, VHF. Everybody was fair game if they got in his way or didnae pay the protection money on time. Nobody could catch him as they didnae know what he looked like and the army gave him free rein. He made the SAS look like the Boys Brigade. Ah don't know how they managed tae stop him but he was eventually brought under control and given a very honourable discharge."

"You seem to know an awful lot about his guy considering the ex army guys didn't want to talk about him" said Kenny.

"Kenny, for all ma faults, ye know I'm not bothered about religion. In the 70s in Glasgow ye had to be a bit nimble on your feet with these characters in Ulster. There was a lot of money to be made and ye had to have an open mind. Business is business. Unfortunately wi Alison's mother ah wasnae quite nimble enough" Kenny remembered Alison had only ever once dropped her guard about her dad. She had told him her mother was killed by a car bomb in 1972. It had been meant for her dad but her mother had taken his car early one Sunday morning to get fresh rolls and was blown to smithereens.

"As ever, I don't have a clue what you are talking about Harold" said Kenny whose levels of concern about his personal well being were going right off the scale.

"Look, ah had tae deal with a variety of people who didnae all have the same viewpoint regardin Northern Ireland. That's all ah can say. Ah still have some contacts there and they could provide me with the information on your wee pal Atholl or Andy Muir as ah believe he's now called. The army wish the guy had

116

never been born but they have to look after their own. He did everythin they needed or wanted done if the boys of the old brigade are to be believed."

Kenny was stunned. "I still don't understand how you've found all this out about the guy. I thought he was a journo called Andy Muir. If he was taking out half the IRA and the UDA, I think they might be a wee bit interested in what he was up to these days and they might have looked for him already" he remarked in a urgent voice.

"Keep it down Kenny, we don't want tae attract too much attention to ourselves." said Harold. "These guys were so happy to see the back of wee Atholl they agreed not to take it any further. When Brian was looking into Andy Muir there was a lot o loose ends. No school records, gaps in employment history aw that sort of thing. It was only when he looked into things like whose name his house was in and other areas it became apparent Andy Muir didnae exist, but a certain Atholl McClackit did. Ah've also got a wee laddie who's a bit o' a computer whizz. He came in tae one o' ma massage parlours near the uni the first day he got his student grant. Blew the load in a week on blow-jobs and tit-fucks. He approached Willie the manager wi a proposition as he had no money but he could order white goods over something called the internet using fake credit cards. Could we accept them as payment? You know, a fridge for a fuck sort o thing. Talk about the appliance of science. Well, when ah heard about his skills ah got him on a retainer. He's managed tae hack, ah think that's the word, into the personnel records of the company "Andy Muir" works for and it's all there. The company is an international security consultancy and Atholl McClackit is their risk assessor. It's owned by some ex-army contact o' his and that's where we got his personal details."

"But what's all this got to do with me?" said Kenny who felt close to a nervous breakdown.

117

Harold paused to take another sip of his coffee. Kenny's head was nipping, Mau Mau, IRA, UDA, somebody actually with a first name of Atholl, it was all getting too much for him.

"Ah don't know Kenny, ye'd have to ask him yoursel but I wouldn't advise gettin that close to him" replied Harold.

He looked at Kenny and wondered if he'd told him too much. He was concerned for a variety of reasons and with all he had planned, this was one distraction he did not need, not now at such a crucial time with regards the wee job lined up for tomorrow. He didn't know what Kenny had done to rattle this boy's cage but he knew one thing. From what he'd seen, Atholl was one dodgy wee fucker you didn't want to mess with and, unfortunately for him, his chump of a son-in-law had managed to do just that.

"Anyway, gettin back to the here and now, the thing is, ah've a bit of business going on tomorrow and ah need a bit of a diversion about 3 pm. We're thinkin o' gettin the game moved from an evening kick off to an afternoon KO. Ma pal here has contacts and they've brought in some dodgy floodlights for the game. Apparently the stadiums a shitehole and they've no permanent floodlights. The Estonian Football Association's got these stage lights in but we've made sure they're about as powerful as a 2 years old fart. To put the cherry on it ah've a couple of sets of negatives of a couple of blazers from the association committee gettin up to things in one of my saunas that their wives might be interested in. So ah will be having a word and tellin them to propose to the high heid yin fae the UEFA or FIFA the lights are fucked and we'll get an afternoon KO."

Harold opened his arms out wide and smiled.

"Job done, eh? What ah need you to do is to go there this afternoon and make sure for me they're as bad as the boy says. Ye know more about the game than any o these locals so ah just need a second opinion. Ok?"

Kenny's head was spinning. Get a game moved? Get a world cup qualifier moved as a diversion to a crime? It is madness. Complete and utter madness.

"Aye ok Harold. No problem," he replied.

CHAPTER 10

Kenny and Dominic were sitting round a table in the Nimita bar with some other fans talking about the Under 21 game which was going to kick off in a couple of hours. Earlier on they had been to a memorial service for those who died when the SS Estonia sank in the Baltic Sea two years before. A few fans had been on the boat itself the week before it sank, so it definitely was a case of there but for the grace of God go I.

It had been a grey old morning in Tallinn with a bit of a chill in the air. There had been a get together outside the town hall first thing where the Scotland fans who had been able to surface had met the mayor to express their condolences. There had been a few murmurs of discontent when a well-known face in the TA had handed over a City of Glasgow plaque and insinuated it was only right and proper as most of the fans were from Glasgow. They'd then walked along the main drag near the old town wall to the memorial site. Kenny had had the misfortune to fall into stride with the attache from the British Embassy whose conversation had been nearly as miserable as the weather. It didn't help that the diplomat's presence reminded Kenny of the last time he had met a member of Her Majesty's Diplomatic Corps just a few days earlier in Riga.

At the ceremony itself, the lament played by the piper had made Kenny feel even more depressed, especially as the piping coincided with the start of a light drizzle. It was all a bit much, coming on top of his earlier conversation with Harold. He'd also had a bit of trouble coming to terms with the monument itself which looked like two pieces of liquorice, one of which was coming out of the ground in an arch and the other was protruding out of the side of a raised banking. One guy was astute enough to get the symbolism. It was, he thought, meant to represent a wave crashing into the prow of a boat. Kenny could see it now but the subtlety of the monument had initially been lost on him. Gus had left part way through the ceremony as he couldn't take it. Drizzle probably making him homesick for Dumfries thought Kenny.

120

Gus walked into the Nimita bar, his face tripping him. As he approached the table where they were sitting, he exploded into yet another rant. "Ah've had it with this place man. The Russians might have gone but it's still a police state, like. The freedom of the individual counts for nothin here. Ah thought they had an open mind, boundaries that previously existed were being taken down and replaced with a new open-minded view on life, like. This is the most blinkered shower of twats ah have ever come across. If this is the free world, they can fucken keep it. Ah cannae wait tae get back to the west where life is for the livin and you're not restricted by petty rules and bureaucracy, like."

"What's gone wrong now?" Kenny asked, wondering exactly what could have got him going so badly.

"Ma photos that's what's gone, never mind gone wrong." replied Gus

"Why what's wrong with them? I thought you put them into that photo shop off the square to get developed?"

Kenny could see the wee man was upset and he was trying his best to placate him.

"Ah did. The bird in the shop, who looked a right old witch, by the way, said they would be ready in an hour. Ah've been for a wee walk, had a freshener in the Hell Hunt and then went back to collect the photos, like."

"So, what's the problem?" enquired Dominic.

"So, what's the problem?" Gus mimicked Dominic's voice in a sarcastic tone.

"The problem is ah get the photos of our sex session in Riga developed and ah'm goin through them thinkin there's somethin missin here, like. Ah remembered it was 36 spool film that ah put in ok? As ah'm walkin down the road ah count the photos and there's only 14 of the bastarts. So ah go back tae the shop and point this out to the old cow. By the way, I'm 22 shots short here Doll. Whit's the jackanory like?"

"So what did she say? " asked Dominic.

"Well the Wicked Witch of the north says "Yes, this film I remember. In Estonia, we not allowed print photos of more than two people in the sex."

"Ah said "more than two people in the sex, what are you on about?" "You, with two men and woman in the sex in photo" she replied. Then I realised the boy wi the camera had obviously got a bit creative while we were on the job, like, an put the lot of us in the photo, no just the odd shot o' me and Greta. Whit a nightmare, like."

"Fuck me, I never realised it was a wide angle lens on that camera. It would be a struggle to get her in one photo never mind the four of you" said Dominic. "Then again, I suppose it was an intimate wee group pose."

"Shut it you, what does a virgin know about erotic art? So ah'm in the shop and ah was a bit embarrassed as you can imagine so ah had to leg it but the more ah think about it, the angrier ah get like. They're ma photaes and ah'm bein' persecuted by the petty rules that govern this country!"

"Have you thought about bribing her?" asked Kenny.

"What the fuck are you on about? Bribing her? To do what exactly?" erupted Gus. It had clearly been a crap start to the day so far and it didn't appear to be getting any better from where he was sitting.

"Well, you know that there is a low wage in Estonia compared to the west, you could go back and offer her some money to be a bit flexible with the rules. You were complaining we didn't offer a big enough bribe when we came through the border, now you're bottling it" said Kenny.

"There's a difference between a border guard and a lassie that works in a photo lab," replied Gus who nevertheless appeared to be considering it a serious option.

"What's the difference? They're both probably paid peanuts and in her case she might be able to do something on the side for you. Go back and explain those photos had sentimental value for you as it's the first time you've ever kissed a man's cock. I can't wait to tell Cammy you've gone bi."

"Do that and it will be the last thing you do, ya bastard. The idea of the bribe's a good one though. Where do you get those brains fae, Bradley? Good work. Ah'm away to have a word wi' her now. See yous cunts at the Under 21s."

Gus bounced out of the pub after they agreed to meet him later.

"What we doing about getting to the game Kenny?" asked Dominic.

"Just cab it. Want to go now and see what's happening?" replied Kenny.

"At an Under 21 game? What the fuck ever happens at these games except a bunch of malnourished youngsters, the future of the Scottish game, I should add, get humped," was Dominic's reply.

Kenny laughed at the all too accurate description of the young Scotland team.

"I'm going out anyway, I might have a word with Frances Fairweather when I'm out there. See how life's treating her."

"Ok I'll see you there. If you see her tell her I was asking for her. Tell her I'm looking for a big interview for the fanzine"

Kenny left the bar and turned right towards the taxi rank. He said hello to a couple of familiar faces en-route and took the first taxi available. Hardly anybody was moving towards the ground yet as it was still an hour to kick off. If what Harold MacMillan had said was true, the whole thing was going to go tits up the following day and there was nothing he could do about it. He couldn't honestly believe Harold and his contacts would get the game moved, but if he could speak to Frances, he might be able to find out if she knew anything about the possibility of a rearrangement and where that would leave the fans. What she knew about football you could write on the back of a stamp in capital letters but when it came to handling Scotland supporters she was in a class of her own. He'd never understood how she got into the job but whoever had appointed her had got extremely lucky. Maybe he should be picking the team.

As for his other problem, he didn't know what he was going to say to Andy or Atholl or whatever the fuck his name was when he saw him but he was sure he would think of something. Would he even be here? Kenny hadn't seen Atholl again in Riga so fuck knows where he was now. Better to start thinking abut the floodlights thought Kenny but his mind kept drifting back to the meeting with his father-in-law earlier on.

Towards the end of the conversation this morning, Harold had asked him how many Scotland fans died on trips. Kenny had known it to happen before but had no hard stats. Harold had then gone on to point out that in the last two away games, a fan had died on each trip. Weren't those stats a little higher than average? All this had started since Atholl had begun trailing Kenny Bradley. Kenny was getting a very uncomfortable feeling in his chest and realised he needed to do something to calm himself down and not create any greater panic than he had already created for himself. He then realised he was going to a Scotland Under 21 game so it was clear the only foreseeable emotion in the future was depression, especially if it had been as bad as the 0-0 draw in Riga.

His taxi pulled up at the entrance to Kadriorg Park and Kenny got out, trying to come to terms with the fact that within this public park was a ground that was capable of hosting an international football match. Aye right. He walked through a heavily wooded section of the park before arriving at the ground. The pitch had a couple of walls but was mainly surrounded by chain link fences. There was a small main stand but apart from that, the whole ground was open to the elements. He saw immediately what Harold had meant regarding the floodlights. The bottom light was barely four yards off the ground and there was hardly twenty feet between the bottom row of four and the top row. Whoever in the Estonian FA had gone for this option, as opposed to playing in daylight, had fucked up bigtime. He was wondering what to do next when he heard a female voice behind him say "Mr. Bradley, what a pleasure to see you. As ever, it is fantastic to know you have arrived in good time to get into the ground and find your seat before kick off."

Kenny turned to see a slight woman in a tan raincoat. Her blonde hair was immaculate and she wore a big smile on her face.

"Alright, Frances. How ye doing?" asked Kenny.

"Very well Kenny. And yourself? Is young Mr McSween not with you today?" enquired Frances.

"No, he's had a problem with getting some photos developed that he took in Riga. You should ask him about them when you see him, I'm sure he'll be glad to explain it to you. You might even be able to help him, given your expertise with a camera."

"I'll ignore that last remark" said Frances with a knowing look in her eye. Frances Fairweather was renowned amongst fans for being appalling at taking photos. A number of times fans had given her their camera to get a photo taken with a player only to see a collection of headless torsos or vast tracts of sky on display once the photos had been printed.

"So any new ice cream parlours in Tallinn?" asked Kenny. Along with her photographic ability, Frances was also noted for her sweet tooth and love of ice cream.

"Sadly not, but they have a new pastry chef in our hotel who makes the Estonian equivalent of caramel shortcake so there's been no withdrawal symptoms so far. And what about you? How's the lovely Alison?"

"Aye great, no problem. I see they've done nothing to this place since the last time I was here," said Kenny gazing around at what he thought was a disaster waiting to happen.

"No, they haven't done much to it have they? It's hard to believe this a ground that is fit to hold a World Cup qualifier," said Frances. "But I am sure everything will be all right on the night."

"Are you absolutely certain about that?" Kenny was trying not to let his panic show, but it was a bit of a struggle.

"Why shouldn't it be?" enquired Frances. She could play the innocent very well when it suited her. Most of the time she took on a naïve outlook to save fans from themselves but Kenny knew beneath her, at times girlish demeanor, there was a razor-sharp brain.

She was also aware of his family connections and whilst never being so crass as to ask what his wife did for a living, he was certain she knew all about the MacMillan dynasty. In fact she knew too much, as any fan would verify. Many fans had come away from a first meeting with her wondering how on earth she knew so many details about them and their personal lives.

Kenny looked up and pointed to the floodlights. He'd barely had to raise his arm to make his point as they were so low.

"Well, I was having a look at these floodlights before you turned up and they don't exactly look international class. You'd be struggling to light up a Subbuteo pitch with these" replied Kenny.

"Funny you should say that as one of our committee members has just said exactly the same thing"

Kenny quickly turned to face Frances and she was giving him what could only be described as a funny look. Not funny ha ha but funny as in "If you know something and don't tell it to me pal, I will make sure you never get a ticket for another Scotland game."

Kenny realised he had to get a grip, "Eh well, don't want to take up too much of your time Frances. I'm sure you've got a lot more meeting and greeting to do. Ah'll see you in the ground" said Kenny who started to walk backwards whilst saying his goodbyes.

"I'm sure you will Kenny, I'm sure you will," said Frances, the knowing look never leaving her eyes for a moment.

Kenny walked up to the ground and was directed into it by a couple of bored looking riot cops. You didn't actually have to pay to see the match as the fencing was, at best, inadequate. If you put up with looking through a chain link fence you could save a big 75p. Kenny was sure there would be a few who would do it as well.

126

He climbed up the steps to the area which was to the right of the main stand as you looked at the pitch. The word "main" could easily be substituted with "only". There were maybe twenty five rows under cover with approximately fifty seats in a row. Whilst the roof protected the fans from the elements, there was little to protect members of the SFA from the verbal abuse that would fall on their ears. The teams were warming up. As usual, Kenny could barely identify three of the Under 21 team. If these were meant to be the prime of a nation's youth, Scotland was fucked big time. Small and slight was the most positive spin you could put on the appearance of most of them with their bleached skins, wasted shoulders and a smattering of acne thrown across half their faces. More like Junkie U21s than Scotland U21s thought Kenny. As the Scotland fans slowly drifted into the ground, Kenny was greeting a few familiar faces. A couple of guys appeared with local women in tow, including, a few rows down, a face Kenny hadn't seen for some time which belonged to Jamesie Cresswell.

"Jamesie, how's it going son? Long time no see. No since where? Moscow? Helsinki?" shouted Kenny.

Jamiesie looked up with a less than impressed expression. "Alright Kenny how you doin? Aye, havnae seen ye since Moscow. I'll catch you later" He then turned back to his female companion and re started his conversation.

Kenny was a bit perplexed by this as he couldn't understand the cold shoulder treatment. He walked down the stand until he was in the same row as Jamesie and wandered up to him.

"You alright, Jamesie?" he enquired.

"Aye, brand new Kenny. It's just ah'm wi company and ah don't want her to feel neglected, ken?" Jamesie was looking at him with a rather pleading look on his face. Kenny realised now would be a good time to do the decent thing and walk away so not to cramp another fan's style. Then again, when did the decent thing and the Tartan Army ever walk had in hand so he ploughed on.

"No going to introduce me to your new friend then, Jamesie?" said Kenny, a broad grin on his face.

"Eh, oh aye, Kenny. Eh, this is eh, eh, Mingo." said Jamesie, who could not look Kenny in the face as he said the girl's name.

"Mingo!" said Kenny, managing to stifle a guffaw as he offered the girl his hand.

"Hi, nice to meet you" came a muted reply from the small Estonian blonde with a name no Scot would ever forget.

"Eh, ok, Jamesie, I'll just leave you to it" said Kenny.

As he turned to leave, Jamesie grabbed his arm and whispered in his ear "You mention her name to McSween and I'll never forgive you. That wee bastard finds out I'm wi a burd called Mingo, ah'll never hear the end of it. Ah'm beggin ye."

"Aye, ok Jamesie, your secret is safe wi me" said Kenny and he walked back up the steep steps to where he was originally standing. Ten minutes later Dominic and Gus turned up and stood next to him.

"See Frances?" enquired Kenny.

"Aye ah did and if it hadnae been for the result ah had in the photo shop, courtesy of your good idea, like, ah would be well fucked off wi you at this moment in time, by the way" replied Gus.

"What's wrong now? Did she ask about the hair transplant?" said Kenny.

"No she didn't, smart bastart. She asked about my photos, like. What the problem was. Were they o' Riga tourist sights and could she see them sometime as she hadn't got much o' a chance to see the city when she was there. You grassed me up to her, didn't you?"

"I merely pointed out you had a wee problem and she might be able to help," replied Kenny.

"Fuck off man. She knows as much about photography as ah do about nuclear fusion. But ah'll forgive ye as that's the sort of man ah am, like. Ah'm bigger than your petty vindictiveness."

"Aye but no much" interrupted Dominic.

"One more crack out of you, Fraser!"

"So what happened at the photo lab then?" enquired Kenny.

"As it happens the old McSween charm worked a treat, like. Ah went back in and told her ah'd forgotten to leave a tip for her. Ah said the quality of the photos that were developed was excellent and ah only wished we had somebody like her in Glasgow. We got chattin and the end result is ah've to meet her tomorrow at 3 pm. She'll do the photos herself tonight when the boss has gone and ah'm taking her out for a wee pre-match meal, like. If it goes alright, she might come to the match wi' me and then we'll see where the night and the music take us. Bit of a result, eh?" Gus rubbed his hands together. His sense of expectation was off the sexual Richter scale.

"Whatever happened to the Wicked Witch of the north bit?" asked Dominic trying to do a bit of a spoiler on Gus' joy.

"Well, maybe I was a wee bit hasty, like. If ye took the horn rimmed glasses off and she let her hair down, she would be a real looker. What's that song "That Old Black Magic Cast a Spell on Me", aye the wee man might just be in love again, like."

"Aye if she's a real witch, maybe she can make that photo of you kissing Hughie's cock disappear" quipped Dominic.

"See you, Fraser, you're getting right on ma tits. As if watching this heap of pre-pubescent shite disgrace the jersey isnae bad enough, ah have to put up with your so called humour".

"Calm down for fuck's sake. Where's your famous Scottish sense of humour" said Kenny trying to cool the situation. "Try and concentrate on the game. Then again..."

It had been a turgid first half and as the light began to fade it took little to deflect Kenny's attention from the game and onto the floodlights. They were struggling to see the far side of the pitch by the time the game ended. Kenny realised that blackmail or no blackmail, somebody somewhere could make a legitimate complaint. They would have a very good case for getting the game moved or, at worst, postponed. It really did not bear thinking about.

"Anybody up for shepherd's pie in the Hell Hunt" suggested Gus.

"I thought you hated dill and vowed never to eat anything apart from McDonalds once you were here" Dominic retorted.

"Aye well, ah suppose ah can make an exception this time, like. That shepherd's pie o theirs is the "chiens ballons". You coming Kenny, or you going to see Frances and leave me with this miserable bastard Fraser for company?" asked Gus.

"Aye, I'll see you in there. Just got a wee bit of business to sort out first" said Kenny as he wandered down the aisle to the front of the stand.

Kenny made his way out with the rest of the crowd. It was a muted scene as it had ended up a 1-0 victory for Scotland but the overall performance was poor, bordering on complete shite. You had to feel for Alex McLeish managing this lot. They had been gubbed 4-0 in Austria where it looked like 11 proles versus 11 specimens of the master race. You looked at the guys in the Scotland shirts and thought, Scottish football has no future, they would be better giving up now. However, the bigger picture could wait as he was more concerned with the "here and now" or to be more precise, the "here and tomorrow".

He found Frances dealing with a couple of irate fans who had bought tickets for the full game in a ticket shop in Tallinn and were complaining that the price charge to locals was a lot cheaper than the SFA's price for match tickets. Do these pricks never realise it's not the SFA that set the price but the home team he wondered. He lingered on the fringes until he caught her eye. In a way only she had, Frances gave these guys a polite fuck off by asking them what their supporters club membership numbers were. This cut the legs from their argument as they were not members and could never have bought tickets from the association anyway. Ah, the lost Scottish art of complaining for the sake of complaining. Driving a taxi had exposed Kenny to more than a couple of these sorts, so Frances had his full sympathy.

Frances walked over to Kenny with a fierce look in her eye "Is there something you want to tell me?" she demanded.

"Nothing that I can say for sure but did you not think those floodlights looked a bit dodgy for a night game?"

"I hadn't thought about it. Surely they have been approved by FIFA as they've played night games here before."

"Yeah but at what time of the year? This is the land of the midnight sun and from what I can see at the moment, they're just not up to it."

They were now standing on the opposite side of the pitch from the main stand which was barely visible in the early evening Estonian gloom, even with the floodlights on.

"As I said before, is there something you want to tell me?" asked Frances.

At that moment the lights were turned off and the stadium fell under a blanket of darkness.

"What's that quote from the First World War?" asked Kenny. "The lights are going out all over Europe"

"We may not see them on again in our time" said Frances completing the quote.

"You said it," said Kenny.

CHAPTER 11

Harold MacMillan was nervous. He normally got nervous before a job, but this time he was in a foreign country relying on a guy he'd met on a golf course in the Caribbean. Not only that, they were depending on the moving of a World Cup qualifier kick off time to act as a distraction for the authorities. He couldn't believe it when the two prats from the SFA International Committee said they had done it. It was only later, after he'd handed over the negatives, he'd established from Kenny it would have been called off anyway, the floodlights really were that bad. The relevant individuals would be contacted at a later date to be informed of his dissatisfaction regarding their claim on achieving what he'd asked of them, when they had had hee-haw to do with it, but that was for back in Scotland. The ongoing situation was another matter.

Harold and Leo, his Estonian partner, had planned everything down to the last second when he'd brought up the issue of Atholl. His plan had not gone down well initially with the Estonians but he'd pointed out the benefits and they had calmed down. They had been planning to use contacts on the inside to help them pull the job off. What Harold proposed would allow them to take the heat off those inside, pointing the authorities in completely the wrong direction. As far as he could see it, which admittedly wasn't very far given his false eye, it wasn't so much a win/win situation as a complete doing.

The boys were in their element. They had endured a bonding session with Leo's bodyguards in a local brothel and it was all brotherly love in the bodyguard world. "The team that drinks, shags and snorts coke together, wins together" could be a new motto above his desk at work. Just as long as it didn't affect their performance on the day, he didn't give a flying fuck. He wasn't sure how things would pan out with the local police after this but Leo seemed confident he could placate them, leaving Harold to make an easy exit. He had to admit this game turning up had been a stroke of luck. He had come in as a fan and could leave as a fan, or at least appear to. From what he'd seen the locals would be sad to see the

Scots depart. He hadn't been on one of these sort of trips since a Wembley weekend in the early 1960s and he'd forgotten just how much money Scots were keen to throw about.

It had been an incredible sight at times. Guys who, back in the wilds of Fife, would have cut off their right arm rather than pay for a cab were getting taxis willy-nilly and, even more incredibly, they could be seen to be tipping. God knows how the Estonian men treated their women as some of these guys were getting laid on the offer of taking a local girl out for a meal.

He'd met one guy who worked in the council offices in Ayrshire. The guy was called Craig and had stumbled into Harold in the hotel bar. The boys had offered to remove him from Harold's company but he'd calmed them down as the guy had been quite amusing. He'd admitted he was nothing, had a shite job in a shite place as he so quaintly put it, but these trips allowed him to be somebody. He only went on the Eastern European trips because the bevvy was cheap and he felt like superman as he could afford to buy anything he wanted. He'd got to know a local burd and she was keen on coming over to see him if he paid for her ticket. He was sure it wasnae a passport job as he knew the look of love when he saw it and she'd definitely got it when she looked at him. More likely when she looked at your wallet, thought Harold but good luck to her. Once she'd had a look at Cumnock and its environs, she'd be on the first flight back to Tallinn. They say love is blind but no that blind.

Harold had pulled Kenny out of the swimming pool at the Hotel Sport earlier on that morning. They'd got the word from FIFA that the game was to be brought forward to 3pm which fitted perfectly with their plans. He had explained to Kenny what would happen, giving him the minimal amount of information. The less he knew the better for him. Harold didn't have any problem with what was going to happen to Atholl. He'd tried to kill a member of Harold's family and whilst there was once a time he might have encouraged him in his task, he'd come to see just how much Kenny meant to Alison. Christ, listen to me, I'm getting totally fucking sentimental thought Harold. Nothing like a wee job to put me back on the mean and callous track. He'd arranged for the boys to keep an eye on Kenny as he thought Atholl would be around somewhere and this time Atholl would maybe get more than he bargained for. He'd asked Leo to see if he could find an Andy Muir registered in any of the Tallinn hotels and, if he did, keep an eye on him.

*****

Kenny had been amazed it had all come off. He didn't want to know what Harold was up to but he knew it must be big for him to come all the way here in person. A gesture of faith to the Estonians? He lay floating in the pool considering what Harold had told him half an hour ago. A dip first thing was the perfect cure for a hangover and, after his night in Club Hollywood, he was enjoying every minute of his pool time. He and Gus had ended up in the nightclub after a couple of hours in the Nimita after the U 21 game where they had been forced to suffer various minor Scottish media celebrities belting out Beatles hits over the PA system. The band in the nightclub had been little better. Their stage wear was reminiscent of the Clash circa Combat Rock but their music had barely moved past 1960. Kenny had been highly amused to see a number of Scots get local girls up to dance only to watch them lumber about, even worse than they usually did, when they heard they would be dancing to Estonians doing a cover version of "Blue Suede Shoes". As he lay back in the refreshing waters, he realised he'd better tell Gus about the KO time being moved. He wouldn't be happy as it cut his pre-match drinking down to three hours. Maybe less if he didn't get his arse into gear. He put on a robe and wandered over to a house phone. After twenty rings he heard a croaky voice go "Whit?"

"It's me Kenny. Look, I know you won't believe this and I am not winding you up. They've moved the kick off to 3pm. The floodlights are sub standard so FIFA have told them to move the game forward" said Kenny.

"Whit?" groaned Gus a bit more force creeping into his voice this time.

"The game's kicking off at 3pm. It's 11.00 now so you'd better get your act together and have a shower and get the battledress on as the game's this afternoon, not this evening."

A quick "No problem" and the phone went dead. Christ, that was easy thought Kenny. He'd decided not to go back into the pool as knew this hotel had a big fuck off sauna somewhere. He was sure this would remove the last remnants of the hangover. He hung up his robe and wandered round the pool looking for the sauna. He finally found it at the far end and wandered in. It was blasting out steam full throttle in a large room with 12 plastic bucket seats around the edges of the room. Now this is what I call a sauna thought Kenny, no like some of those lukewarm garden sheds back home wi a bucket of fake coal in the corner. Kenny could only make out a couple of pairs of ankles which he presumed were male given their thickness, then again he'd seen a couple of Scottish girls here with their boyfriends earlier on so he thought he'd better keep his speedos on, just in case.

Pity nobody else was here for a wee chat but he wondered how long he would last it was so hot. One of the locals got up and started stretching a bit. He gave it a few arm swings and then walked out of the sauna and stepped straight in the plunge pool next to the sauna. Seems like a good plan thought Kenny and got up. At this point a shape appeared out of the mist and said, "Hello Kenny. Fancy bumping into you here." It was Atholl.

Oh fuck thought Kenny. Before Kenny could say anything Atholl had his hands round Kenny's throat and was applying maximum pressure to his Adam's apple. Within seconds Kenny was seeing bright silver lights flashing through the steam of the sauna. Bastard he thought and tried to fight back, but it was useless. Too many lagers and too many curries had reduced him to a pathetic state. He really is trying to kill me thought Kenny but why? So many questions and no fucking answers. Kenny flailed his arms around but resistance was pointless. As the steam parted for a brief second, he glimpsed Atholl's face, pent up with anger. But why me thought Kenny as he started to black out. At that, the pressure was suddenly released and as he staggered back, he could make out Atholl falling to the ground through the steam. He looked up to see the boys looming large through the clouds.

"All right Kenny?" asked Alec, the friendlier of the two.

"Aye, aye, just about. Where have you been sittin?" spluttered Kenny as he tried to massage some feeling back into his throat.

"We were in the corner. Got a tip off fae Leo's minders this wee cunt was in the hotel and was watching you. We beetled over just in time, by the looks of things. Don't know what he would have done if you hadnae come in here but he's a game wee cunt. Had to hit him three times before he went down. Once on the napper and then once behind each knee. Most impressed but still, he went down."

"What are you going to do now?" asked Kenny.

"Don't worry, Kenny. Harold's got plans for this wee shite" said Tony the other "boy". He smiled which to Kenny was equally as uncomfortable as Harold smiling. He realised then that whatever happened to Atholl was going to be quite, no totally, unpleasant.

"Alright Tony, I'll get the laundry bag and the trolley. If he comes round and tries anything just smack him again."

"No probs Alec. Want to disappear Kenny?" enquired Tony.

"Could be an idea. Thanks, that's one I owe you" said Kenny as he stepped over Atholl and prepared to leave the sauna.

Tony was shaking his head in a bemused fashion.

"One you owe us? Ha Ha. Did you hear that Alec? Robert de Niro here owes us. Aye right. Catch you later, Kenny. Now fuck off out of it!"

That fucking Robert de Niro crack yet again. Alright, the bastard might have saved his life but ever since Tony had seen Taxi Driver he had been needling him, going on about when was Kenny going to get a Mohican and asking how Cybil Shepherd was doing. Still what was he going to say in reply that wasn't going to get him killed. Thinking of that, what the fuck had he done to wind up this Atholl guy so much?

He quickly legged it out of the pool area and into the changing room. He had a quick shower and dried himself off. When he got back to the room, Gus was pulling on a Timberland boot and whistling.

"What's up wi' you?" enquired Kenny.

"Dominic's just been on the phone. The Estonians are threatenin tae no turn up. It's an inter-fucking-national incident. We're going to be the centre of the known world this afternoon pal, you'd better believe it. And you know what *the* really good thing is?"

"What's that?"

"We'll be there. What a game to be at. Ah'll be telling ma grandchildren about this one" said Gus who started whistling again to the tune of Oasis' "Champagne Supernova".

"What the fuck has "Champagne Supernova" got to do wi this state of affairs? And I'm sorry but when do you plan to have children never mind bloody grandchildren?" said Kenny.

"We'll be drinkin champagnski the night if they don't turn up, won't we? If they bottle it, they've forfeited the game and we get the three points. What a double header this is, like. Two clean sheets and six points. The Austrians and the Swedes will be spewing. Parlez vous francais, Kenny? Ya beauty, France 98 here we come. Grandchildren? Ye know ah've always wanted to have kids. How long have we known each other? Don't tell me you don't see me as a responsible parent?"

"I give up" said Kenny and lay down on his bed. "No game and now you're telling me you want to become a father. The world's gone mad."

"Come on you, pull yoursel the gither. Ah said we'd meet Dominic at half eleven in the lobby. We'll get a cab into town to make sure everybody else knows the score. How did you find out anyway?" asked Gus.

137

"I was in the pool and Harold came and told me the game had been moved. I've a lot to tell you but it'll need to wait until we're back home" replied Kenny in a muted tone.

"Harold came tae tell ye? Why am ah no likin the sound of this? Harold came to tell you? Oh fuck. What's going on?"

Gus had turned paler than normal. Kenny looked at him and wondered if he should tell him the whole story but decided against it. Gus must have been in a hurry in the shower as he'd let the hair transplant get wet. It was now in a state of complete collapse having absorbed too much water. It looks like ginger seaweed draped across his scalp thought Kenny.

"Nothing we can do about it so come on, let's get into town and see what the story is" mumbled Kenny trying to move the conversation back to a more comfortable topic.

"Hey, were some guys no coming over on the ferry from Helsinki and Stockholm today. They'll be donald ducked if they don't know about it. Fuck me, what a game to miss" said Gus ruefully.

At that moment Gus was looking distinctly uncomfortable but Kenny didn't think it had anything to do with the earlier conversation about Harold.

"Have you got any o' that pile cream?" asked Gus "The Duke of Argylls are playing me up something rotten."

"Aye, it's in my toiletry bag in the bog. Help yourself" replied Kenny.

Gus disappeared into the toilet for a minute before coming out looking a bit puzzled.

"Did you get it?" asked Kenny

"Yeah, it's fine. I just don't understand why they need tae put mint in it," came the reply.

"Mint?"

"Aye, it was smellin spearminty."

"Have you put your contact lenses in?"

"No, what's that got to do with anythin?"

"Because I think you've just pushed a finger full of toothpaste up your arse. Still, puts a new meaning on the term ring of confidence," said Kenny with a wry grin on his face.

"You bastard. This goes no further, right. Ah've been the butt o' enough jokes on this trip, ah fuck, what did ah say that for, ach do what you want." Gus looked like he was going to explode with frustration as he flung the tube of toothpaste at Kenny.

"Go on, brush your teeth with the Anusol for piles of smiles" came Kenny's reply.

"Look, come on" said Gus. "We've barely got three hours pre match drinkin time so get yer finger out, just like ah did a minute ago."

Kenny smoothed out the bed and sorted out his gear for the match on it. Unlike a lot of fans, he preferred to wear jeans to a game as opposed to a kilt. He knew the main attraction of the kilt for most guys was its attractiveness to the opposite sex but he had Alison and crap chat up technique. Besides even he knew the kilt wasn't going to do that much for him. Plus Gus was not the only person in the room suffering from Farmer Giles. A pair of jeans and a snug pair of boxers helped keep Kenny's piles under control and he was fucked if he was going to let the remote possibility of a shag mean he would be wandering round Tallinn with a sweaty arse. He also had to get his match kit ready and was taking into consideration the weather conditions. T-shirt under the top for this he thought and a jacket. He also found the Think Scottish baseball cap from the other night so stuck it on. He rounded it all off by tying a Lion Rampant flag round his neck in the form of a scarf.

"There you go, no quite the extra from Braveheart like some of yous but it'll have to do" he said as he looked in the mirror before going into the corridor to catch up with Gus. They made it downstairs in the lift only to find Harold waiting for them.

"Beat it, Gus. Ah need a word in private wi Kenny." Harold issued his command with a curt nod of the head for Kenny to follow him into the coffee bar. Harold looked as if somebody might have rained on his parade and Kenny had a fair idea who that somebody might be. Gus had followed Harold's orders straight away and was now outside the hotel with a concerned look on his face, watching through the window as Harold broke some bad news to Kenny.

"Ah knew that wee shite Atholl or Andy or whatever the fuck he's called was a nasty wee piece o' work but it looks like ah never really impressed it enough on the boys. They got a bit cocky when they were puttin him in a laundry bag and turned their back on him for a minute too long. As o' now, Tony is in Tallinn A+E getting treatment for a broken nose, two black eyes and a fucked jaw, courtesy of Atholl smackin him in the puss with a fire extinguisher. Fortunately as he tried to do Alec he slipped on a pair of dirty tights and Alec was able to do the wee cunt first. The bad news is, this leaves us one man short for the job"

Kenny made a large mental leap to a very uncomfortable conclusion.

"Wait a minute, Harold. Don't think I'm not grateful but come on. You don't mean you want me to……." stuttered Kenny.

"It's no a case of "want", mair like "need" ye to put in an appearance wi us this afternoon. As far as ah see it, ah've saved yer life this mornin and ye owe me. Bigtime. In fact, had it not been for you, ah wouldnae be in this position o' being a man light on the biggest job of ma career so far. So from ma point of view, ye're in it up to your eyebrows, Kenny, and before you even think about saying "What about the game, Harold?" ah've no come all this way to call it off now because my son-in-law is worried about missin a poxy fucken football match. Be back here at 2pm on the dot."

*****

Where had it all gone wrong, thought Atholl as he lay in the back of a Mercedes van, parked in the car park of the Grand Hotel. It wasn't meant to be like this but come on, pull yourself together. You've been in civvy street too long if you start thinking like that he told himself and tried to take a more positive viewpoint. He had taken one of them out and if it hadn't been for that pair of tights causing him to slip on the wet tiles, he'd have taken care of the other one. Lucky amateurs or what! Still they'd given him a fair whack to the legs earlier on and that was one trick he would have to remember for the future.

To add insult to injury the pair of tights that had literally caused his downfall were now being used as a gag. Even more worryingly, despite the pain in his legs, his bound hands and ankles plus the throbbing at the back of his neck, it was another kind of throbbing which was now causing him concern. How on earth could he be getting turned on by a pair of dirty tights in his mouth, the state he was in? A stiffy in his state was unthinkable, especially as his body's position gave little or no room for manouevre for any kind of hard on. He had to admit they'd trussed him up like the proverbial Christmas turkey, binding his hands and ankles then using a pair of handcuffs to connect the two sets of rope. Thus, Atholl looked like he was touching his toes but at the same time, trying to find room for his penis to reach full maturity. Whoever had these tights before must have been one dirty bitch, thought Atholl as the taste brought back memories of a series of sexual encounters he'd previously managed to lose deep in his subconscious. He tried to remove all thoughts of sexiness from them by imagining their owner as some old Estonian crone who suffered from mild incontinence but it wasn't working. Still, at least the pain in his groin as his prick struggled for some space, like a mole trying to burrow through concrete, took some of the agony away from his legs.

He also felt something odd around his ears when he moved his head. He couldn't put his finger on it but then his head touched the van panel and he realised what the weird feeling was. They had shaved his head completely!

The back door of the van opened and a man Atholl didn't recognise got in. His captors had made no effort to hide their faces so Atholl presumed this was it. He'd had a good innings, especially when his time in Northern Ireland was taken into consideration, so no complaints. Just a pity the Laird would never know.

141

"Awright wee man?" came the voice drenched in a Glasgow accent. "Are we havin fun yet? Ye've caused me a wee bit of grief on a very important day in ma life Atholl and to put it mildly it is just not on. Ah would have been slightly upset if ye'd topped my son-in-law as he is, regrettably, family but to get in the way of business is somethin else. Then again Atholl, from what ah know about ye, ye're somethin else yourself."

All of a sudden Atholl's erection had vanished. How on earth did this piece of Glaswegian dogshit know his name? This was not right, not right at all.

"Anyway, come on. To show you ah'm not all mean-hearted ah've brought ye a wee drinky-poo. Nothing fancy like ye'd be drinkin in the Atlantic Bar or Quaglino's, but ah'm sure ye'll appreciate it enough."

Harold MacMillan produced a water bottle like the type used by cyclists on the Tour de France. He pulled the pair of tights in Atholl's mouth to one side and squirted the bottle hard. The liquid went up through the flexi straw and burst into his mouth. Atholl was reluctant to take the drink, but he'd been thrown by the fact the guy knew his real name and he was completely parched. Harold gave the bottle a couple of generous squeezes and the liquid dribbled down Atholl's chin where it had not been forced down his throat. "Oops silly me" said Harold. "Ah should have said it'll be like the Atlantic Bar cause ye've just had a wee cocktail. Sorry there wisnae a paper umbrella or a cherry wi it but where ye're goin ah don't think it would make much difference. Sweet dreams, wee Atholl, sweet dreams."

The fucker thought Atholl, the complete and utter fu..........

In the taxi into the centre of Tallinn, Gus had started to ask Kenny about his conversation with Harold but one look from Kenny had shut him up. Better keep schtum on this one he thought as Kenny looked totally pissed off. This was in stark contrast to the mood in the old town. Everywhere Scotland fans were running around telling other fans what they already knew. The game had been moved and the kick off was at 3 pm. Rumours were circulating over whether the

Estonians would turn up or not. Some people thought they would, others believed there would definitely be no game. Nobody thought about asking any Estonians, as that would have been too obvious.

Kenny had bumped into a couple of Scots guys in their mid 40s in a café. He'd met them once before but had been hacked off by their patronising attitude. He also knew them to be jazz fans, which probably explained why they saw themselves as superior. These were the last people he wanted to meet at this moment in time. Gus, unaware of this, bounced up to them on entering the café and informed them the game had been moved to 3pm. He was casually informed they had known since 9 am and had already done a radio interview with a friend who worked at BBC Scotland.

"Just wanted to make sure you knew, like," he said before he turned back to Kenny whilst making a face that showed just what he thought of them.

"Eh, I've got to go back to the hotel to help Harold with something. I'll see you at the game" said Kenny who got up and walked out of the café before Gus could say anything. Gus knew this was bad news but couldn't think of anything to do. He decided to find Dominic and take it from there.

*****

Alec pulled up in front of the Hotel in the white Mercedes van at 2pm. Harold was in the passenger seat and when he saw Kenny he got out and let him take the seat in the front of the van. Harold stood with the van door in one hand and one hand on Kenny's shoulder.

"Now calm down, Kenny. We've got aw this sussed. Yer wee pal in the back has been a bit o' a fly in the ointment but as it turns oot, it's no' all bad news for us. For him, maybe but no for us. We'll just have to wait and see."

At this Harold burst out laughing. "Ah've just seen a wee bit o' irony here. Ah don't know fuck all about football and here ah am, ah'm goin to the game and you, one of Scotland's biggest fans is goin to miss it. Nae luck, son. See ye later"

143

Harold patted Kenny on the face with one hand then slammed the door shut with the other and walked back into the hotel.

Alec put the van in gear and drove off. "Sorry, Kenny, it's nothing personal but if you don't play ball Harold says I've to pull you back in line. By any means. Ok?"

"Aye ok" whispered Kenny. "Why the fuck is he going to the game?"

"A small matter of an alibi, I do believe. He's bribed a newspaper photographer to make sure there will be a photae o him at the match in a Scottish daily tomorrow. Maybe no centre stage but somewhere in a wee corner where he can prove he was definitely at the game" replied Alec. "Look, when we get to the place just do as I say and it will be ok. Harold doesnae pull these stunts for a laugh and it has all been nicely planned. Follow my orders and we'll be in and out in no time. Ok?"

"Aye, ok," came a muted reply.

CHAPTER 12

Alec had left the van radio on some local station before he had disappeared. The sound of the Fugees singing "Killing Me Softly" gently filled the van. There's fucking irony for you thought Kenny. Outside an old woman stood in the doorway of a dilapidated building holding out a cup. Kenny had been surprised at the number of elderly Estonians out begging. He wondered what the new post Soviet Union culture was like for the elderly. How did you survive a crash course in capitalism at the age of 78? Two kids came running down the street one of them wearing a Juventus top, shouting something in Estonian at his mate. Kenny was reminded of the Jam song "Dreams of Children". All he knew was that he was definitely going underground once this caper was over. He sat in the van and wondered how the fuck it had come to this. It looked likely that in the space of 24 hours he would survive an attempt on his life, take part in a criminal offence, sorry, a *serious* criminal offence and to cap it all, miss the one game that people would be talking about for years to come. He turned round in his seat and looked at Andy or Atholl or whoever he was. What have I done to you to deserve all of this you bastard?

"Ok, game on" said Alec as he appeared at the passenger window. He was wearing a collar and tie, sunglasses and a well-cut pin stripe suit.

"What the fuck are you doing dressed like that?" demanded Kenny.

"Get real Kenny, for fuck's sake. What wir ye expectin? A black mask, a hooped jumper an a bag wi "swag" written oan it? Get wi the project, right?" He turned his head back down the van and shouted "Martin, now".

Kenny turned his head out of the passenger window to see a tall well built man in a suit similar to Alec's get out of a Mercedes saloon parked behind Kenny's van. He was also wearing a collar and tie and sunglasses. Behind him two guys dressed in painter and decorators overalls got out of a beaten up van. As they passed the car, a smaller guy also got out of the Merc, again sharply dressed in a business suit.

"Ok, here's how it's goin doon, Kenny. Me, Leo and Martin here are casually goin in tae the bank and wir goin tae the safe deposit room. The two painters are going tae take Atholl in wi us, wrapped up in a sheet. There'll be a wee bit o a kerfuffle as they're no expected so then we make oor move. We dae what we have to dae and then come back out again, nice as ninepence, leaving Sleeping Beauty in there tae face the music."

The bigger of the two locals, Martin, approached the van. "Everything A-ok?" he asked.

"Nae problem big man" said Alec. "Kenny here is the eyes of the operation and if anythin looks like it will go tits up, he'll blow the horn."

"Tits up? Blow the horn? You crazy Scots guys always thinking about pussy" came the reply from Martin who had a big grin on his face.

"No, that's the last thing on ma mind at this moment in time, ah can assure you," said Alec. "No time for fannyin about o any kind. Now, lets go."

The painters slid open the side door of the van and proceeded to wrap Atholl in a dust sheet. Kenny was a bit surprised to see Atholl also was wearing a good suit with a collar and tie as well, exactly the same as Leo. His head was completely shaved. The best-dressed impersonation of Kojak I've ever seen thought Kenny. What the fuck was going on?

Alec took one last look round and said "Remember Kenny, eyes and ears ok? Ah've jist realised, this goes well enough, ye might even make the second half!" He winked at Kenny and headed off across the street with the two well-dressed Estonians. The painters slammed the side door shut and headed off carrying a neatly wrapped sausage roll with an Atholl filling on their shoulders.

The next twenty minutes were the longest of Kenny's life. The radio station was now playing "Three Lions on a Shirt" by Baddiel and Skinner. This just gets better and better he thought. The old woman was still in the doorway. Could she be a police undercover agent, waiting to call in some elite squad of Tallinn cops? Where had that boy in the Juve top gone? Could he be a Jimmy Clitheroe type waiting to pounce with a .44 Magnum hidden under his baggy top? His paranoia was getting too much for him and this music wasn't helping any. He would turn the radio off but he didn't have a clue how to do it. Knowing his luck he'd turn on the emergency lights, triggering the van alarm at the same time. He kept his eyes peeled for any sign of a police car or security staff but there were no flashing lights, no sirens and best of all, no alarm bells.

Despite his state of high anxiety, he found himself looking disbelievingly as Alec and Martin, plus the two painters, casually strolled across the road from the bank. What he didn't understand was why were the painters carrying the same size bundle as before they had gone in? Where was the wee guy in the suit that had gone in with Martin and Alec? Where was the swag bag?

Alec climbed into the drivers seat and turned to Kenny with a big smile on his face, "Awright big boy? Ye did terrific pal, really great. Ye might jist o hae found yourself an openin in the business. Once Tony can actually see out of his eyes again, he might find his position under threat. Harold's always looking to add to his squad. Do you fancy a three-year contract? The win bonuses won't always be guaranteed like this one but you never know." Alec burst out laughing but Kenny failed to see any humour in the situation.

As Alec was talking the two guys in the painters get up had climbed into the back of the van and had gently laid down the bundle they were carrying.

Kenny's eyes bulged as he saw Leo, the smaller of original three suited guys clamber out of the dust-sheets. As he sat up he cried "Why the fuck are we still here? Let's go!!"

Alec put the van in gear and headed off. "No problem Leo".

"Could someone please tell me what the fuck is going on and why this seems to have passed off so easily?" asked Kenny in a bewildered tone of voice.

"Take it easy, Kenny" said Alec. "Everythin's goin to be fine. As far as the cameras are concerned three robbers went into the bank and two left. Unfortunately the third was clubbed by the security guard and sadly for him, had to be left behind."

"So where is it then? " asked Kenny.

"What? The swag bag?" asked Alec in mocking tone.

"Don't fuck me about, Alec, you know what I mean."

"Calm down, Kenny. Everythin's under control. We've got nothin on us as we've stolen nothin fae the bank." Alec took his right arm off the steering wheel and placed his hand on Kenny's knee.

"No way. We've been through this fucken charade and you're going to tell me you've done nothing but leave that wee bastard Atholl in the vault?" protested Kenny, a definite note of hysteria creeping into his voice.

"Look, we've slightly re-arranged things. Atholl turning up is a peach as it diverts attention fae us. They have a collar and we're away from it all the morn wi the rest of you football guys. "Scot-free" you could say," Alec burst out laughing at his own joke.

"I'm still no gettin it" said Kenny.

"Look, it's a long story but tae cut tae the chase, Leo here owns the bank."

"He what? He's just robbed his own bank?" shouted Kenny struggling to come to terms with what he was hearing. He turned round to look at Leo who was undoing his tie. Leo gave Kenny a very laid back grin.

"Aye, it's his bank. How can ye launder dodgy money if ye huvnae got a washin machine? Yesterday he took delivery of two million quids worth of diamonds fae the mines in Siberia en-route tae Antwerp. We've gaun in an moved things aboot so it looks like somebody has trousered the gear, when in fact it's in a safe deposit box a few drawers along, owned by Harold. He set it up a few months ago on his first visit out here. We've smashed a few boxes open and thrown stuff about. Normal villainy, eh? Leo's goat insurance and we've goat the diamonds. Get what I'm saying? We've left Atholl in there wi a belt round the lughole from the security guards truncheon and when he comes round or rather down, he'll be able to tell them fuck all."

"Harold's been here before? What do you mean when he comes down?" asked Kenny. He couldn't keep up.

"Harold made him one of his special cocktails before we went in. Two thirds LSD and one third sleeping tablets. When he wakes up he'll be seein lizards and Betty Boo crawlin up his cell wall. Good luck to the cunt as it's more than he deserves."

"But really, you're telling me I've been used," cried Kenny. "Harold didn't need any cover or any help at all. He's already been here! Unbe-fucking-lievable!"

"Take it up wi him when you see him, Kenny. Ah'm sure he'll understand your point of view. He's an easygoing kinda guy." Alec was smiling from ear to ear. Kenny turned round to see Leo trying not to laugh too much at Kenny's frustrated cries of outrage.

They were now approaching the old docks. Kenny had been through this area in 1994 when he got off the ferry from Helsinki. It was being modernised but there were still a few areas of grim warehouses where it would be unwise to go without a formal welcome.

Alec pulled the van into a large vaulted warehouse. Two men were waiting for them and as Alec and Kenny got out, along with the three guys in the back, they jumped in and drove off. As they were driving off, Kenny noticed for the first time the van had Latvian number plates.

"Not a bad wee tickle as it happens. What do you reckon Kenny?" asked Alec, a broad smile on his face. "Want to say thank you to Leo for arrangin aw this? In a roundabout way he's saved your life as if it wasnae fur him, we wouldnae be here and you know where that would have left you, don't you?"

"Aye, lyin on the floor of a sauna wonderin why it was so cold," replied Kenny. "Somehow, I think I'll pass on the thank yous until I'm safely back home."

"Alright. Have it your way, you fucking Dumfries ingrate."

Kenny suddenly looked at Alec as he had normally been friendly towards him. Alec broke into a big smile.

"Just a wee wind up, Kenny. Take it easy. As Liam Gallagher says "Don't Look Back in Anger". You'll still make the game. Come on we'll give you a lift up the street and you can get a taxi to the stadium."

CHAPTER 13

Kenny got out of the taxi at the park and wandered up towards the Kadriorg Stadium. It was 3.30 and he was a bit puzzled to see a stream of people walking towards him, all of whom appeared to be Scots. He saw Gus and Dominic both of whom looked rather hot and sweaty for some bizarre reason.

"Well hello stranger!" said Gus. "Have you missed yourself or what? Fuckin' Estonians never showed up, man. Doddsy passed it to Collins and the ref blew the whistle. Ye just had tae be there."

"What happened Kenny or can you no say?" quizzed Dominic in a low voice. "Gus said you'd been speaking to Harold."

"Got held up at the bank, if you must know. I'll tell you later. Why are you two so fucking sweaty? Don't tell me there's been more group sex in the changing rooms." Kenny was trying to lighten the mood but it was a sore one.

"Nah, better than group sex. We've just had the kickaboot tae end all kickaboots. After the team went off, this fat wee ugly guy in a kilt ran on to the pitch with a ball from the touchline, dummied a security guard and slotted the ball home. Cue mass invasion by Scotland fans. Ah nearly scored but was taken out by some guy fae Burntisland. It was absolutely magic." He'd never known Gus to take uppers but Kenny could swear he was high on something now.

Kenny looked at them both and they looked radiant. Dominic was absolutely crap at football but he'd still got on and it had made the trip for him. The lack of a game wasn't an issue as they'd both been there. Scotland would get the three points for one kick of the ball but more importantly these guys had been at an event that would echo round the world of football for years to come. He'd missed it. He was alive but he'd still missed being there. What a complete and utter bummer. Whoever said life was more important than football had got it wrong.

"Everythin' alright wi Harold?" Gus asked, a concerned note in his voice.

"Aye, sweet as a nut. Everything's sorted" said Kenny. "I think I'll go up and have a look so that at least I can say I was in the ground. I'll catch you back in the pub. What one are yous going to?"

"Hell Hunt as per usual. The Nimita will be mobbed" replied Dominic.

"Ok, catch you in there" muttered Kenny as he turned away.

Kenny continued his walk up to the ground. It was a trickle of fans that were coming out now and most of the fans looked a combination of delirious and knackered. The average consumption of alcohol by a fan before a game went against having a mass kickabout five minutes after kick off when most people expected to be still queuing to get in. He was able to walk into the ground without showing a ticket as they'd opened the gates to let the fans out. He was astonished to see there were still some people on the pitch until he realised it was the Scotland team going through a training routine.

He was watching the squad go through its paces when a familiar voice called "Mr Bradley, still here I see." Kenny turned round to see Frances Fairweather walking up to him with a quizical expression on her face.

"No, just got here Frances" The words were out of his mouth before he could stop himself. Oh fuck, shouldn't have said. Frances had been a teacher before joining the SFA and he knew straight away she could smell out a lie the way Gus could smell out a slapper.

"Just got here? And why is that? Don't tell me you missed all the action?" she said, her eyes fixing a steely gaze on his.

"Yes, one of those things. Forgot my ticket, had to go back to the hotel and then got caught in traffic. Did I miss much?"

"From a footballing point of view, no, but you did miss the Scotland fans serenading me when I was making an announcement over the tannoy."

"Oh aye, what was it? Flower of Scotland? A wee bit of Neil Diamond?" asked Kenny with a smile on his face.

"No, it was that well known Scottish ballad that goes something like" and here Frances took a deep breath to gently sing "Get yer tits out, get yer tits out, get yer tits out for the lads, get yer tits out for the lads."

Kenny burst out laughing.

"I saw Mr McSween singing it quite lustily so tell him that I am looking forward to him giving me a personal serenade soon. I never realised he was such a chanteuse." Frances had a mischievous look on her face.

"I'll be sure to mention it to him" said Kenny.

"But what about you Kenny, is everything ok in your life?"

Ah, the classic Frances Fairweather sting. Lull you into a false sense of security and then get you right in the guts with a swift upper hook. He knew she didn't believe a word he'd been saying but there was no way he was telling her what had just happened that afternoon.

"Never better Frances" replied Kenny, "Never better. Six points from two games, two clean sheets and a memorable day in Tallinn all round. Can't complain. Think I'll be heading back into town. You flying back tonight?"

"Yes. Once they've finished this session, we're off. And yourself?"

"The morn's mornin."

"You flying back with your father-in-law? I saw he was at the game. I thought you might have told me he'd become a bit of a Scotland fan with him joining the supporters club as well."

Oh fuck, he was on the ropes now. He'd taken the earlier body blow but she was going for a knockout with that last comment.

"I expect so but Harold's a bit of a law unto himself if you get my drift" he managed to reply. "Well is that the time? I've got to go and meet the rest of the guys, so have a safe flight home and I'll be in touch."

"You take care Kenny. Have a safe flight." Frances had that knowing look on her face yet again and Kenny couldn't get out of that park quick enough.

He caught a cab to the Hell Hunt and immediately regretted it. This was the first western style pub opened in Tallinn after the Estonians gained their independence. It had been decorated in mock Irish pub style but at that moment in time looked more like a mock Irish funeral parlour. The late afternoon gloom from outside was being absorbed by the dark, heavy Irish furniture. To make matters worse Christy Moore singing some dirge-like Irish ballad was playing through the pub's sound system. Gus and Dominic sat at a table, two empty bowls in front of them. Kenny had expected a few more fans to be in but it was deadly quiet. Kenny looked at his two pals and realised the adrenaline of this afternoon's events had vanished. They both looked quietly contemplative and Kenny's appearance seemed to wake them from some kind of trance.

"Awright Kenny?" asked Gus. "We've just been talkin about you funnily enough." Dominic shot Gus an angry glance but Gus ploughed on. "We can't work out what you've been up to and we don't want to know. All we're saying is, like, that we're here for you pal. If Harold and his heavies want to start anything, they'll have to get past Dominic and me first."

This was all said with a confident tone but Kenny knew the facts of the matter. Gus and Dominic couldn't fight sleep. God knows what Alec, Martin or Leo would do to them.

"Calm down for fuck's sake. You've been watching too many kamikaze films on cable. It's all sorted and nothing else is going to happen to us from Harold."

"Oh aye," said Dominic with a quizical tone. He nodded at a TV in the corner.

"Can you explain that to us then?" The screen showed the front of the bank where Kenny had been parked earlier on. A couple of police cars were parked outside with the lights on the roof flashing merrily away. Two policemen were standing outside the entrance to the bank and another two had just left carrying Atholl McClackit between them. The three fans looked at the screen transfixed as Atholl appeared to try to point to something then shrieked with laughter. Another policeman came from behind and grabbed his ear to try and control his head. By the time he'd got a grip Atholl had calmed down and appeared to have passed out. The screen then cut away to a newsreader sitting behind a desk. She continued reading the news about the diamond robbery with a still photo of Atholl being held by two policemen, hovering just above her right shoulder. Dominic asked the barman what the news report was about. The barman turned the TV up and listened intently. He then put his lips together and blew out a small whistle.

"Big diamond robbery at bank. 50 million kroon in diamonds taken by thieves. Guy in photo captured by security. He face long jail time."

Gus and Dominic turned to Kenny, bewildered expressions on their faces but all he could say was "Don't ask. Just don't fucking ask, ok?"

CHAPTER 14

Kenny was standing in Tallinn airport's duty free shop trying to work out what perfume to get Alison. The shop wasn't much more than an enlarged kiosk and the range was pretty small. His mind was all over the place as the events of the last week raced around in his brain. He felt a presence standing next to him and turned to see Harold MacMillan standing before him with a big smile on his face. Behind Harold was Alec, a knowing grin on his face and next to him Tony. Well he thought it was Tony. There were so many bandages on his face Kenny had difficulty identifying him. Atholl must have caught him good style with that fire extinguisher thought Kenny. Looking back to Harold, Kenny could see his false eye was glistening somewhat and for some reason he had this bizarre image of Harold putting eye drops in his false eye.

"Alright, Kenny. Never had you doon for the Chanel type masel. A bit too classy for you, is it no?" teased Harold. He had caught Kenny in what could loosely be described as the Chanel section of the duty free shop in that Kenny was standing next to the one shelf containing the one bottle of Chanel No 5.

"Fortunately it's not for me, Harold. It's for Alison. I think you might be a wee bit disappointed yourself mind."

"Oh aye, how's that?"

"They seem to be out of Brut 33."

"Very fuckin funny. Just as well ah'm in a good mood wi ye at this moment in time. Ah heard ye didnae let the boys doon so ah've got a wee memento fur ye."

"A diamond? Oh Harold, you shouldn't have. People will talk. I'm a married man" replied Kenny a big grin on his face.

"Will ye do the right thing for once and just shut the fuck up. Here, ah'm almost tempted no to gie it to ye now but ye've done ok considerin you're a lippy fucker." Harold shoved a carrier bag in to Kenny's chest. Kenny opened the bag and found himself looking at a Scotland top. Not any Scotland top but one worn by one of the players the previous day. There was a number on the back and the SFA badge was embroidered into the material.

Kenny was stunned. He'd always wanted a genuine top but the prices had gone through the roof as the football memorabilia market took off.

"Where did you get this?" he asked Harold.

"One o the players was gettin in a bit too deep at ma casino. Ah told him ah would look kindly on his debts if he could come up wi a top fur me. When it's yer achilles tendon or a poxy bit of 100% polyester eh, it does focus the mind a wee bit? Just hope it fits. It's no exactly goin fae one athletic frame to another, is it?"

"Eh, aye, you're right there. Thanks a million, Harold. If there's anything I can ever..." Kenny's voice trailed off as he realised what he was saying.

"Don't worry, Kenny. Ah didnae get where ah am takin unnecessary chances. Once is enough for you, as far as ah'm concerned. Have a safe flight home. Ye goin via Copenhagen?"

"Aye, what about you? You no doing the same?"

"No, ah've got a couple of business opportunities croppin up in Moscow with Leo so we're goin to visit some acquaintances there before it gets too nippy. Ah'll be back home at the weekend so tell Alison ah'll see her on Monday mornin. Ok?"

"Aye, ok. Take care." Kenny was relieved to see Harold walk away towards the boarding gate for the Moscow flight. As he turned away with Harold, Alec made a gun out of his right hand and pointed it at Kenny. He had a big smile on his face all the while. Kenny grinned back at him. As for what Tony was doing with his face, Kenny had no idea, but hoped it was painful. Miserable fuck.

Kenny looked up at the departures screen only to realise he still had another 45 minutes before the SAS flight to Copenhagen was due to leave. Kenny was wondering what to tell Alison when he got home but decided silence was the only option. She'd probably find out about his adventures when Harold turned up at work with six million Estonian kroons and asked her to take it down Thomas Cook's for a decent rate of exchange.

He looked around the departure terminal and saw Gus trying to chat up the girl working the till in the cafeteria. As he approached Gus, Kenny saw he was just in time to see her give him a piece of paper.

"Come on you, can you not give it a rest for five minutes?" Kenny sighed.

"These burds love me man, it's in ma endolphins or ma fairy gnomes. One or the other." boasted Gus as he pocketed the bit of paper. He blew a kiss to the girl on the till and she giggled. They walked off towards the seated area to await the call for their flight.

"What happened to the one in the blue dress last night?" asked Kenny.

"No problem. Clinched the deal back at hers, like."

"She was pretty good looking apart from those boils on her arm," replied Kenny, a trace of a smile playing on his face.

"For the last time they werenae boils. It was a nervous condition," claimed an exasperated sounding Gus.

"Well that's understandable."

"What de ye mean by that?" asked Gus.

"Well I'd definitely be nervous if I was going to shag you. They might come in handy those boils you know. You run out of KY jelly, you just pop a boil and there's your lube."

"Aw get tae fuck man. That is one of the most disgustin things I've ever heard. You're one sick bastard Bradley, you really fucking are." Gus' face contorted as he thought back to what Kenny had said.

In an effort to regain the high ground, Gus continued, "What we had last night was beautiful, like. A man and a woman doing the most natural thing in the world and you've got to spoil it for me. The poetic beauty of life just passes you by at times pal. You're a bitter, bitter man, Kenny Bradley."

"Oh fuck off, "What we had last night was the poetic beauty of life"? You're having a laugh. If it was so beautiful how long did you stay after you had sex. 5

minutes? 15 minutes? or did you push the boat out and stay for half an hour's post-coital pillow talk?"

Gus had a resigned look on his face.

"Ok smart bastart. It wasnae quite five minutes but there was mitigatin circumstances, like. She lives wi her mother in one o those Russian built estates, no hot water, black and white telly that sort of thing. She normally shares the bed wi the mother so when we get in, we're getting down to it on the rug in front of the fire like. Everything's goin well, till the family dog appears from nowhere and starts lickin ma arse. Now ah've had a few funny experiences on the job in my time. Burds sticking their middle finger up ma ring, that sort of thing, but nothin like this dog. It had some tongue on it by the way. So this is really gettin me goin, you know what ah mean, like"

"No, sorry. As I've never had a dog lick my arse whilst I've been having sex, I don't quite know what you mean. But do continue. I suppose it puts a new meaning into the term doing it "doggy style"" said Kenny struggling to believe what he was hearing.

"Aye aye, ok, don't get clever. So there ah am in full stride like, a real buckin bronco, givin it laldy and this dog's tongue is the biggest turn on ah've ever had like. So you know what happens. I shoot ma load, start mooin like a cow and this dog goes absolutely mental. The burds right into what we're doin but then realises the dog will wake her mother up. She puts her hand over my mouth to shut me up but this just gets me goin even worse. Then the bedroom door opens and the old crone comes out to see what's goin on. Fuckin bedlam ensues like, wi the dog barkin, the mother pullin me off the daughter and the poor wee lassie trying to cover hersel up. So that's me donald ducked in more than one sense ah can tell you. One minute ah'm havin the best sex of my life courtesy of a dog lickin ma arse, the next minute I'm gettin barked at by the dog and huckled oot the door by the lassie's old dear."

"So did you get her number?"

"Who? The mother?"

"No, did you get Lassie's number?"

"Aye, ah got it in the nightclub"

"That's no quite the Lassie I was thinking of. I know you've been out with a few dogs in your time but this is a new one to me. There's never been one that's licked your arse."

"Aw, get tae fuck. That's no funny ya mad bastard."

"You really are incredible at times. Dragging Dominic into it as well. That boy will never be the same." Kenny was shaking his head in disapproval.

"Aye right. He didnae look too unhappy at breakfast when I saw him last. I think he might even be meetin her fae last night later on. He's no flyin back till tomorrow, like."

Kenny thought back to the previous night's events. After they had left the Hell Hunt they had made their way through the old town square to the Nimita bar. The place was jumping with Scotland fans who couldn't believe what they had experienced. A crowd of Estonian fans had come into the bar but had quickly left as the whole bar sang at them "Where were you at three o'clock?" and "One team in Tallinn, there's only one team in Tallinn."

Kenny had spotted two women in a corner, one of whom was a bit of a looker in a blue dress but her pal looked like a million dollars, in loose change.

Gus had charged straight in but had hit a major stumbling block in that the girl in the blue dress spoke no English and it was clear her pal, who did speak English wasn't going to play the role of interpreter without a bit of male company herself. Luckily for Kenny he had been paying a visit to the Gents when this had initially kicked off and, in a time of emergency, Gus had to enroll, if not endure, Dominic in the role of wingman. Gus was paying a high price for his companionship as it was only the promise of free lager all night that ensured Dominic's continued attendance.

Kenny had come back to the surreal sight of the four of them sitting round the table, with Gus saying to Dominic "Get her tae ask her what she does." Dominic then asking Anna what her friend does for a living in English and Anna asking her friend in the blue dress who was called Svea, the question in Estonian. Svea would say something to Anna who would then tell Dominic, who would then say "Gym instructor" to Gus. It was one of the most pathetic sights Kenny had ever seen so he went off looking for somebody to talk to about the day's events and he didn't mean a bank robbery.

Gus had bounded into the room around 4 am commenting that, like Santa Claus on Boxing Day, his sacks were well and truly empty. Kenny had asked about Dominic but all Gus had done was cackle in an evil manner, then made some comment about "sending a boy to do a man's job" before falling on his bed, fully clothed and passing out.

They were called for the flight to Copenhagen. The whole plane was full of Scotland fans trying to put their brains back in order. A few were sporting Russian military caps and hats bought in the Tallinn flea market. I bet Gorby never thought he was going to set up an international market in military memorabilia when he removed the iron curtain reflected Kenny. A couple of guys had gone the whole hog and bought jackets with medals to accompany the hats.

They boarded the plane and Gus had no sooner sat down than yet again he passed out. Kenny sat back and looked out at the clouds below them. The Baltic was occasionally visible through gaps in the steely grey clouds but there was nothing to see below. He thought back over the events of the last six days thinking this had been the trip to end all trips. He was still at a loss as to why Atholl or Andy or whoever had tried to kill him. He'd never ever heard of the guy. Maybe Harold could get a bit more info for him but he hoped he would be seeing less rather than more of Harold over the next few months. So, considering the last few days, he'd seen Scotland win once, the U21's were undefeated in two games, he'd missed a game people would be talking about for years to come, somebody had tried to kill him. Twice, if he thought back to Riga. He'd taken part in a diamond robbery where the diamonds hadn't left the bank and he'd got a genuine player's top.

All of a sudden he felt a surge of anger. The hotel electrics in Riga. He'd told that wee bastard Atholl they were dodgy and he'd legged it out of the bar not five minutes later. To think Jock Paisley died because of the wee shite. He couldn't be certain but it all made sense now, all the drinks on expenses, my God, maybe even Tadger Currie was murdered by him. Kenny was struggling to come to terms with what he'd just realised. He ran through what he could put together. The question that came back to haunt him was from Harold. How many Scotland fans normally die on trips? He couldn't pin Tadger Currie's demise on Atholl in the same way as Jock's but the wee bastard had definitely been in the bar prior to Tadger pegging it. Whatever was happening to Atholl, it wasn't enough in Kenny's book.

Gus was still fast asleep when all of a sudden he awoke with a start exclaiming, "Ma photaes, ma fuckin photaes" and immediately Kenny realised what he meant. With the excitement of the previous day, Gus had forgotten about his 3 pm appointment with the lady from the photo lab. At the time he was due to meet her, Gus had been standing in the Kadriorg Stadium singing "get your tits out for the lads" as Frances Fairweather made an announcement to the Scotland fans asking for calm.

"Looks like you'll just have to arrange another trip to Tallinn then Gus" said Kenny.

Gus' face relaxed into a smile as he said, "Could be an idea big boy. Could be an idea."

*****

Dair McClackit tied the last French tricolour round Sally McChisholm's ankle and the post of his bed. He had his Napoleon outfit on and had tried to tie her up as he would have imagined the man himself would have until he realised it was a physical impossibility with only one arm. Fortunately for Sally she was lying face down on the bed so she couldn't see his embarrassment. Fortunately for Dair, she was also stark naked and he was looking forward to a good afternoon's entertainment.

"Are you finished Dair?" she asked with an impatient tone. He had taken ten minutes to tie the last two, starting off using only one arm as a kind of experiment, till he realised it was taking too long and the effect of his pills might start to wane. Her earlier gentle snores had also been a bit of a prompt for him to hurry up.

"Sally, how many times have I told you it's Napoleon when I'm in uniform, not Dair," he said with an exasperated tone of voice.

"Sorry, Mon General but is there any chance of Napoleon wielding his grande baguette this side of Christmas? I've got high tea with the rural at 5pm so if you don't *allez vite* we're going to have to call a halt just when it is getting good."

"Ok, we're all set. I'll just put the tape on"

Sally sighed heavily. "Do we have to Dair, sorry Napoleon. Just for once, I would like to have sex without the 1812 Overture blaring in my ear."

"Calm down, Sally. It all adds to the effect. I just have to hit the play button. Dair McClackit was halfway across the bedroom when there was a knock on the door. He'd told Potter he was not to be disturbed under any circumstances. The man knew better than to interrupt him when he was with Sally McChisholm.

"Yes, Potter. What is it?" he bellowed across the room.

"A phone call Sir, Master Atholl. It's most urgent." came the muted reply through the door.

"Wait a minute" shouted Dair as he walked across the room. He had been in numerous battles with Potter who had served him loyally for 40 years and there was little they didn't know about each other. However, this Napoleon get up was a bit of an embarrassment despite their comradeship so Dair took his cocked hat off and opened the door just enough to take the phone. He picked up the receiver and held it to his ear.

"Atholl? Atholl, what's wrong. Why are you crying? Atholl? Atholl? What's happened? What have they done to you?"

SECOND HALF

CHAPTER 15

Gus and Kenny were standing at the bar of a pub at Charing Cross. It was a Friday lunchtime some four weeks after the trip to the Baltics. The pub was busy with workers having a leisurely lunch of Scottish staples such as lentil soup or steak pie and potatoes as they looked forward to the weekend ahead. In one corner, a raised seating area hosted a leaving do that was being wrapped up by the presentation of a card and a joke present. The boss making the presentation was clearly keen to get back, whereas his workers looked more reluctant. The smile on the face of the guy leaving spoke volumes for the working environment or maybe that was just the four pints of Belhaven weaving their own brand of alcoholic magic.

"So how are the Nobby Stiles these days then," asked Kenny, taking a sip from his pint of lager.

"No' too bad now ye come tae mention it, like," said Gus McSween, hitching up his jeans and then scratching his balls as an afterthought.

Kenny looked askance at Gus who was calmly drinking from his pint of Stella, one foot on the railing beneath the bar, not a care in the world.

"Ah got a really good tip from a boy at ma work. You keep your suppositories in the fridge. That way, when you've got to, eh, pop one in shall we say, they're nice and firm and there's minimal mess, like."

"I take it pop one in means what I think it means?"

"Exactly. Let's just leave it at that shall we?"

Kenny nodded quickly and stared at the gantry.

"So is that you finished for the week?" asked Gus.

"Aye, I'm finished but what about you? That's your third pint. Are you going back this afternoon?"

Gus put his pint down then raised his hand to stifle a burp.

"Excuse me. Aye, ah'm goin back. No problem. You just trying to get out of buying me another pint, like?"

"No, no, I just thought the three pints of Stella you've downed might affect your performance this afternoon."

"Don't worry about it. Go back a bit. So you were sayin, that wee prick Atholl got ten years then?"

"I think so. I bumped into Dominic the other day. He's kept in touch with the boy with the bar in Tallinn. Apparently Atholl's trial was rushed through. He was found guilty in less than two hours by the jury and banged up for ten years. Pity it wasn't life."

Gus looked at his watch.

"Will make the next my last. It's your round. Sounds like the Estonian justice system is something to be proud of, like. No messin."

Kenny waved over the barman and ordered a pint of Tennents for himself and another Stella for Gus.

"How can you drink this stuff at lunchtime, man. Four pints of Stella and you'll able to work? You'll be spending most of the afternoon in the Gents."

Gus shrugged and looked around the bar.

"Who owns the problem, Kenny? Eh? Not you."

"Aye, well. Talking of Estonia are we on for Monaco?"

"Aye, sure. Just one wee problem."

What's that?" asked Kenny.

"Ah might have gone a wee bit over the top yesterday."

"How's that?"

"Ah phoned Lennart Johanssen at home."

"You what?"

Ah'd had a couple at lunchtime and when ah got back tae the office, his home number was in the paper so ah called it."

"So you just thought you would phone the secretary of UEFA at home. Was he in?"

"No."

"Thank fuck for that."

"But his wife was."

"Please tell me you didn't have a go at her."

"Eh, no. It was a bit more than a go. More like a bit of a rant."

"Seriously?"

"Aye, a sort of anti-Brazilian rant but more anti-Swedish."

"Anti-Swedish?"

"Aye, well a bit more specific. Anti Swedes called Lennart Johanssen."

Gus took a mouthful of Stella and held his hand out in a placatory gesture.

"Kenny, he's brought it on himself. He could have stepped out o that meeting reviewin the game in Estonia and done the decent thing, like. He had a vested interest there man and did fuck all apart from re-arrange another fixture for us against fucken Estonia in bastardin Monaco. Have you heard how much a pint is there, like? A fucken fiver man!"

"I suppose he had a lot of pressure from the Estonians to get the game replayed."

"Get the game replayed? Why? They couldnae get a decent set o' lights for that fucken public park of pitch, so they forfeit the game. End of story, like. I don't see what the problem is? Do you?"

Kenny shook his head.

"I agree 100%. They fucked it. It's their loss. Why should we replay them?"

Gus looked at his pint for a couple of seconds and then turned to Kenny with a serious look on his face.

"Speakin o' Estonia, have you spoken to Harold lately?"

Kenny shuddered.

"I've been trying not to think about him to be honest. I don't know what was worse, missing the three-second game or being involved in a jewel heist with your father-in-law. No, wait a minute, I do know what was worse - him helping to save my life in that sauna. I am likely to be paying back that debt for a long time to come. "Better off dead" is the term that springs to mind."

"So you've not seen him at all?"

"No, I saw him last weekend when I got back from Ibrox. Alison had him over for Sunday dinner."

"Oh fuck, and how was he?" Kenny could tell Gus was concerned, as he hadn't touched his pint for thirty seconds.

"Well, he barely spoke to me and when he did he ripped the juice out of me."

"Back to normal then?"

Kenny laughed. "Oh aye, back to normal. But it begs the question, what is normal when you're Harold MacMillan? Do you ever think we think about life too much, Gus? You know - over analyse things? There's Harold, just goes out and does it, doesn't let anyone or anything get in his way."

"Aye, ah see where you're comin from Kenny. Though ah see masel in pretty much the same alpha male group as Harold, like."

Kenny looked around the bar to check he was still living in the real world.

"Fuck off, you're about as much an alpha male as Lionel Blair. How the fuck are you an alpha fucking male?"

"Kenny, ah see a beautiful woman and ah go for her. Ah don't let anythin stop me in my pursuit of beauty."

"Dear God, this just gets better and better. Do me a fucking favour. Most of the women you go out with have to be moved about under cover of darkness in case they scare children. Anyway, shouldn't you be going back to work?"

Kenny finished the dregs of his pint and picked his coat up off the back of the stool.

"You no' want another?" asked Gus.

"Seriously?" Kenny put his coat down.

"Oh aye," continued Gus, waving a fiver in the general direction of the barman.

"If anyone sees us in here and asks you who you are, you're a union member with a gambling problem and ah'm helping to counsel you." Gus was still waving the note in the general direction of the barman.

169

"You still on Tennent's?" he asked.

"Eh, go on then. They're still falling for these excuses of yours on a Friday afternoon then?" Kenny sat back down on the bar stool and looked around the pub. The clientele had thinned out considerably as clearly some people had a bit of a conscience when it came to work. The rump of the leaving party had disappeared back to work leaving the departee with a couple of close work mates. As for Gus.....

"Aye well, ah had a bit o' a result the week after ah came back fae Tallinn, like. You've met big George from Stirling. He's been on a couple o' trips."

"Oh aye. Nice guy, real family man" said Kenny thinking back to a decent bloke who insisted on showing you photos of the wife and kids every time you met him.

"Well he's had a few financial problems with his wife leaving him and then spending a lot of time in the bookies trying to win money to win her back. So ah block-booked a Friday afternoon to meet him. The big boss hears about this and came round to check, as he knew we were pals. He bursts into the office just as George has broken down. It was utterly pitiful, truth be told, but when the boss saw the state o him, he told me to take as long as necessary."

Kenny took a large mouthful of lager from his pint and set the glass back down.

"Brilliant, so I'm a devoted family man whose wife has left him, I have gambling problems and am, subsequently, on the verge of a nervous breakdown."

"If you put it like that then yes. Thinking about it this will need to be my last actually. Ah've got rehearsals later."

Kenny placed both hands on the bar pretending to steady himself from a fainting fit.

"I thought you were joking when you said you were joining Shawlands Amateur Dramatic and Operatic Society, what is it called again? SADOS? Too fucking right, the biggest bunch of sad bastards going."

Gus had quickly finished his pint and wasn't biting.

"Kenny, these actress burds are well up for it. Well the ones that arenae lezzers, are right up for it, even wi ugly bastarts like me."

"Must be the alpha male about you Gus. You, Errol Flynn and Warren Beatty. Stars of stage screen and the Shawlands Community Centre. How does that song go "Don't put your daughter on the stage Mrs. Worthington, Gus McSween's after his hole."

Gus sniggered along with Kenny.

"Just as well you weren't on Stella, son. That Tennent's pish has gone right to your head. Kenny Bradley, Scotland's answer to Noel Coward."

CHAPTER 16

Denise Bradley rolled off Harold MacMillan and focused hard on the hotel room ceiling. She tried to make something out in the pale blue paint but there was nothing she could see. She could have been staring at a summer sky. That in itself was something of a relief as she tried to compose her thoughts. In the last fifteen minutes she had been informed of three attempts on her son's life on Scotland trips and had, essentially, been ravaged by a man possessed by a sexual hunger the depths of which she had not realised existed until this afternoon.

"By Christ Denise, you know how to move a man. Ah could feel that one coming up from my ankles."

Harold was lying on his back panting.

As she turned her head Denise could see his false eye watching them from the bedside table. She had to admit she found it a bit of a turn on being watched having sex, even if it was just a bit of glass. It was on the table as it had a nasty habit of popping out of Harold's eye with surprising force as he climaxed. She'd once had a bruise on her forehead for a few days which took a bit of explaining when Kenny dropped in for a surprise visit.

She turned to look at Harold. He was in good nick for a man his age, the scars of his lifelong career in crime only adding to the mystique. She had never dared ask about the long scars on his back and thigh. She imagined the small ones near his shoulder to be bullet wounds. He did like to have them stroked but the eye was the main piece of damage.

"You're not so bad yourself Harold!" she replied. "Life in the old dog yet, eh?"

"Woof, fuckin woof" said Harold as turned on his side and reached over her to pick up his eye. He put it back in and looked down at her.

Denise pulled up the duvet as she felt self-conscious when she was being looked at by him. Almost as if she was being examined for flaws. The eye on the bedside table was one thing but when he had inserted it in the socket, both it and the man himself appeared to grow in stature.

172

"Ah thought ah was having a heart attack back there. I'll need to get back down the gym or back on the golf course to do some exercise. Then again, was this just no' the sort of aerobic workout the doctor recommends?"

She smiled up at him, trying to put on a convincing face.

"If you're happy, I'm happy, Harold."

She lifted her head and re-arranged the pillows then pulled both herself and the duvet up so she could assume a position of comfort when she was really trying to gain some control of the conversation.

"So let me get this straight, Dair McClackit thought Kenny was his son and sent his other son out to kill him?"

"Got it in one, Denise."

"So what are we going to do now?" she asked looking directly at Harold.

"Well, ah was kinda hopin' for a cuppa tea and maybe a chocolate digestive," said Harold with a mischievous look in his good eye.

"No, you daft fool. What are we going to do about Dair McClackit?" exclaimed Denise.

"His son being put away makes no difference. He won't let that stop him if he's anything like the Dair McClackit I knew."

Harold lay back and closed his eyes.

"At this moment in time ah don't know what to do - so ah'm going to do nothin."

"Do nothing? Typical bloody male attitude!" snorted Denise. "I want to know my boy is safe and if there's any chance of him being in danger, I want you to protect him, please!"

" Aye, OK, OK" Harold held his hand up in mock surrender. "You're a demandin woman at times Denise but you have your moments just like ah like to think ah have mine."

"Oh aye, you have your moments Harold. Like when your trying to get into my good books so you can get me back in here." She pointed at the bed with her index finger to emphasise the point.

173

Her face was flushed and it was not just the sex.

Harold ran his hands over his face and through his hair.

"Hmm, you have a point and ah'm going to agree with you for one simple reason."

"Oh aye, what's that?" said Denise, who by this stage was brushing her hair with aggressive strokes, almost hitting her head before pulling the brush through her brunette mane. She pointed the brush at Harold.

"Let's hear it, and I want the truth"

Harold was lying on his back, with his right forearm covering his eyes. Denise thought he was trying to protect himself as much as hide his feelings.

"Ok, here we go" he started.

"After ah left Kenny in Tallinn, ah went to Moscow with the Estonian boy Leo, the boy ah met in the Caribbean. He had arranged to meet a big mafia boss in Moscow at a restaurant, somewhere near Red Square. When we got there ah just felt it was wrong. Ah've been in this game all ma life so have got to know when somethin's just no right. As soon as we walk in ah knew there was going to be grief so ah said ah had to go to the toilet as ah'd had somethin dodgy on the flight. Ah'm escorted to the bogs, sorry Gents, wi this Russian boy. Ah do the necessary but all the time ah'm trying tae work out how ah can get out of this mess with limited damage to yours truly."

Harold sighed.

"Funny how certain things come back to ye at certain times in your life. It was simple. Ah'd done it before so it just fell into place. After ma time at the urinal ah go tae the sink. Ah call the boy over and ask him to hold onto my eye while I wash my hands and face. You should have seen the look on his face. He looked even worse when ah kneed him in the baws and smashed his face off the taps a couple of times. Ah shut him in a cubicle and legged it out through the kitchens. Do you know how difficult it is to get a taxi in Moscow when ye're running for your life?"

"Funnily enough, no!" Denise had stopped brushing.

174

"So anyway ah tell the driver to take me to the domestic airport. Ah reckon the first thing they'll think of is the international departures so ah end up taking in the sights of St Petersburg airport after the flight there. Excellent wee bar on the right as you come out of the Gents in domestic arrivals, by the way. Ah got a train to Helsinki and a couple of flights later ah'm back in the bosom of my lovin family, all safe and sound."

He took his arm off his face and looked at Denise.

"Satisfied?"

"And Leo?" asked Denise.

"We were dead men walking as soon as we went in there. If the main man had played it a bit cooler we would both be worm feed. He was way too happy to see us. What's the word ah'm looking for? Effusive. There you go. Fuckin effusive. These guys normally treat you like something they have found on their shoe."

"Language! That boy of mine is bad enough."

Harold closed his eyes and put his arm back over his face. Maybe coming clean wasn't the right idea as part of a big build up after all.

Denise poked one his wounds on his right shoulder.

"Don't ignore me, Harold. Where is this all leading? I can't remember the last time you were this open."

"Ah'm trying to explain something if you'll just give me a chance for Christ's sake!"

Denise shrank back into the pillows.

"Go on then, say your piece" she said in a muted tone.

"The escape from Moscow, and ah don't use the word escape lightly, gave me a bit of time to think. Ah'm fifty six. Ah don't think ah'm too old to be pullin jobs but ah'm definitely too young to die."

"Harold, you don't need to do this. You've made your money. Why can't you just leave it?" Denise had her own eyes closed as she said this. She had never spoken to the man lying across from her in this tone before.

175

"Leave it? Interesting point Denise but as soon as word gets out ah'm giving up on the life, ah'm dead meat. There is a possible compromise to be reached, a kind of handin over o power if you like but ah'd need a convincing reason to do it."

"What…"

Harold slightly raised his hand from his face and stretched it out but Denise did not flinch.

"Hear me out Denise, if you please." He lowered his hand.

Harold was trying to find the words to ensure the conversation went the way he wanted, no, needed it to go. He wanted to have a bit of fun in his retirement and if there was one woman who offered you fun like no other, it was Denise. He'd had experience of young bimbos in the past. The sort who can't see past their own eyelashes without being dazzled by their stupidity. That stage of his life had gone. Denise was a self-made woman and, alright she had some baggage, namely the waster prick of a son who was married to his daughter, but all things considered he loved her deeply.

"Give me a minute and I'll tell you." Harold patted the bed with his left hand and reached over to the bedside table and took a small box from the drawer.

He sat up in bed, looked Denise in the eye and said "Denise Bradley, will you marry me?"

Denise sat upright "OK, ya bugger. Yes, I will."

"Fantastic," said Harold and reached over to kiss the newly engaged Denise Bradley.

"Excellent. Ah can tell you what ah need to tell you now."

"Tell me what? Is it to do with Kenny?" a concerned tone entered Denise's voice.

"No, not directly. When I said I planned to do nothing over Dair McClackit, it wasn't strictly true."

Denise fell back on the pillow, the joy of the proposal immediately forgotten.

"Harold, don't tell me. What have you done?"

"Nothing bad, don't worry but I got a couple of the lads to drive up to the

McClackit estate and make enquiries about any jobs that might have needed doing."

He sat right up in bed with his hands on his lap, looking at Denise.

"I assure you it was nothing heavy. They were trying to find out the lie of the land but they said some mean looking ex-army type in his mid 50s had appeared with a shotgun and so they'd legged it. By the sounds of things the guy was more interested in protecting the castle than launching another attempt on Kenny's life, but you never know. Would that be this Dair character?"

"No he would be too young. Did they describe him anymore? Height? Moustache? Build?"

"No they said he was a well built bloke in his mid 50s, handled the shotgun like it was very familiar to him. Looked ex-military with the 'tache."

Denise took the pillow from behind her head and put it over her face. Harold heard what sounded like a low moan coming from beneath it.

"Denise, what's wrong?"

"I can't tell you just now" came the muffled reply.

She took the pillow away and looked up at Harold.

"Trust me when the time is right, you'll be the second to know."

"What are you on about? Second to know? Who's going to be the first?"

"Kenny" came the reply as the pillow was replaced over her face.

CHAPTER 17

The next day, Harold took Denise for a drive up north. They took the road up to Inverurie, as Harold was looking at investing some money into a luxury golf club development. Denise asked if she could take the car and as she had a spa afternoon planned in another local hotel.

"OK, Doll. No problem. I am going to be in meetings with these financial pricks all afternoon, so come back for about 6 and I'll see you then. Drive carefully."

As Denise left the development, she drove along the road for 100 yards before parking up. She got out the road map and quickly found the location of Castle McClackit. Thinking about the distance she realised it was doable in the time available so put the map on the passenger seat and headed off in the direction of Dair McClackit.

As she approached the castle a wave of memories swept over her. She couldn't deny she'd had some good times there and the only bad thing that had happened was falling pregnant with Kenny which had been the making of her. She knew she'd been badly treated on her departure, but what's that nonsense about what doesn't kill me makes me stronger? Aye, that was it. A minor setback on life's long journey but now she was back to sort out a few things, one way or another. At times she often felt she would not have done as well in life but for the dismissal from Castle McClackit so in a funny way, she owed Dair McClackit more than he would ever know.

Coming up the driveway, Potter appeared at from the front door with a shotgun.

"Don't tell me you're going to marry me after all these years, Frank," said Denise as she got out of the car.

"Denise? Is that you?" Potter lowered the shotgun and stared back at a face he'd not seen in over thirty years. The last time he'd seen her he'd put her on a train at Aberdeen. Here she was, driving a BMW 5 series and looking like a thoroughly well groomed affluent middle-aged woman.

"Not much of welcome but then this place was never the friendliest to me," said

Denise as she walked up to Potter and planted a kiss on his cheek.

"Eh, aye well, you know how it is," said Potter an embarrassed look on his face.

"So, are you going to invite me in?"

"Aye sure. Come on in. You won't see many changes, mind."

"Surely the old goat's spent some money on the place in the last thirty odd years?"

"Not as you'd know it. I sneak the odd bill past him but there's no central heating, the roof's done and there's damp everywhere. What do you want, Denise?"

"I want to see the Laird if that's alright with you Frank. I think you know why I'm here and what it concerns."

By this stage they had wandered from the drive to the hallway.

"Good God, this hasn't changed a bit," exclaimed Denise.

"No, nothing different here. What do you mean when you say I will know why you're here?" Potter had had enough surprises in his life to be happy with the plain and ordinary of normal life. The sight of Denise Bradley had been a not entirely unwelcome one as she was looking very good for her age, but she'd brought something with her. He couldn't put his finger on it but there was a determined air about her for some reason or another and determined women made him feel slightly uncomfortable.

"Come, come Frank. I'm sure the Laird wouldn't have dreamed up a scheme to kill my Kenny without discussing it with you first?"

They had made their way in to the kitchen, Denise noting the unchanged shabby décor of old. The same carpets, the same tables and chairs, even the same drying horse form 1959. She sat down at the kitchen table and was looking up at Potter with a severe expression.

"Kill your Kenny, what are you on about?" Potter was holding on to the back of a chair as he said this and was glad of the support.

"Kill *your* Kenny? Why don't you try "Kill *our* Kenny, Frank?""

Potter mumbled a couple of words as he stared at the seat of a chair.

179

"Frank, don't be coy. You could never hide your emotions from me and don't think you can start now."

"Hide my emotions? I don't have the foggiest what you're on about woman. What's the old devil been up to?"

Potter felt distinctly uneasy with the way the conversation was going. This sudden appearance was bringing emotions to the surface he'd repressed for a number of years. He had always been good around women but Denise brought something to their relationship that made him feel defenceless. At times she was more man than woman.

"Well, how can I put it Frank? I have it on very good authority from my fiancé, note the "fiancé" bit, that young Atholl is currently banged up in jail in Estonia. Prior to his arrest he tried to kill my son three times and failed each time. Now, I don't know why he wanted to kill Kenny, but I imagine a certain old rogue in this building has a good idea about why Atholl was trying to harm my, sorry our, poor wee innocent boy."

Potter grasped the back of a kitchen chair for support.

"Denise, God's truth! I don't know what you're talking about. He's hardly spoken to me since Atholl was locked up and he's at death's door anyway. He's been taking these drugs to boost his sex drive but with their side effects and the news on Atholl, he's gone right downhill."

"OK, well if you can't give me answers, he's going to. Where is he?"

Denise stood up staring hard at Potter. He could not look her in the eye but gestured weakly to a door at the far end of the kitchen.

Denise had formulated a plan on the drive up and was now wondering if she could go through with it. She'd done a lot in a life of more downs than ups, but somebody had tried to kill the one thing she had to show for her life and they were going to pay.

"Come on, he's in the master bedroom. He's not well so go easy on the man. It's been a long hard life and his heart is on its last legs."

They left the kitchen and climbed the back stairs to a landing giving a view out on to the glen. As she paused to look out, she saw the gardens were still immaculate. If the Laird wanted the place to go to rack and ruin it was clear Potter was still trying keep up appearances. They then walked along the wood-paneled corridor, a smell of dampness adding to the sense of decay Denise had felt since entering the house. As she walked behind Potter, the memories came flooding back. The unrelenting boredom of living in the small castle based community where the only thing people had in common was their fear of the Laird. The curtains looked the same drab design that was popular sometime in the 1940s. She could even see the same damp patch in the ceiling underneath the one bathroom in the attic that was meant to be shared by six servants. She had a bad feeling the first time she saw Castle McClackit, a chill had seeped into her bones then but she was not cold now. Anything but.

Potter pushed the bedroom door open and beckoned Denise inside.

"Sir, there's someone here to see you. Sir? Are you awake Sir?" Potter spoke in hushed tones hoping that he would find the Laird fast asleep or dead. He had a bad feeling about letting Denise in here and wondered what exactly she had in mind.

"Let me in, Frank. I want to see the old fool," said Denise as she brushed him out of the way.

Dair McClackit was pretending to be asleep. On hearing the female voice he turned over and raised his head. "Who's that? Potter, who is this woman you've allowed into my bedroom?" To Denise's ears the voice sounded exactly the way she'd remembered it. Arrogant and used to being obeyed.

"It's Denise, Dair. Denise Bradley. I was in the vicinity so I thought I'd pop in for old times sake."

"Denise? Denise who? Potter, who is this woman and what is she doing in my bedroom? Remove her at once."

Denise by this point had moved to the other side of the bed from where Potter was standing.

"Oh there's no need to be like that Dair. Think back a few years to when we were both a bit younger and friskier."

She stood over the bed and took her coat off, folding it neatly and placing it on the bottom of the bed.

She put one knee on the bed and swiftly moved her hand under the covers. She'd had little idea what she planned to do once she saw Dair McClackit, but it had suddenly hit her what she could do and more importantly, how she would get away with it. She leaned in close to the Laird's ear and started whispering.

"Come on, Dair. Think back to that hot summer of '59. You'd just finished in Kenya and were back here, roaming the grounds like a caged lion desperate for some relief. Remember how I gave you that relief, Dair? Remember those hand-jobs in the toolshed, in the pantry or the greenhouse? You couldn't bring yourself to get that close to a woman Dair, but you needed some relief. Well I'm here to give you that relief once more. Only, this time it is going to be a hand-job you'll never forget. Why did you tell Atholl to kill my boy, Dair?"

"Who are you? Denise? Not that trollop from Dumfries that was sent away in disgrace after you'd engineered some bastard from the seed of my loins?"

"The one and only!" By this time Denise had found what she was looking for under the sheets and was frantically working Dair's cock with her left hand. She was surprised at the alertness of the member - then remembered what Potter had said about the drugs.

"I remember so much from that time Dair. I remember being forced to give you hand-jobs or you said you'd sack me and I would go home to Dumfries. I remember hot passionate nights in the gatekeeper's lodge with Frank here. But forget about my memories, why did you want Kenny dead?"

"Denise, don't say it" interrupted Potter.

"Don't say what Frank? Don't say that I loved you more than any man I'd ever known? That I would have done anything for you? That you are the father to my

182

only son? Not this deranged old fool who always thought better of himself than anyone else did?"

"I thought he was mine," exclaimed the old man whose cock was being worked very hard. "I thought he would want the castle and the estate when I was gone. Atholl should be the only successor to the Clan McCla… Oh, don't stop, girl. Don't stop!" By this stage he was holding on the edge of the mattress either side of him. He stared at Denise his milky eyes displaying an intense glee.

Denise swapped hands and then moved back to throw the sheets off the Laird and to get a better grip.

He was really enjoying it she thought - as she brought the pillow down on his face with her right hand. Potter took a step forward but she stopped him with one look.

"Keep away, Frank. He tried to have my Kenny killed for God knows what reason, but it's his time to pay. He always knew his time would come and - oops, hasn't it just."

An arc of sperm flew from Dair's cock as Denise maintained the firm downward pressure on the pillow. Dair thrashed as his air supply dwindled and his body finally gave up the battle.

"Wait, wait a minute" cried Potter as Denise got off the bed.

"What? He's gone Frank. There's nothing you can do."

Denise was breathing deeply as the realisation of what she had just done sunk in.

"You can't leave him like this," said Potter.

"Why not," Denise asked?

"If you leave him like this they'll know he was murdered. There will be a post mortem and they'll find he's been suffocated. You need to try and disguise it a bit better. I've done this before so leave it with me. I'll sort it. Denise, we need to talk. I never knew about the boy. I wish you'd contacted me. We could have worked something out."

"Don't worry Frank. I worked it all out. I was so angry with you when they threw me out. I thought you would have come with me. But let me guess, it was duty, eh?"

"Duty," exclaimed Potter. "If only. I was scared shitless. I'd done so many bad things in weird places that the idea of actually settling down somewhere and building a family was beyond me."

He pointed at the corpse. "He was convinced the kid was his. Which shows you what a complete fool he was and what fools we were to allow him to believe it. Leave him the now and come downstairs I'll sort it later and phone an ambulance once you're gone."

They went back down the stairs and into the kitchen.

"I could do with a drink after that," said Potter.

"So could I," said Denise. "Milk and one sugar, please."

Frank Potter stopped in his tracks.

"Tea? You've just given a geriatric the hand job of death and all you want is tea? Bloody hell woman, they broke the mould when they made you."

He turned to pick up the kettle as Denise settled herself at the kitchen table. She looked at the old range and a memory of burning her forearm taking a roasting pan out of the oven suddenly sprang to mind. She looked at her forearm to see if the scar was still there but there was nothing. She looked further down at the hand which had been instrumental in the death of Dair McClackit but there was nothing there either. She didn't make the rules but she would play by her own if that's what it took.

"Frank, how can I put it this? I know what you were like before we met so I can only imagine in the years after I left you continued in the same vein. Death, destruction, mayhem, all caused by you or people you were working with. Am I wrong? I rid the world of one piece of human trash and you think I am the hard one. So what do you see when you look in the mirror, eh?

Potter was taking the lid from a tin of biscuits as he listened to this.

He put some on a plate and placed the plate on the table.

"Rich tea?" exclaimed Denise. "Sums this bloody place up."

"Christ, you've landed me with a bit of a mess to clear up Denise so please don't mind if I am not too upset at the lack of gypsy creams or vanilla bourbons to go with your tea."

"It's chocolate."

"Eh?"

"Chocolate bourbons."

Potter banged the teapot down on the table.

"Look, I don't care if it is gold-plated bloody bourbons, what are we going to do about that upstairs?"

Denise had poured herself a cup of tea and was calmly staring at Potter as she stirred her sugar in.

"Five minutes ago you told me you could sort it. Do it. How many dead bodies have you disposed of in the past Frank? Use your imagination. Be creative. Make it happen!"

She sipped her tea and looked out the window.

Potter vigorously snapped a biscuit in two and gave it a couple of quick dunks in his mug.

"As you wish, My Lady. I suppose it is only fair you get your way this time. You've never asked me for anything before."

"That's very kind of you Frank. Also very accurate - so don't you forget it."

"However, there is one small favour I would like to ask in return."

"Tread carefully Frank as you are walking in an emotional minefield. One false step and BOOM!" Denise had turned her gaze back to Potter.

"I would like to meet my son." He was staring at the table as he spoke. He could not look her in the eye anymore.

"Well. That's not an unreasonable request but I can't guarantee he'll want to meet you. I will leave you my card. Give me a call when this has been cleared up, say a week or so, and we'll take it from there. No promises but I'll do my best."

185

Denise had opened her handbag and was foraging for her purse.

"Card? Get you!" said Potter in a poor attempt at a posh English accent.

"Frank, get with the programme. We are on the verge of the 21st century. You are going to have to come out into the big bad world now the Laird has gone. Women have business cards, women drive nice cars and lots of women could buy or sell you."

She stood up and pinched his cheek with her left hand.

"Good luck Frank. I think you're going to need it."

As she drove away from Castle McClackit, Denise had the strange sensation she was being watched. You can watch all you want Dair, as you can't touch me now.

She couldn't promise anything to Potter about meeting Kenny, as God knows Kenny was a law unto himself, but she'd try and persuade him to give it a go with Potter. Lately he'd not asked about his dad which was not like him, but maybe she'd surprise him the next time he brought the subject up.

She parked up in the golf club car-park and wandered into reception. Harold was sitting reading the Financial Times, moving his lips as he tried to come to terms with words he did not normally come across in the Daily Record.

"Oh, get you. That reminds me of the old joke," said Denise, a broad smile on her face.

"Eh?"

"What's pink and hard?"

"What are you talking about, woman?"

"What's pink and hard?" - a more determined tone in her voice this time.

"I don't know, what is pink and hard?" said Harold thoroughly confused by the conversation.

"The Financial Times crossword. Boom, boom!"

"Jeezo, that spa did the trick. Jokes and a healthy glow about you." He looked her up and down.

"What's that on your skirt? Moisturiser?"

Denise looked down to see where some of Dair's sperm had landed on a small patch of her skirt.

"Oh aye. That stuff is deadly."

"Any free samples?"

"No, that was the last of that line. They have a related range but it's a bit nasty so I passed."

CHAPTER 18

The rain beat against the patio windows of Denise Bradley's house in
Dumfries. Her lounge was tastefully decorated in what Kenny believed people in
the design magazines referred to as "muted tones". The carpet was a dirty-grey
beige. He remembered his mother describing the colour as "pale ash bark" on
one of his infrequent trips to Dumfries with Alison.

The two leather settees, set off at a right angle, were another colour shade he
remembered - strong tobacco. Who came up with these names? Whatever
happened to light brown and dark brown?

The curtains blended in with the carpets and settee. An expensive looking Sony
TV dominated one corner in an otherwise tasteful and understated room. His
mum had moved here about two years after Kenny married Alison. It was not the
house he had grown up in and he found it hard to love. He also had a sneaking
suspicion someone had helped her with the purchase but it was nothing he could
put his finger on, just something that felt not quite right.

As he continued staring out the window from his vantage point on the settee,
wondering if the Queens game would be called off, his mum appeared from the
kitchen carrying a tray with a teapot, two mugs and a packet of Jaffa Cakes. As
Denise put the tray down on the coffee table, another tasteful piece of gear now
Kenny looked at it more closely, she looked up at him.

"Sorry, Kenny. I am still not going to tell you who your father is. Why don't you
just leave it?"

Kenny was taken aback by this turn of phrase from his mum. "Leave it", was
normally her last word on a matter. Essentially she was saying "Don't push your
luck, pal." They had spent the last twenty minutes arguing about her refusing to
reveal who his father was. Her disappearance into the kitchen had clearly been to
buy time for herself, but Kenny had taken as much as he could take.

"Leave it! Bloody leave it!" shouted Kenny.

Kenny could not believe he had sworn in front of his mother but was in no mood to apologise. He stood up from one of the "strong tobacco" couches.

"It's OK for you to say that but you've not had some nutter trying to kill you in an Estonian sauna!" By this stage, his face had reddened in the cheeks. Spittle had sprayed from his mouth with the last comment and he thought he might have overstepped the mark.

His mother had retaken her seat and was pouring the tea.

"OK, look. I've heard about your problems so give me five minutes till we've both calmed down."

Kenny immediately fell back on to the couch. "Heard about your problems"? How could she have heard about what happened in Tallinn? Gus? Dominic? He looked at her but she was concentrating on pouring him his tea. She produced a coaster from a drawer in the coffee table and placed the mug of tea down on it before sliding it over to him. She then took another one out for herself before pouring her own tea.

She handed him a plate then offered him a Jaffa Cake which he accepted.

"No Hobnobs?" he enquired.

"No, just Jaffa Cakes. They were on special offer and to be honest, I wasn't expecting you. Right, are you calmed down?" asked Denise as she poured milk into her tea. She picked up the mug and settled back into the couch, the leather upholstery making a soft ruffling sound as she moved back into a comfortable position.

"Aye, just about," said Kenny quietly. "Sorry." He had poured milk into his mug and was slowly stirring the brew.

"Now look Kenny. No mother who has brought her son up on her own likes to think they owe the father anything but, thinking about it, I suppose I owe you an explanation of who your dad is."

"Right, fine. Progress at last." Kenny turned on his part of the couch and looked his mother straight in eye.

"So, who's my dad then?" he asked.

Denise took a deep breath.

"Your father is a man called Frank Potter. He used to be the in the special forces, serving under Dair McClackit."

"Frank Potter!" exclaimed Kenny.

"Yes, Frank Potter."

"Not Dair McClackit?"

"No, not Dair McClackit." His mum was now looking down at the mug of tea in her hands. She looked up at Kenny abruptly, a fierce determination blazing her eyes.

"I never had an affair with Dair. I pleasured him occasionally. God, that sounds awful but Frank Potter is your dad. We were lovers when I worked at Castle McClackit."

"Whoa, whoa, whoa," said Kenny who was now up and pacing round the room like a lab rat who'd been given some speed as part of an experiment. "That's more than I really need to know."

He had put his tea down to prevent it spilling onto the pale ash bark carpet and was now rifling his hands through his hair as he walked round the room. It was that or tear his hair out.

"So, wait a minute. You're telling me that wee shite Atholl has been trying to kill me over nothing?" asked Kenny. He was now past caring about his language in front of his mum.

"So it would appear," said Denise, who shrugged her shoulders in Kenny's direction.

"Funny how life turns out, eh?" said Denise as a small tight smile broke her face. Kenny kept pacing round the room like a caged lion. Un fucking believable. Two guys had died, he'd been scared witless on that bank job and all for sweet FA. Wait a minute though. This still doesn't explain how his mum knew about these events.

"OK, I can just about get my head around all you've told me but what I want to know now is, who told you about all this stuff that went on in Estonia?"

He heard his mum groan and he realised she'd overplayed her hand.

"Kenny, sit down as this will come as a bit of a shock. Do you want a drink? I'm going to have a small brandy. I need something to steady my nerves."

She was walking over towards a unit where Kenny knew she kept a small but select collection of drink. As she opened the door of the cabinet, he could see a couple of bottles of Glenfiddich, Harold's favourite tipple if he remembered correctly, a bottle of Tanqueray gin, a bottle of Smirnoff Blue Label and a bottle of OVD rum.

She picked out a bottle of Hine cognac and offered it in his direction.

"No, I'm fine. I've got the car. I need to get back tonight after the game."

This was definitely getting heavier by the minute if his mum was having a drink during the day. Denise had poured herself a small stiffener and was warming the glass between her hands as she returned to her seat.

"Kenny, I've always brought you up to question things and be interested in life but you've got to realise that such inquisitiveness might sometimes come at a cost. You've got to be braced for some unpleasant answers at certain times if you keep on asking questions."

Denise took a sip of her brandy and sat back down on the couch.

"I have formed a friendship with Harold Macmillan, your father-in-law." She said it so quietly Kenny could hardly hear her.

"Formed a friendship? Formed a friendship?" He shot up from his seat. "It sounds more like the axis of evil to me," said Kenny as he once more paced around the lounge at an even greater speed.

"Sit down will you, please? This carpet's not long laid and I don't want you scoring big ruts in it."

Given her friendship with Harold, Kenny was wondering if the carpet was not the only thing in the house not long laid but he put that thought as far out of his mind as quickly as possible. The word *pleasured* was still wreaking havoc in his head.

He sat back down on the couch. His mind was racing. How long had this been going on? Harold was laughing at him behind his back as he maintained a "friendship" with his mum. The fact was his mum was dating Harold. That was the only word he could bear to use when thinking about the two of them. A man he neither liked nor trusted, a man who had saved his life but that was by the by, given this latest news update.

"Are you sure you don't want a brandy, Kenny. You look like you could do with one." She stood up as if to go to the drinks cabinet but Kenny stopped her with a curt wave of his hand.

"How long has this been going on?" Kenny quietly asked.

"We started seeing each other a couple of years after your wedding. He's a lovely man who is very kind to me. I thought you'd be upset which is why I never told you. I think you're taking it quite well actually."

"I am too stunned to speak. Frank Potter and Harold MacMillan in the space of ten minutes. Talk about too much information."

Denise took another sip of her brandy. Kenny could see she was a bit more relaxed and didn't know if it was the drink or the fact she had finally unburdened herself of the great secret affair between her and Harold. For fuck's sake, what was going on here?

"So what do you think?" she asked.

"Think about what?" By this stage he was lying back on the couch with his hands over his face.

"Kenny, sit up and look at me. You would think you were about five the way you're acting. What do you think about Harold and I?"

Kenny sat up properly and looked at her. He wanted to take his leather jacket off. In fact he wanted to take himself off, anywhere but this lounge, this house, this town, this planet.

"Eh, very good. Delighted for the pair of you. If you're happy, I'm happy. And any other bloody cliché you can think of."

192

He was up off the sofa again but not pacing. He stretched his arms out above his head, trying to free himself of a tension that had gripped his body over the last ten minutes. Denise took another sip of the brandy and looked out the windows into the garden.

A cold tone was in her voice as she said, "Thank you, I knew you'd approve."

"Aye, because if I didn't I wouldn't have any kneecaps left by five o'clock."

"Now, now, being bitter doesn't suit you son. Have a Jaffa Cake."

CHAPTER 19

"So tell me Andee, what will you do when you get out of here in 2006?" Atholl put down the pan he was cleaning and turned to face the guard, Viktor. The one guard that could speak English in this godforsaken hole and he wanted to practice it all the time.

"No time off for good behaviour Viktor? That's a bit harsh"

"No time off for good behavior, Andee. Slight possibility before Alexi die in shower. Now, how you say, no chance. You have long time to plan future. You plan, yes?"

"I don't really know, Viktor. Maybe open up a cafe after all my cooking experience in this jail. A small bistro in Provence. You could come and be my waiter. Decent money, decent food and better bloody weather. You won't have been to the south of France I take it? It's my favourite place on earth"

Viktor smiled at Atholl.

"Sat would be really nice, Andee. Sank you very much for sinking of me. What sose guys say about you and Alexi, sats all how you say in English – bullshit! No way a small nice guy like you kill big Russian prick."

"Not a problem old boy, sank, er, thank you for your kind words and I look forward to you joining me. Remind me not to put broth on the menu, though."

Atholl picked up another pan and began scrubbing it with a vigour that surprised him. When I get out of here, he thought, the cafe in Provence can wait, as the first thing I intend to do is find Kenny bloody Bradley and make him suffer.

He looked past Viktor to take in his surroundings. If someone had told him six months ago he would be a kitchen assistant in an Estonian jail he would have laughed in their face. He was alone with Viktor as they left him with the worst jobs to do at the end of the day but he could not be left unattended. So here he was with Viktor, dreaming about the south of France whilst living a complete nightmare.

To pass the time in his mundane kitchen duties Atholl thought about little else than what he would do to Kenny. Sometimes he thought about what he would do to Harold McMillan who was largely responsible for his current predicament but, no, Kenny Bradley was "number one with a bullet" as the song said. As he mopped the floors, as he peeled an endless mountain of potatoes, vengeance spurred him on.

"Viktor, are you sure there is no way you can get me back in the Governor's office?"

"Andee, what can I say? I ask the assistant governor, I mention to him bribe, I tell him sat you have more money san se whole Estonian people but no, how you say, joy!"

"OK Viktor. It's bitterly disappointing to me but I believe you and thank you once again."

"No Andee, sank you. I very much enjoy seese conversations sat we are enjoying togeser."

Atholl put the last of the pans on a drying board.

"Can I go back to my cell now?"

"Sure sing Andee, I will come back wiss you. You have no knives on you sen? Ha, Ha. I joke."

As they walked along the corridor back to the cell, numerous inmates who had been loitering outside their cells went back in like rats up a drainpipe. Atholl had had to take certain measures to establish he went unmolested in his time inside the Estonian jail and no prisoner wanted to get on his wrong side after the incident with Alexi.

"OK, Andee, sweet dreams tonight. No more nightmares?" Viktor looked at him with a concerned expression.

"I can't promise anything Viktor. The dreams, the nightmares, they come from nowhere."

"OK, but try to keep se noise down, eh?"

Atholl knew where the dreams and nightmares came from all right, but he wasn't telling Viktor. They came from that cocktail of drugs Harold McMillan had given him on that day in October. Six weeks later he was still getting flashbacks and cold sweats most nights. As a foreign prisoner he had a cell to himself, but his screams and wails were getting on the nerves of other prisoners though none of them dare take issue with him.

On his arrival at the jail, Atholl had spotted an immediate opportunity for escape but the timing needed to be right. He was still shaking off the effects of the drugs so it would best to cleanse himself before he was all set. When the second escape route appeared he thought he would square the circle of escaping and disappearing at the same time.

Lying on his bunk, he was collecting his thoughts on the best way to dispose of Kenny Bradley's body, when Viktor re-appeared at the cell door.

"Andee, the Governor wants you. Guy from British Embassy here too."

Atholl sat bolt upright. The guy from the embassy? They'd washed their hands of him long since. He thought he had more chance of getting a Red Cross parcel than any of those pen-pushing dimwits putting in an appearance.

"Sure, Viktor, right away."

As they entered the Governor's office, Atholl saw the jumped-up clerk from Blackpool who was passing himself off as the British Consul these days. Christ, if this man was the personification of Her Majesty's government we were all fucked!

The Governor was a large ex-Communist party official. He had been appointed just before the wall came down and was clinging to the post like a drowning man clinging to a lifebuoy.

"Mr Muir, good to see you again," came the greeting from the clerk who remained sitting opposite the Governor. Don't bother getting up you little fuck you thought Atholl.

"Moor, pay attention" said the Governor "Meester Borthwick has bad news. Please, Your Excellency."

196

The Governor gestured towards Atholl with his right hand.

"Your Excellency?" thought Atholl. The only thing this guy excelled at was mediocrity.

"Ah, yes. Thank you, Governor. I have some bad news from home for you Mr. Muir. There's no easy way to say it but we have been informed by a Mr Bryce Sutherland your father died last week of suspected heart failure. It is thought it was brought on by, how can I best put it, a certain method of arousing oneself, if you catch my drift."

"Don't worry I catch your drift with both hands. The dirty old bugger was trying to make himself come by a dangerous means. It came back and bit him on the bum?"

"Eh yes, quite. If you want to put it like that." The clerk shifted uneasily in his seat.

The Governor sensed that something was not quite right between the two.

"Father dead is very bad news. Son in jail very bad news. How father die?"

"A sporting accident governor," said Atholl before the clerk could answer. "Physical jerks. He should not have been trying to exercise so hard. His heart failed."

The governor patted his large stomach and said "Exercise, very bad." He shook his head in a manner that suggested to Atholl that he had little for sympathy in the plight of his father and even less for Atholl. No trip home for the funeral then Atholl supposed.

Atholl felt little or nothing. He'd badly let down his father when he had failed to kill Kenny Bradley and his father had not been backward in coming forward with his thoughts on the matter when he'd had his one phone call. Suddenly a sense of disappointment gripped his body to the extent he wondered if it would ever leave him.

"Can I make a special request, Governor?" asked Atholl.

"Special request?"

197

"Yes, I wish to phone my solicitor back in London to arrange for the funeral."

"Don't you think you're being a little hasty?" asked the embassy official.

"No, I need to speak to him straight away." Atholl had raised his voice; he knew the moment had come to act and to act fast. He needed to press this bureaucratic nobody into doing something for him, something that was going to make everything right but only if he got to a phone straightaway.

"Is not problem," said the Governor. "Please, use phone in office where you used to work." The governor gave Atholl a knowing look. Atholl excused himself and Viktor came out.

"Please Viktor. Five minutes privacy?"

"I sink Andee you need personal moment. Sorry to hear about fasser."

Atholl watched him go out of the room and then spent a moment composing the number in his head for the security company he'd worked for.

He dialed the number and asked to be put through to Bryce Sutherland.

Bryce here, how can I help?" came the confident voice from the office in St James.

"Bryce, it's Atholl."

"Atholl? Atholl!! Where are you?"

"Still in jail in Tallinn, sadly."

"What happened?"

"I can't talk about that now Bryce but I need two things. Firstly, I need you to start to get an op together to get me out of here. Secondly, I have just found out my father has died. I need you to speak to our solicitors, McKenzie Bell in Edinburgh's new town, and tell them to wrap up the estate. They are to put it on the market immediately. I am the sole beneficiary and everything is to be transferred to my Coutts account once the taxes have been paid. Is that clear?"

"Couldn't be clearer, old boy. Sorry to hear about your pa. I am just glad I was able to pass on the message to the embassy. Any date for this op?"

"The middle of next month. It will require you and a team. I will need a passport and a ticket out of the country. I would appreciate it if you could visit me first and I will finalise the details."

"Shouldn't we be saying the black swan flies at midnight or something? It all sounds crazy."

"Sorry Bryce, I am past crazy. I just want out."

CHAPTER 20

Kenny suddenly felt a presence at the table. He looked up and saw

Harold MacMillan grinning down at him. Kenny looked past Harold and saw at the

far end of the bar the lads from Tallinn. Alec raised his pint to him whilst Tony

scowled, his broken nose reminding Kenny of a day he would happily forget. They

were standing next to the pub's Christmas tree but Kenny did not feel particularly

festive at this moment in time.

"Alright Kenny?" said Harold. "Are ye no going to introduce me to your dad?"

Potter stood up, pulling his shoulders back. He extended his hand to Harold.

"Frank Potter. And you are?"

"Peter MacMillan. But as you're family you can call me Harold."

"Interesting. I always believe you don't get a second chance to make a first

impression" said Potter extending his right hand.

As they briefly shook hands Kenny was surprised. He had expected them to be

locked in a macho handshake battle until one of them wilted and came away the

lesser man. Maybe they were past that sort of thing.

"Family?" asked Potter looking quizzically at Kenny. Before Kenny could answer,

Harold chipped in.

"Aye, this waster boy of yours has married my lovely Alison. My only child and

she goes and picks this specimen as a husband." Harold rolled his eye in disgust.

"I am sure he speaks highly of you" said Potter still looking puzzled by the

encounter.

Kenny tried to regain some kind of control of the situation.

"What are you doing here Harold?"

"Just came to make sure you were Ok. Protectin the family interests so to speak.

Alison was a wee bit concerned after your disaster of a first meetin so ah thought

ah would maybe drop by and see that everythin went off nice as ninepence. Ah

never knew ma dad so ah'm very happy for you tae finally, what's the word they use these days….?" Harold stared up at the ceiling then jerked his head back down staring at Potter.

"Bond. That's the word I was thinking of. Ah hope the pair of you bond."

He sat down at the table and held up his hand with a small gap between thumb and forefinger.

"Aye, like two wee pieces of a broken vase, re-united by super glue!"

He turned as Alec put a gin and tonic in front of him.

"Feel free to join us, you and Rudolph the red nosed reindeer over there." said Kenny in a muted tone.

"I'll catch you later Kenny. But I'll pass on your good wishes to Tony." Alec winked at Kenny and moved off back to where he'd been sitting.

"I was just about to offer to buy you a drink as well" said Potter who was looking completely bemused.

Kenny place both hands on the table and prepared to stand up.

"If you don't mind I need to pay a visit. Excuse me Harold."

Harold was staring at Potter and never realized Kenny wanted out.

"Harold, excuse me please."

"Eh, oh aye. Where are my manners?"

He stood up and let Kenny out.

Harold and Potter watched Kenny walk off in the direction of the Gents.

Harold turned and immediately raised his right hand and pointed his finger at Potter.

"Ok you, cards on the table time. Are you after money?" asked Harold, a harsh tone in his voice.

"You do realize when you point the finger at someone, there's normally three pointing back at you?"

"What?"

"No."

"No, what?"

"No, I am not after money."

"Are you after somewhere to stay? Expecting them to put you up?"

"No, I've just bought a flat in the Merchant City."

"Ok, nice area. Lastly, are you after Denise?"

Potter leant back and gave a gentle laugh, still looking at Harold. He took a sip from his pint and then smiled.

"Am I amusing you pal?" Harold had both hands on the table and looked like he was about to leap at Potter.

Potter looked down the bar to where Harold's boys had put their drinks down and also appeared poised to jump into action. He pointed at them.

"Do us both a favour and call the attack dogs off."

Harold turned and made a chopping motion with his right hand.

"So. We finally get to the heart of the issue." Potter took a deep breath. "You don't give a flying fuck about Kenny or any bonding. You're worried about Denise and I getting back together? Does Kenny know about this?"

Harold shook his head, avoiding Potter's gaze.

"Well, Denise is an attractive woman for her age. Intelligent, self made, still pretty trim but don't worry Harold."

Potter, quickly put his hand on Harold's left shoulder out of view of the boys at the bar. He casually pinched a nerve through Harold's jacket causing Harold to screw his face in pain.

"That ship has sailed. I had my chance and blew it. That said, if you ever do so much as harm a hair on the head of my son or his mother, you'll have me to answer to. Am I clear?"

Harold tried to stare Potter down but the pinch pressure on his shoulder was increased.

Harold curtly nodded his head and Potter took his hand away.

Harold moved his hand up to massage his shoulder where Potter had held him.

"Point well made. Nice move, by the way. I'll be looking out for that one in future."

Potter stared at Harold across the table.

"Don't worry there's lots more where that came from."

"I don't doubt it" Harold replied. "Drink?"

"Pint of Guinness please. Very kind of you, Harold."

"You getting a round in then Harold?" said Kenny re-appearing from the Gents.

"Oh for fuck's sake. Have you been hiding in there til ah was goin tae the bar?" He looked at Potter.

"See what ah mean?"

Potter shrugged.

Ok. Lager is it?" Harold had waved over to the bar and the barmaid came over and took their order.

"I never knew they did table service in this place" said Kenny.

"They don't," said Harold "But as it's ma pub, they know who tae look after."

Kenny looked up to see Gus giving Harold's boys at the bar a wide berth as he walked down the bar to their booth.

"Oh and here's Gus. He'll probably want a pint as well."

"For fuck's sake, this just gets better and better. Bad enough ah have to drink wi you, now the poison dwarf wants in on the act."

"Oh no" cried Gus. "I didn't expect to see you here as well Harold. We should have sold tickets. Live tonight, round two of the emotional train wreck, as Highland father meets long lost Lowlands son."

"Would you like to sit down and just shut the fuck up ya ugly wee prick!"

Gus immediately squeezed in next to Potter.

"Eh, s-s-sure Harold, eh, Mr MacMillan. No problem" he stammered. He looked at Kenny with frantic eyes.

Kenny shrugged his shoulders.

Harold was holding on to the table with both hands, trying to control himself so he could calm down.

"Right, are ye wantin a pint Gus?"

"Well if ye insist, ah'll have a Stella."

"What's the magic word?" asked Harold.

Gus looked at Kenny and winked.

"Now!"

Kenny groaned.

"Look here ya wee shite, you'll be wearin a pint of Stella not drinkin it if you don't stop windin me up."

"Eh, sure Ha, eh, Mr MacMillan. A pint of Stella would be lovely please."

"Ok, ah'm off to the Gents. Ah'll tell the girl to get the wee prick a Stella."

Gus had taken his coat off by this stage, a big smile on his face at the thought of a free pint off Harold.

Kenny looked him up and down.

"Why the fuck are you wearing a black capped sleeve t-shirt with marble wash jeans?"

"Kenny, you know I have two wardrobes - classic and everyday, like. Most of my every day gear is in the wash so I had to pick out a couple of pieces from the classic section of my wardrobe."

"Classic is another word for gear you are too tight to throw away? You look like a gay refugee from East Germany in that get up."

"Marble wash jeans will never go out of fashion, Kenny." Gus had folded his arms across his chest on top of his bulging stomach and was intent on holding his ground.

"If that's the case are you still sprinkling your love letters with Blue Stratos?" asked Kenny.

"What?" exclaimed Potter.

"When we were teenagers in Dumfries he thought it would be romantic to write love letters to his latest crush describing what he would like to do to her. For the extra wee bit of romance, he'd spray each letter with Blue Stratos. God knows what the postman made of it."

"Look here, we've all made mistakes in our youth, Kenny. Unfortunately, ah cannae think of one your classics from that time but give me five minutes, like, and ah'll be back at you pal. You'll get yours!"

"Aye right. And then that girl's dad found the letter you'd written and came round your house, threatening to boot your balls if you went near his daughter again."

Gus shook his head then smiled up at the barmaid who had appeared with his Stella.

"Oh aye, poor bastard. Ma dad had been going through a phase of thinking ah was gay for some unknown reason, like, so when this guy came round complaining about me and his daughter, ma dad went through him like a dose of salts."

"Marble wash jeans? asked Potter. "Were they no popular for about ten minutes ten years ago?"

" Aye the last time he fitted into them properly" chipped in Kenny. "How tight are they? Are they not cutting off the blood supply to your nether regions, wee man. I always thought you had a peri pathetic style of dress to be honest, Gus."

Pottered looked at Kenny quizzically.

"Don't you mean peripatetic?"

"I know what I said!" came the reply.

"Look here you two, ah'm no here to be taken the piss out o'. Ah'm here to rub the pair of yous noses in it, like. But in a gesture of friendship here ah will take the slings and arrows of outrageous fortune if it means getting you two together. That's the size of the man ah am, by the way."

"Shut the fuck up" said Harold who had heard the last of Gus' statement on the way back from the Gents.

"Ah'm just saying, ah'm a friend of Kenny's and ah'm here for him in this moment of emotional turmoil, like."

Harold looked at Gus as he took a sip from his gin and tonic. He put the glass down and looked at Kenny.

"Christ, when Alison married you I never realized it was buy one idiot get one free. Ah never realized you two came as a package."

Kenny shifted in his seat and stared at his pint. He would leave the provoking of Harold to Gus. Why stifle a natural talent for annoying people?

Kenny remained to be convinced this getting to know his dad was a good idea. This was the second meeting and a struggle to put it mildly. The first hadn't been much better as he'd failed to generate any connection with Potter to the extent he'd taken him to meet Gus and Dominic to take the pressure off the encounter. Apart from Potter threatening to kill Gus at one point after the wee man had asked him if his nickname was Pansy, that evening was a definite success compared to this.

Slaughtered by Harold, Gus adding to the general feeling of discomfort and Potter saying barely fuck all. He must be scared of Harold, thought Kenny. Fucking military hard man my arse. He'd let that one eyed prick walk all over him.

CHAPTER 21

As Atholl landed in the van, Bryce Sutherland clasped him by the shoulders and stared down into his eyes. "Atholl McClackit, Laird McClackit of McClackit, Clan Chieftain of the Clan McClackit, welcome to freedom."

"Thank you, Bryce, but I will be a lot happier to accept your welcome when we are sipping cold champagne in warmer climes."

Despite the freezing December night, Atholl felt a sudden warmth all over his body. He turned and helped Bryce bring the various sections of the metal ladder into the van. They laid it flat out and Atholl stowed the rope Bryce had thrown him moments before when he himself was on the ladder on top of the prison wall.

"Outstanding" said Bryce who reached forward to bang on the front panel of the van interior. At once the van moved off and both men swayed, clutching each other. Bryce grabbed Atholl round the neck and rubbed his hair with his gloved hand.

"You silly little Scots twat. How did it come to this?"

He let go and reached up to pull a grey tarpaulin across the top of the van roof so that no one from a higher vantage point could see inside the van.

Atholl slumped down against one of the van walls. He looked around at what he presumed was the interior of some kind of Baltic Ford Transit. The smell of diesel was overpowering but was almost perfume like compared to the smell of Partmui prison.

As Atholl took in the wooden panels, the mattresses, quilts and a small hamper he suddenly burst out crying. This was not what he wanted but the question from Bryce had triggered a wave of emotion he had been bottling up until now. Self-pity was the preserve of the weak as far as he was concerned but the simple question was, how had it come to this? Breaking out of an Estonian prison like a common criminal, putting the lives and livelihoods of close friends in danger all because he had allowed himself to be caught up in some madcap scheme of his father's. Even worse, being stitched up like a kipper by a Glasgow hood who had escaped scot free whilst Atholl was left to do time, short but hard time in one of the rankest, smelliest institutions he had ever been unfortunate enough to visit. They didn't need to march people across the Brecon Beacons to see if they could get into the SAS, let them try and survive two months in Partmui prison.

"Here." Bryce had opened the hamper and produced a small bottle of cognac. He had produced two brandy goblets and poured a generous measure into each, proffering one to Atholl.

He raised his glass to Atholl.

"Savour it. If you knock it all back in one you'll throw up. To the regiment."

Atholl clinked his glass against Bryce's and rolled the brandy around the glass. He sniffed the brandy then took a small sip.

"Hine VSOP?" he asked.

"Well it is not everyday you get to break your best friend out of jail so why not push the boat out, eh?" Bryce smiled and knocked back his measure in one.

He put his glass back in the hamper and turned to Atholl.

"So the riot was a success then? What were those bangs I heard earlier?"

Atholl took another sip and scratched his right ear. He looked sheepishly at Bryce.

"Old habits die hard Bryce. I had a petrol can, 95% petrol and 5% sugar, sitting in each of the deep fat fryers in the kitchen. One in each of the ovens just for good measure. God, I hated that place. I reckoned I scrubbed over one thousand pans in my time there."

The van had slowed.

"Traffic lights." came the voice from the drivers cabin.

"Understood." replied Bryce, a look of concern disappearing from his face.

"So, everything went as expected?" asked Bryce who proferred the bottle.

Atholl shook his head.

"It went as well as could be expected. I started off low in terms of what I offered the riot leaders and the final price came in on budget. Ten thousand US is a small price to pay for freedom. They kicked off at the expected time and that drew the attention of the rest of the guards apart from one. I'll come to that in a minute."

"But it was a success with the fake escape?" Bryce had by this stage opened a large brown bag and was offering Atholl a sandwich.

Atholl reached in and produced a roast chicken and tomato sandwich.

"Cognac, roast chicken sandwiches, you really are spoiling me Bryce."

"Not a problem. So you were saying?

"Yes, I had to take out a guy called Tomas as he was the only inmate in the whole place who was of a similar build to me. So, I removed him from the equation and put him in cold storage in the freezer room until the time for the op. I cobbled together a sheet rope and slung it over the wall at the opposite end of the jail. It was a poor attempt to make it look like an escape but it gave them something to ponder." Atholl took a bite of his sandwich.

"I don't suppose there's any salt, old boy?"

"Just a mo" said Bryce as he reached into the hamper and came out with a salt-shaker.

"Just the ticket" said Atholl as he liberally covered the chicken in his sandwich.

 "So they didn't catch on?"

"No, I had a cushy number to begin with. The governor put me in his office to help him practice his English. I switched my dental records with Tomas. He had been cooking the books in state run enterprise. By the way, it is land of the bloody giants in there. I managed to do that just before an incident in the showers with a Russian called Alexi. I think somebody on the outside wanted me removed from the equation but sadly for them I managed to thwart his best endeavours. That incident rather blotted my copybook with the governor so I was moved to the kitchen."

"But why only decide to escape once your pa had died?"

"I was full of drugs Bryce. I needed a clear mind. I had to get clean. By that stage I was just about back to normal and father's death gave me one final push."

Atholl was a bit taken aback by Bruce's interest. He decided to pour himself another brandy and considered his answer. He had thought Bryce would have been more concerned about getting out of Estonia but then he remembered Bryce's love of planning and plotting. Setting up the op was his main skill. The actual execution he was normally happy to delegate or manage at a distance.

"So once I arranged for Tomas to disappear they knew something was up but they couldn't quite figure it out. Only fly in the ointment was Viktor."

They both froze as a police car with it's siren blaring whizzed past them.

A voice from the driver's compartment shook him from his thoughts.

"No threat."

Bryce acknowledged the comment with a curt "Roger that."

"Viktor? Who is he?" Bryce enquired.

"Sadly the closest thing to a friend I had in there. He was a guard. Loved to practice his English on me. I was just pulling Tomas' body from the freezer room where I had stored it when he ran in to the kitchen to tell me about the riot."

Atholl paused for a moment thinking about his actions of the evening.

"All you could hear was the sound of a riot not that far off, the noise of breaking glass and alarm bells. A few yells. I presume Viktor had come running back to tell me to go back to my cell as there was a riot. When he saw what I was doing he started shouting."

"Andee, what is happening? What have you done? What is happening?" he cried.

"I'd told him to get out but he kept coming towards me, kept shouting "Andee! Andee! Andee" until I realized he would attract attention despite the noise of the riot. The look on his face as I put the knife in his throat will stay with me forever."

"We're here" came the voice from the driver's cab.

"Excellent" said Bryce. "All going to plan. Have you any idea of the price of hiring a light aircraft in this country old boy? Bloody arm and a leg."

Atholl looked at Bryce.

"Have you been listening to a word I have been saying?"

Bryce reached down to help Atholl up.

"Yes. Prisoner killed, guard killed. Here we both are. Atholl, what was your objective? Escape, freedom, the whole ten yards. When I visited you last week, you were desperate. If I had told you there was a requirement for you to kill two people to get your freedom you would have agreed instantly. You can find time for regret when we are finally out of this frozen hellhole. Let's get our act together and complete the op."

Bryce sharply closed the lid of the hamper.

"It has been a long day Bryce" said Atholl. He rubbed his face with both hands as a shudder passed through his body.

"Shall we?" Bryce pointed at the rear door that had just been opened by the driver.

"Just the two of you?" asked Atholl.

"Yes. Decided at the last moment to keep it lean and mean. I was a bit concerned until I met you last week. I have two others on standby but I reckoned Ken and I would suffice. We are also leaving in the same plane as you so that was another consideration. Immigration has been cleared at both ends through a contact in the FO."

Bryce handed Atholl a brand new British passport.

Atholl opened it up under the light from the van interior.

"Oh for God's sake," He exclaimed. "Michael Lazarus Jackson!" He looked at Bryce waiting for an answer.

"Thought the middle one was a bit obvious as you're back from the dead but who could ever forget you dancing to Billie Jean in the mess ten years ago. Bloody hysterical. Think of it every time I hear the song."

They had left the vicinity of the prison at dusk and on getting out of the van Atholl saw they now stood at the edge of an airfield in the pitch dark. About two hundred metres away there was a small control tower and a couple of hangars.

They were poorly lit by a few small dim lights coming out of the side of the hangars. A chill December wind cut across the large expanse.

Bryce shivered.

"Forgot to say. You might want to change into the gear in the back of the van. Kept it simple. British tourist standard issue. Be a bit warmer than your jailbird outfit. Admittedly the aroma will be less, shall we say, industrial but I am sure you will manage."

Atholl jumped back into the van and emerged five minutes later in a Helly Hansen waterproof, checked shirt, jumper, jeans and hiking boots.

"Ready for the off?" asked Bryce.

"Roger that" came the reply from Atholl.

They set off across the tarmac towards the hangar. Ken had produced a large torch from a small knapsack. Atholl followed him and Bryce turning over the events of the last week in his head, trying to ensure there had been no chance he had given away his plans to anyone in the prison. He had been badly affected by killing Viktor. He then remembered Viktor bemoaning the disappearance of Tomas just after Atholl had killed him. They were both keen chess players. Bryce, from the very beginning, had been highly amused by the whole affair, much to Atholl's distaste. He wasn't the guy scrubbing pans and having one shower a fortnight. Bryce's comment "it is a bit whiffy in here old boy" on his prison visit had not been particularly well received either, given that Atholl had been breathing the stinking body odour of 230 Estonians for the last two months. Atholl had also met with the clerk from the British Embassy the day before who had passed over some books and a couple of magazines. Stitched inside the covers of the books were ten thousand US dollars.

"I meant to ask Bryce, how did you get the clerk to bring the book with the dollars to me in jail?"

They were approaching the hangars and a strong external light had been switched on, totally illuminating the front of the hangar and the light aircraft.

"Quite easy in the end. I met him as he left the embassy one night and told him I represented MI6. I mentioned a few names and asked him to call them to verify my credentials. Long story short, some old pals turned up trumps and he thought he was James Bond. I mentioned Her Majesty would look favourably on anyone who helped assist in your release. Clearly we couldn't go as far as a K but an OBE or an MBE should be in the offing. He was like a dog with two dicks at that one. Ok, here we are."

As they approached the hangar two men emerged from a doorway.

One moved towards the plane as the other approached Atholl and the others.

"Michael Jackson?" he asked with a smile on his face.

Atholl stepped forward

"Yes."

"Let me show you the way to go." A muffled laugh came from the man standing next to the aircraft.

As they walked over, the man clapped Atholl on the back.

"Excuse me. Your friend asked me make joke with you."

Atholl sighed but realized if a couple of crap jokes were a price to pay for getting out of Estonia then so be it.

Bryce stepped up to the man with Atholl.

"Ok Sergei, as agreed, the second five thousand dollars on departure. Want to count it? I made sure the notes are crisp and new."

He handed Sergei a thick padded envelope.

"Is ok Bryce. Last packet good. No problem. We speak soon?"

"Definitely. Spaseba Sergei. I will be in touch."

The pilot had opened the plane door and as Atholl was about to get in Sergei stepped forward.

"One moment please."

Atholl tensed, unwilling to accept that it might suddenly all go to cock at the very last moment.

213

Sergei took an object from a pocket inside the large military style parka he was wearing. He handed Atholl a book.

"Some reading for your flight" he announced.

Atholl was taken aback by this gesture.

"What is it?"

"A thriller!"

CHAPTER 22

Alison and Kenny entered Gus' flat. Alison looked around and nearly burst out laughing. Essentially the place was unchanged since she'd last been there for New Year some six years ago. That wasn't strictly true, as Gus had at least managed to blow up a couple of balloons this year. She didn't know why they had "Happy Birthday 50" printed on them, but at least he'd made an effort. The curtains, the carpet, the leatherette settee, all had been around since her last visit, all having merged into a dirty beige colour. Apart from the black stuffing coming of the sofa where the fake leather had split.

"Still not got round to dating Laura Ashley then, Gus? asked Alison. She took a couple of wary steps into the lounge from the hallway, hoping that the smell was not what she thought it could be. It was a heady bouquet. The combination of used sports socks, soured milk and rotting fruit. Well, there was no way it could be rotting fruit given the diet that Gus survived on so that left only.... and no, she just didn't want to go there.

Gus followed them in.

"Naw, Kenny tells me you know all about her and that I should get you to set me up. He said she works in shop in the city centre." Gus wandered off into the kitchen.

Alison smiled. It was she and Kenny's little private joke. "Well, the next time I see her I'll make sure to give her your number."

Gus' voice came though from the kitchen. "Aye, you do that Alison. You know I'm a guy that normally dates women with professional careers but I am prepared to drop my standards if she's a friend of yours."

"It's a done deal, Gus. It will be my New Year's present to you."

Gus had re-appeared from kitchen with a large bowl of crisps and a can of lager each for him and Kenny.

"Aye, well that's the buffet sorted, eh?" Gus said as he put the bowl down on heavily stained coffee table.

215

Alison looked at the bowl of crisps and realised he wasn't joking.

"I don't get a drink then, Gus?" she asked.

"Oh, aye where's ma manners? Sweet sherry is it Alison?" said Gus heading back into the kitchen.

"No chance of any wine?" She called through. "Pinot Grigio? Even a Californian chardonnay would do?" She looked at Kenny who was picking at the crisps, doing his usual trick of going through the bowl looking for the small burnt ones first. She shook her head.

"Naw," came a muffled voice from the kitchen. "Wait a minute though......"

Alison had tried to avoid this moment but decided to venture into the kitchen to see what had happened to Gus. Surprisingly she found it neat and tidy as he'd clearly made an effort to clean the place but sadly the clean spots on the work surfaces only served to highlight their grubby natural colour, emphasising the stains on the wall and cupboard doors, which had remained untouched. To put the cherry on it, Gus was kneeling with his head in the cupboard under the sink, showing a builder's cleavage that looked like it could manage a Harley Davidson parked in it, never mind a bicycle.

Gus pulled his head out from under the cupboard before Alison had a chance to look at the underwear below the crack. Wait a minute! Was he actually wearing underwear? Alison felt her stomach turn.

"There you go. Ah knew I had a bottle of wine somewhere. Austrian Riesling, 40% proof with a wee dash of anti freeze to take the edge off. That OK?"

"Aye, that'll do fine," said Alison who turned and hurried back into the lounge.

"Everything OK?" asked Kenny as she shot him a vicious look.

As she sat down she thought the sofa was going to swallow her up. Is this Groundhog Day she wondered as the self-same thing had happened on her last visit. She managed to right herself and tried to focus on Gus as she thought he was speaking to her directly for once. This made a change to his usual strategy of completely ignoring her unless he made a joke about Kenny therefore needing someone to laugh with him.

"So Alison, maybe you can settle an argument I had with fuck face, sorry, Kenny here?"

Gus settled on the one chair that looked vaguely new. Alison remembered some story about Gus waking up in a skip and finding a usable chair next to him.

"Eh yes, Gus. What is it?"

"Do we have to," said Kenny.

"Aye, we do. It is a point of principle, like."

Alison had heard this all before but as she was in his flat, she thought it best to humour him. Anyway, focusing on him might be distasteful but it was a lot better than looking at the damp patch on the right hand corner of the ceiling. She also congratulated herself on going to the Ladies before they left the Italian restaurant Kenny and her had eaten in earlier.

"That wee flower a bloke wears in his lapel at a wedding, like. It's called a bouquet garni, isn't it?"

"What do you mean?" Alison looked at Kenny who shrugged and bit his lip.

"You wear a bouquet garni in your lapel at a wedding if you're a man," said Gus with a worryingly confident tone.

"No, it's called a buttonhole."

"Told you," said Kenny. "That will be five pounds please."

"The fuck it is," cried Gus. "The bit o' the flower is like a mini bouquet and the garni bit comes from the fact it's garnishin the lapel."

"No, sorry Gus. It's called a buttonhole."

"No, no, no. Ah can see what's happenin here. You two are gangin up on me. There's a Steward's Enquiry needed here. You Bradleys are like the Corleone family and ah'm Mo Green. No, ah'm no' havin it."

At that the front bell rang and Gus went to answer it.

"Right that's it Kenny. I don't care if he is your best pal; I am never coming to this flat again. Look at the state of the place! It's like going back in time. What a mess.

There's a paper on the floor over there dated 1994."

"Aye, it's compact and bijou without the bijou I suppose. Bit disappointed in the buffet, he might have pushed the boat out and got cheese and onion – ready fucking salted. Just as well you suggested we go for a meal first."

"Aye, and we could have still been there if you hadn't insisted we come here."

"Shoosh, here he is again."

Gus had re-appeared with a concerned look on his face. He ignored Alison and looking at Kenny went, "Harold and your mum are here, Kenny. Is everything alright?"

Alison looked at Kenny who was halfway through stuffing his mouth with crisps. As he went "What?" Alison was covered in a shower of half eaten potato crisp crumbs, the shoulders of her little black dress covered in a flurry of crisp dandruff.

A smartly dressed Harold McMillan walked into the room rubbing his hands, a big smile on his face.

"Alright, young lovers. All set for the bells?"

Alison got up and kissed her dad on both cheeks.

"Where's Denise?" asked Alison.

"She's decided to take her life in her hands and use the facilities," said Harold, shuddering as he looked around the lounge. "Never realised it was your birthday today, Gus?'

"Eh, it's not," said Gus in a muted tone.

"What's wi' the happy birthday balloons then, ye balloon?" Harold smiled at his own joke as Kenny grimaced.

"They were left over from a work party for a guy who was 50."

"As usual, all expense spared wi' you, wee man." Harold rolled his eyes and went to sit on the couch before thinking better of it.

Denise Bradley walked in to the room "Hello boys. Hi, Alison. God, what has happened to your hair Alison? What's that on your shoulder?"

Alison always wondered how Kenny's mother got a march on her. She could never do anything quite right by this woman and yet again she was forced to make excuses over something.

"Kenny, thought it would be nice to express his love for me by showering me in crisp crumbs, didn't you darling?"

"Come on into the bathroom dear and I'll help you clean them off. I need to tell you something anyway. I've used the dregs of a bottle of Domestos so it doesn't smell quite so bad."

"Any chance of drink, wee man?" asked Harold. "Some fucking host you are!"

"Aye, there's a tray of Tennent's in the fridge, like. Can you get it, I need to speak to Kenny about somethin'."

"No problem," said Harold and he smiled at them both as he sauntered, yes, that was the word, sauntered into the kitchen.

"What the fuck's he doing here?" hissed Gus at Kenny.

"How the fuck do I know? I didn't invite him. Why the fuck would I want to invite Harold McMillan to anything?"

They heard the "psst" of a ring-can being opened in the kitchen.

"Shoosh, here he comes," said Gus who sat down on the settee trying to look normal, calm and relaxed and in the process and failing miserably.

Denise and Alison re-entered at the same time as Harold. Harold and Denise exchanged looks as he went "Well, shall you tell or shall I?"

"You tell them, dear," said Denise.

Alison looked at Kenny and gently shook her head. That was the best signal she could give him that his world was about to come tumbling down. Whilst Denise had been, rather aggressively Alison thought, removing the crumbs from her shoulders, she had imparted some news.

"OK, firstly, sorry for gatecrashing your party, wee man, but I have news that Denise and I are bursting to tell Kenny and Alison."

"Here we go," thought Alison. Brace! Brace!

"Denise and I are engaged."

For the first time in her life Alison experienced a stunned silence. She looked at Kenny who appeared to be staring into space, his mouth moving but no words coming out. If anything, Gus looked the worse of the two as his face had drained of colour. The normally purple infused veins on his nose as a result of years of alcohol abuse had faded to a light lilac from their normally vibrant crimson.

"Holy fuck," went Gus.

Kenny was still standing moving his mouth but unspeaking.

"Hey manners you wee cu.. - eh, idiot you." said Harold. "Ah take it there's no shampoo in this flat? No' even the hair washing kind?"

"Eh no, Harold. Ah don't like taking two bottles into the shower," Gus tried a weak joke to lighten the mood but the clouds of darkness that appeared on the horizon when Harold turned up at the front door had suddenly swept into the room and had submerged him and Kenny in their gloom.

Alison tried to get things back to normal. "Kenny, are you not going to congratulate your mother. I've already done so when she told me in the bathroom. Dad, I'm really happy for you. You'll be great together." She walked across the room and embraced her father.

"Come on, Denise. Let's leave Kenny to come to terms with the news," said Harold. "We'll get the champagne from the car. Lucky I brought my own eh, wee man?"

Alison saw her chance to get out of the flat for even a few minutes. "No, stay where you are dad. I'll help Denise get the bottles."

"Good girl," said Harold. "I might have to give Kenny the kiss of life - he seems dumbstruck. If I'd known it would have this effect on him, I would have told him five years ago your mother and I were an item."

As the women left Kenny finally came to. "Fucking brilliant, when did this all come about?"

"A few weeks ago, we thought we'd make it official tonight." Harold was revelling in the effect the announcement had on Kenny.

"Excuse me, but can I ask something?" Gus came back in from the kitchen after getting another can of lager each for Kenny and him.

"Ask away, Gus. I'm feeling generous."

"How do you know where I live?"

"There's a lot I know about you, wee man," said Harold. "Still drinking Bacardi and coke after you've filled up on lager? Still shagging that married burd from your work on the first Thursday of every month when her husband's at the lodge meeting?"

"Nice try, Harold. Kenny been blabbing after a couple of sweet sherries has he?" said Gus in an unconvincing tone of voice.

"Oh no, wee man," replied Harold, a very knowing smile breaking across his face. "I make it my business to know a lot of things that go on in this city. Some for business reasons and some for personal reasons but sometimes, just for the sheer joy of seeing the face on the wee man in the street when I tell him I know his life inside and out. Ah'm lucky to get a "Hello" out of Kenny when ah see him, so he's no' ma Deep Throat on Gus McSween. Got that? Excellent. Think it's time I had a wee drink to celebrate ma engagement so ah'll have a small lager, my good man. Go on, pick your jaw up off the ground and get me a drink."

Gus trudged back to the kitchen like a man with the weight of the world on his shoulders.

Half an hour later, Alison found herself standing at the fire with Gus. He had his Christmas cards up on the mantelpiece, all six of them. She picked up a big 6 x 9 card that had a traditional Dickensian scene on the front. It featured a sleigh party driving through the snow wearing top hats and frock coats for the men and large dresses for the women. She looked at the back and was surprised to see it was produced by Harrods. Harrods producing quality tasteful cards was not so much a shock as the fact Gus knew someone who could be bothered to send him one. She asked Gus who he knew in London and he raised his eyebrows.

"That's from ma brother. Likes to give it the "big I am" with the Harrods Christmas cards every year. Aye, he's the one that got away to London and made it big. So fuckin' big he lives in a one bedroom flat in Penge. Fuckin' Penge! You ever heard of a place that sounds more like a cross between penis and minge? He got the usual fae me."

"Sweet FA?" Alison waited for confirmation.

"Exactly." A pathetic electrical buzzing filled the flat once more.

"Is that the bell?" enquired Alison, her facial expression trying to suggest to Gus he might want to actually answer it.

"Aye, ah'll get it," said Gus, reluctantly, as he turned away from Alison towards the hallway.

He opened the door to two somewhat sozzled revellers.

"Alright Gus?" said Cammy "I heard you were having a party. I take it my invite got lost in the post but I thought we would drop in anyway."

"Oh aye, that would be the invite that said no poofs allowed." Gus stood back from the doorway. "Well, now that ye're here come on in but remember no arse sex in public OK. Ah know what you poofs are like."

"Oh aye, where did you read that? The gay section of the Daily Record? Calm down, we're keeping the lively stuff for the club." He turned to his companion. "Gus, this is Myke."

Gus extended his right arm very slowly as he tried to work out if Myke would do anything untoward with his hand.

"Mike, OK?" said Gus, tentatively moving his hand up and down with Myke's.

"Aye, with a y."

"Is that no Mikey?"

"No, it's M-Y-K-E."

"Oh right – "Myke". What do you do like?"

"I'm a hair stylist." In a disinterested tone he continued, "Sorry, what was your name again?

222

"Gus, with a G, a U and an S. Rhymes with puss."

"OK Gus, play nice," said Cammy. "Look we've brought some bevvy and a curry as we were starving and you can never get anything to eat after the bells. Can we use your kitchen?"

"Aye sure, just remember what ah said about arse sex. No BJ's either come to think of it!"

"A hand job be OK, Gussy Wussy?" asked Myke in a sing-song voice as he wandered past Gus towards the kitchen.

"No, it fucking would not. Come inside and we can make the introductions before you eat."

Gus showed them into the front room and promptly gave up on the idea of introducing them to anybody. He looked at his watch.

"Kenny, it's half-ten, see if there's anything on the telly. The one thing ah must do is tape "Scotch and Wry". See me through the year that does. Good old Rikki Fulton, the man's a genius, like."

"There's fuck all on Gus," said Harold. "Best waiting for Scotch and Wry. For the first time in your life ye've got something right."

The electrical buzzing filled the flat once more.

"Oh for fuck's sake," said Gus. "If ah'd known this amount of folk were going to turn up ah'd have bought another big bag o' crisps."

CHAPTER 23

Atholl sipped on his cognac in the restaurant of the Hotel du Sud in Monte Carlo. The New Years Eve ball in the hotel was reaching fever pitch now the meal had ended and 1997 fast approached. It was a black tie affair which Atholl thought might allow him to blend in but dining on his own always made him feel like a social leper. Not quite untouchable but not a kick in the arse off it. Large groups of couples dominated the event. One all-female couple had made a couple of sorties past his table but he wasn't paying for it and didn't really feel in the mood. Maybe it was something they put in the coffee in the prison as he had definitely noticed a decline in the old libido since being inside.

If his sex drive had diminished one thing to increase was his appetite for good food. The meal tonight had looked slightly disappointing on the menu but had been better than expected, foie gras, sole, duck with black cherries and then profiteroles. Pretty straightforward in his eyes but through expert cooking, every mouthful was delicious and to be savoured. He didn't spend much time reflecting on what the inmates at Partmui prison would be up to. Bringing in the New Year with a piece of black bread and some prison distilled hooch if they were lucky. Blind drunk indeed drinking that stuff.

Earlier on in the day he had tried to prepare for the future by renting a flat in Monaco. He knew it was an expensive introduction back into civilization after the time in jail but the thought of facing January in London was just as depressing as another ten years in prison. He did not care to think what he would do at the end of the three months but it would give him time to plan.

As Atholl finished his brandy, the DJ had started to crank things up a bit so when Billie Jean came on it was too much. Good times in the mess were one thing but being reminded of the escape from Estonia was another. As he signed for the meal, the female couple made one last pass hoping to attract his attention but he kept his head down, concentrating on the bill.

"They've got their eye on you." came a voice from behind him.

He turned round and found himself looking at a well built middle-aged man smoking a reasonably sized cigar. He was wearing a white dinner jacket and had a full of grey hair styled in a 1980s mullet. There were a couple of gold sovereign rings on the fingers of the hand holding the cigar. At first Atholl thought it was Jimmy Saville's brother but then the man stretched out his right hand.

"Barry Jones, roofer from Bolton. How do?"

"Mike Jackson, pleased to meet you." said Atholl who thought it best to stick to the name on his new passport.

Barry nodded in the direction of the pair of women who had just passed Atholl's table.

"I had the blonde when the wife was having a spa treatment. Eight out of ten for looks and effort. Fook all for originality. They see you as easy meat. When you've been around tarts as much as me, you can tell. It's up to you but you'd be best off keeping your hand on your ha'penny." At this, he took a long draw on his cigar before emitting a cloud of smoke that completely engulfed Atholl.

"Thanks for the advice. I'll keep it in mind."

Atholl turned back to the bill.

"Wait a minute" came the voice from behind.

"Mike Jackson. That's short for Michael Jackson in'tit? Wait till I tell the wife, I've met Michael Jackson in Monte Carlo. Michael fucken Jackson. Ha ha."

At this point Barry leant forward and clapped Atholl on the back.

As he turned round Atholl was struggling to keep himself under control.

"You mention your wife but you appear to be dining alone?"

"Oh her? She's upstairs. She knows foie gras binds her but she still eats it. She'll be in't bathroom trying to squeeze one out before she goes to bed. Binds her somethin rotten it does but she can't say no, loves the bloody stuff."

"Binds her?" queried Atholl who was struggling come to terms with this encounter.

"Down below. Blocks her up. To put it bluntly, constipation!"

Barry delivered the last word rather loudly to ensure Atholl understood what he was getting at but it was delivered just as the music died. It painted the picture perfectly for Atholl but also drew some reproving glances from other tables around them.

By this stage Barry had placed his sovereign encrusted hand over his mouth but Atholl could see a big grin on Barry's face, his eyes alight at having said something so loud and out of place in a Monte Carlo ballroom, even if it was in English.

"So how is the roofing business these days?" asked Atholl rather clunkily trying to change the conversation.

"I'm from Bolton and spending New Year's Eve in Monte Carlo. How the fuck do you think it's doing? I'm shitting gold bricks. If only I could say the same for her upstairs."

At this Barry put his head back and roared at his own joke.

Atholl was lost for words.

As Barry brought his head back down to face Atholl, he inhaled on his cigar.

"And what about you lad, what do you do?"

"I've been spending some time in Eastern Europe recently, looking at opportunities."

"Spending or doing?"

Atholl looked more closely at Barry.

"Spending time or doing time?" asked Barry who had had the good grace to lower his voice as he looked Atholl straight in the eye.

"Makes no odds to me, we've all been there mate. Fancy another cognac?"

Not waiting for Atholl's response Barry put his hand up to attract a waiter.

"If you know what it looks like, it is written all over you. Even in this light you look jail pale." said Barry

The waiter appeared at that moment.

"You want one or not?"

*****

226

As Atholl was going up to his room in the lift a feeling of freedom and light-headedness came over him. At first he put it down to the movement of the lift or the brandy he'd drunk with Barry which had been more than just the one but it continued as he entered the room. He lay on his bed for a couple of minutes then stood up and stripped off. The conversation with Barry had been a difficult one for Atholl. They had spent a good two hours talking, New Year having passed by as a sideshow. It was with no little disbelief he realised his telling a roofer from Bolton about the events of the last few months had lifted an enormous burden from him. Who would have thought on first glance, Barry could take on the role of a father confessor on New Years Eve in a Monaco hotel?

Atholl looked around the suite he'd booked overlooking the harbour in Monte Carlo. The lighting by the bed was so subtle he had to turn on the main light if he wanted to read a book. He'd given up on the sound system control handset after a five minute period where the only things he'd succeeded in getting to function, in the vaguest sense of the word, were the balcony curtains opening and closing. He picked up the handset once more but this time only succeeded in closing the curtains when he wanted them open. He wanted a to project his sense of freedom into space.

He finally managed to fight his way through the curtains doing a very good imitation of Eric Morecambe in a Christmas special in the process. In fact, he now stood bollock naked on his hotel balcony. This was what freedom finally felt like he thought. Here he was exposed to the elements without a care in the world. Free of the Laird, free of bloody Scotland and free from prison. Earlier in the day, as 1996 shuffled off the stage to be replaced by 1997, Atholl had thought, "This will be my year. Vengeance will be mine." But then he thought back to his talk with Barry. He had confided in Barry his remorse at the killing of Viktor, the void left by the death of his father and his general aimlessness now he was free of everything he'd hated.

He also now realised whilst embracing the New Year in the buff was definitely a

227

statement of intent, it was getting rather chilly outside despite the more temperate climes of the south of France. The old chap down below was shrivelled up like the last Moroccan date in the box a fortnight after Christmas. As he fought his way back through the curtains Atholl let his mind wander back to the previous year's festivities.

This time last year he had been down in the Cotswolds with some friends to see in the New Year. The Laird had put in his annual request for him to come north to celebrate but he had impolitely declined. He wondered if he would have driven up had he realised it might be the last time they could spend a New Year together.

It could not have been any worse than the cottage in the Cotswolds, thinking about it. Young Tory twats down from Notting Hill, planning their ascent to power, aiming right at the top of the political tree. Atholl remembered making his excuses at quarter past midnight but his girlfriend at the time, Alice, Alison, Alicia yes, Alicia, was all for plotting a glorious new dawn for her and her Oxford chums. By his calculation he'd been out of circulation in London for around ten weeks at the end of the year, yet when he returned to his flat, there was one message on his answer machine and that was from the belly dancer who thought she'd left an earring by his bed. Tough luck, love, no sign of it.

Tonight's conversation, whilst helping him finally express to someone what he had experienced over the last few months had made him melancholy. This was unchartered territory to him. Barry's last words from a song he'd talked about had confused Atholl but now they suddenly made sense. I will survive

Once back in the room, Atholl opened the mini bar and took out a miniature of Glenlivet. The cool air from the fridge reminded him he was still naked. He moved into the bathroom to put on a robe. Having poured himself a drink he returned to the balcony, this time managing to retain both his dignity and his drink in his tussle with the curtains.

As he looked out over the yachts, the floating gin palaces of renown where various members of the Euro trash family were partying the night away, he was only now realising how hard a blow the Laird's death had struck him. His focus on getting out of jail had meant the stark fact of his father's death had been pushed to one side. That he wasn't there for him when he passed away was another uncomfortable thought. He didn't even know what had happened to Potter who appeared to have made his excuses after the funeral and disappeared into thin air. Atholl had only received the sketchiest of details from Bryce regarding his father's affairs but they had been sorted, at least in the short term, with minimal fuss.

Atholl thought back to the rest of the previous year with a feeling he found hard to come to terms with. Disgust with himself had taken on a physical sensation, a dead weight in the pit of his stomach. It was there when he woke up in the morning and then last thing at night as he went bed. He had tried as best he could with the Kenny Bradley mission yet still failed. Failed his father and failed himself. Was it lack of preparation or bad luck? He caught himself at that one. Bad luck as an excuse was a loser's way out. He would have to take the pain and work at it until he had managed to nullify it. Funnily enough that feeling had now gone since the meeting with blessed Father Barry.

But the past was past as Barry had put it so what about the future? He'd tried to think about the future when locked up in his prison cell, but it had seemed so distant. A vague illusion that could be neither imagined nor planned for. He had no family, few friends and ex-wife who appeared to be trying to get in the Guinness Book of Records for banging athletes. On the flight out of Estonia he'd asked Bryce if she had popped up on his radar and he burst out laughing. "Popped up on my radar?" he'd snorted. "I bumped into her on a ski-ing holiday in Wengen in the first week of December. She was trying to kid me into thinking she was running a bar but I think she might just have been working in it. She looked fantastic considering what she's been through. Sorry, that's a bit off." When Atholl had asked what he meant by that Bryce had said it was personal stuff she hadn't really wanted to talk about and she had not gone into details. Atholl thought this was a better snow job than an alpine downhill but declined to push it any further.

He drank his Glenlivet and went back for another from the mini bar. He had invited Bryce out for a bachelor's New Year in Monaco, but Bryce had declined as he was going to pop the question to the lovely Sarah at her folks' house in Cumbria.

The thought of his best friend happily engaged plunged Atholl into an even gloomier mood. Any release that had followed the evening's earlier conversation in the ballroom was now disappearing. As the discos on the boats died out, Atholl finished the last of his second malt. The whisky and the robe generated a nice glow.

The image of the Hotel Sport sauna suddenly came back to Atholl. Had he really intended to kill his half brother in cold blood? All for what? 150 acres in the Highlands that he never visited, a hideous castle he struggled to call home sitting in the middle of those acres.

He stood up from the desk and went back to the mini bar. The malt was finished so he opened a Johnny Walker red label. How was much was he paying for this suite and only two bloody malts in the minibar he thought. He would have a word in the morning.

He put a couple of ice cubes in the glass and poured the whisky over them. He realised this was only making him feel more maudling but he'd been trying to deal with the events of the last few months by putting a brave face on things so why not have a little self pity.

He sipped the whisky.

At times like this a wife could be a help he thought. Would it be worth getting back in touch with Fiona? Extending the olive branch? He pulled back from that one. Self-pity was one thing, self-destruction was another. But would it really be that bad he wondered. What else was he going to do? Who else was there?

Probably one for sober reflection in the morning he thought but what about reaching out to the half brother? Admittedly that might mean a return to Scotland which was to be resisted at all costs. But why not? He could explain the situation, how he had not been thinking clearly and wipe the slate clean.
It would be a fresh start for him and Fiona and him and Kenny. Why not? Was there any Johnny Walker left?

CHAPTER 24

Kenny looked around the pub and, as ever, felt somewhat comforted by being in a bar. The dark colours of the wood paneling, the alcoholic glow on the face of the office party who'd carried on from their post work drinks, it all added up to a feeling of - what was the word the Spanish had – bonhomie! Aye fucking right! It was the French that had that word tucked up nicely. What was Gus' classic line "What's French for deja vu?" Stupid wee bastard. Even the fag smoke from the group of suited office workers next to him added to the atmosphere. He managed to stifle a fart that would have also contributed to the atmosphere but not in a positive sense. Why had he decided to start on Guinness? It was one thing keeping Potter company in drinking the same pint, but it played havoc with his guts.

"Alright Kenny?" asked Potter as he walked up having taken in the whole pub by the time he got to Kenny.

"Oh, hi. Alright, Potter? Guinness is it?" asked Kenny who was still getting used to being in a pub with his dad.

"Excellent."

Kenny looked down the bar to get the barman's attention, to no avail. The barman was chatting up one of the barmaids whilst another barman was polishing a pint glass to within a millimetre of it's life. The first barman was now offering the barmaid a cigarette. It wouldn't be so bad but she hadn't actually put out the one she was currently smoking. Talk about rubbing it in? The second barman had put the glass on the shelf behind him but had now found something else on the shelf that necessitated him turning his back on Kenny completely whilst he delved into the space with his right arm.

If ever ignoring customers was an Olympic sport thought Kenny, Scotland's bar staff would be nap for a gold in that competition. Just as he was beginning to despair of the barman ever seeing him, Potter stepped forward, cleared his throat in aggressive manner and barked, yes really barked, "Two pints of

Guinness please."

Kenny was a bit taken aback with that action from him but was completely surprised when he had the chance to take in what Potter was wearing. Well, not so much surprised as completely and utterly gobsmacked. Kenny clocked Potter was wearing a smart looking black leather jacket, a white Ralph Lauren polo shirt, jeans and, wait a fucking minute, thought Kenny, were they Timberland boots? They're over a hundred quid a pair!

"You OK Kenny?" asked Potter once he realised Kenny was giving him the onceover.

"Aye, eh, fine. You look, eh, a wee bit different from the last time."

Potter gave Kenny one of his knowing smiles.

"What? Are you put out because I don't look like an extra from "Hunting Shooting Fishing Weekly" anymore?"

"Well, if you want to say that but I couldn't comment on fashion really. Thinking back though, the first time I met you were wearing a Barbour jacket, those thick cords posh blokes wear and a deerstalker" said Kenny, trying to get his head around the fact he had a trendy dad. He was still trying to come to terms with the knowledge he had a living dad, so all in all it was a bit of a mindfuck for him.

Potter laughed

"Don't worry. That lot went to a charity shop in the east end. I'm only pulling your leg. I've had a wee holiday in the States over New Year since I last saw you. Went to New York and then down to Washington to visit an old friend in the USAF. Sorry, the American Air Force. She took me to one of those outlet malls they have over there and got me dolled up with a new wardrobe. Couldn't believe the prices. These boots were only £50! I saw them in a shop in Buchanan Street the other day for over £100. Can you believe it?"

"Oh aye, I can believe it," said Kenny who'd noted the old air force pal was a female of the species. Potter clearly had an eye for more than a bargain in the good old US of A.

"In fact it was so cheap, I even bought you something." Potter handed Kenny a navy plastic bag with a large white image of a polo player on a horse embossed on it. Kenny opened the bag to find two navy blue polo shirts inside.

"No offence with the cheapness remark, by the way." said Potter hurriedly.

"No worries. Wow, Ralph Lauren! No' a fake, the genuine article. Thanks very much Potter." He looked a bit closer at the shirt and was disappointed to see it was a size medium.

"That's a pity. It's a bit wee for me," said Kenny in a muted tone.

"Oh, sorry, I should have explained. One's for you and the other is for the poison dwarf. The other one should be an XL. I've got to build a couple of bridges with Gus, I was a bit out of order the night before I left."

Kenny listened with interest to that last statement. He had been fearing something like this since he had brought Potter out and about in Glasgow after their initial meetings. The guy had something about him, call it a presence, call it a male allure but everywhere they went, women, not just middle aged women, all women, seemed to be a bit energised, for want of a better word. He nearly said turned on but he couldn't admit to that. Gus had seen it as well and, apparently, been a victim of it. Kenny had wondered what Gus meant on the phone the other night when he was going on about Potter's endolphins making him a robbing bastard, but guessed he was trying to make the same point. Not wanting to get in too deep, Kenny decided a change of subject might be in order.

"So, how's the new flat?" he asked.

"Excellent. I had no idea the city centre had so much to offer. It's busy most of the time but that's how I like it as I am looking to get back into the real world. The Highlands has the scenery but I am after moving up a couple of gears now my time there is done. Now the Laird has passed on. If you asked me to describe it in one word I would use re-invigorated. You can only spend so much time in the middle of nowhere, probably too much in my case, so I am looking to make up for lost time."

An awkward silence followed as Kenny realised the making up for lost time also applied to him. He tried to re-start the conversation, turning back from Potter's openness of feelings.

"So you bought a one bedroom flat in the Merchant City?"

"Aye, it's all I need at my time in life."

"Your time in life? Christ, Potter. You sound like it should be an old folks' home you're going to, not a bachelor pad."

"Aye, fair point Kenny." Potter had raised his left hand as he took a drink with his right.

Kenny wondered how old Potter was. His quick but dodgy mental sums had put Potter about the same age as his mum, in his 50s. However, the fucker looked a good ten years younger with a full head of hair, greying at the temples, and a build that suggested anyone starting something had better look out, as Potter would definitely be finishing it.

"You got all you need for the home?" asked Kenny, hoping he had, as there was no way Kenny was ponying up for a dining table with matching chairs.

"Oh aye. No problem. I've decorated it myself, kept it calm, neutral tones."

"Neutral fuckin' tones? What the fuck are ye on about, Frank?"

Gus announced his arrival in his usual muted way.

"Christ, it's like that song, "Father and Son Reunion" I see before me."

"And a good evening to you Gus," said Potter with a big grin on his face.

"Aye, ye can wipe that smug look off yer coupon, Frank. Ah want words wi' you by the way. It's one thing coming out for a drink wi' me, it's another pinchin' ma burd, like. Did ye hear about this Kenny? Ah'm away tae the Gents for a moment. Get me a pint of lager and explain to young Kenneth what you did the other night."

"Oh aye, you been a naughty boy, Potter?"

Potter looked at Kenny.

"Cat got your tongue, Potter?" Kenny was trying not to make it look like he was enjoying Potter's discomfort, but it was a rare opportunity to get one over on him.

"That wee bastard McSween. I've been meaning to have a word. He's got no scruples that boy."

"*He's* got no scruples? You're the one that cut his grass!" Kenny was really enjoying this, but unfortunately the excitement of the moment caught up with him and he dropped an enormous fart.

In an effort to hide from those around him in the bar, Kenny turned to the bar and managed to order a pint of lager for Gus. Potter was staring down a couple of suits nearby who had been less than impressed with new atmosphere in the pub.

"Fuck's sake, Kenny, was that you?" asked Gus as he pushed his way past the same couple of guys who turned to shoot Kenny dirty looks.

"Aye, keep it down. It's this fucking Guinness."

Kenny couldn't believe it. He'd got Potter on the back foot and in a matter of seconds it was himself who was on the defensive."

"Whoa, for fuck's sake." Gus waved his hand in front of his face to wave the smell away. "That's Charles Laughton, like".

"Charles Laughton?" asked Potter.

"To Gus, "Charles Laughton" equals "rotten". He can't stand London but keeps on speaking in rhyming slang for some reason."

Kenny took a look at Gus who was wearing his usual clean, but ill-matched ensemble. A bottle green polo shirt was buttoned up to the neck and on top of that was a purple golf jumper with a yellow and grey diamond pattern down the front. This was topped off with a pale blue zip up cagoule. The pale beige chinos didn't really go with the black slip-ons either, but having seen the wee man naked, Kenny thought the clothes, however garish, served a higher purpose. To put the cherry on his outfit, Gus was also carrying an old battered brown leather briefcase, the type Kenny remembered his English teacher at school owning. It had a single handle with the lockable strap coming underneath the grip.

After taking a mouthful of lager, Gus was now standing with an inane grin on his face.

"What's put you in such a good mood?" asked Potter.

"Just been to the printers, like. Picked up ma new business cards." Gus had put the briefcase on a bar stool and had sprung the lock, prior to opening the case.

"Christ, the last time I saw something like that, Winston Churchill was carrying it into a meeting with Stalin," said Potter.

"Shut it you. Nothin' that comes out of that small teuchter brain o' yours can upset me today, Frank as ah've just been tae the printers!"

"What the fuck were you doing at the printers, and why do you keep repeating "Ah've just been to the printers"?" snorted Kenny.

"Ah was gettin' ma business cards printed," said Gus, as he produced a small white cardboard box from the ancient case. He opened the box and produced a sample card, presenting it to Kenny with a flourish.

"A business card?" asked Potter, who winked at Kenny as he asked the question.

"Aye, a business card. Everyone knows ah'm in the business o' love, like. Ah thought it only fit an' proper that ah had a card made up so ah could present myself to the fairer sex in an accomplished an' professional manner. Got a problem wi' it, like?"

"Oh no," said Potter" No problem. Good luck to you. Can I see one, please?"

Gus passed a card to Potter who, as he read it, began to chuckle.

"What's so fuckin' funny, Frank?" asked Gus, a slightly piqued tone in his voice.

Potter looked up from card "Your lumber number?" he enquired.

"I am reading it but not really taking it in," said Kenny. "As Potter says, your lumber number?"

"Exactly, it's a fuckin' play on words, ya daft twats. Ah was watchin' a video ae "Roots" the other night, like, an Chicken George's grandson, wait a minute, was it his great-grandson? No, the grandson, hold on, it was the great, great......"

"In your own time Gus," said Potter.

"Hey, nothin' wrong gettin' the details of a story right by the way. Anyway, where was ah?

"Chicken George's great-grandson!" said Kenny in an exasperated tone.

"Aye right, well this boy ended up wi' a lumberyard, like. And his advertising slogan was the telephone number of the yard, followed by the words "Your lumber number". Immediately, fuckin' immediately, ah thought, "What a great thing tae have printed on a card, like". Get it on a business card and ah'm away.

"Alright doll, fancy a lumber? Well this is your lumber number" Burds always like a man wi' a sense o' humour and if that doesnae crack a smile like, what will, eh? What d'ye think?"

Kenny and Potter looked at each other. Kenny eventually started tugging at his right ear for want of something better to do. Looking around the bar he saw two women in their early thirties sitting in a corner, a large glass of wine in front of each of them and an empty bottle in an ice bucket on the floor. They looked like they might be up for some cheeky nonsense if they were already the best part of their way through a bottle of wine and it was only 7pm.

"There you go Gus. There's a target rich environment," said Kenny, raising an eyebrow in the direction of the two women drinking wine. "That pair look like they're set up for you."

"Well done, Kenny. Good tae see that for a useless bastard your eyesight's no' totally shot tae bits. Watch the briefcase Frank. Ah may be some time."

Gus plonked the briefcase at Potter's feet and set off across the pub.

As he watched Gus walk to his doom, Potter muttered "You cruel bastard, Kenny. These cards aren't cheap to get printed and he's going to get crushed into a thousand little pieces the first time he uses them."

"Life is a learning experience Potter. He's going to get taught a lesson, just like I was last year. It may well be a very harsh lesson but do me a favour? "Your lumber number"? That's tragic!"

They looked across the bar where Gus was giving it his best sales pitch. As the women looked at the cards Gus had presented to them, they turned to look at each other and embarrassed smiles broke across their faces.

Gus was actually standing on his tiptoes as he administered his killer line but he sagged back on his heels as one of the women replied to him, a rather dismissive look crossing her face as she spoke. She turned to her friend and shook her head. Gus took his card back and walked back to Kenny and Potter. Kenny thought he looked on the verge of tears and realised this would not be a good time to take the piss.

"What? A KB?" asked Potter, clearly not sharing Kenny's now charitable take on proceedings.

"What happened?" asked Kenny, as he shot Potter a dirty look.

"Eh. It didnae quite go tae plan, like."

"Go tae plan? Oh for God's sake," said Potter as he looked up at the ceiling. He was biting his lip clearly trying not to laugh at the wee man's plight.

"What did you say to them?" asked Kenny.

"Ah said ah heard good looking women like them liked a man wi' a sense o' humour, so ah then presented them wi' a card each."

"And?"

"One o' them said she thought Laurel and Hardy were funny but she didnae fancy a threesome. Then the other one ripped ma card up."

"She what?" Potter had immediately stopped staring at the ceiling and was now completely focused on Gus with a visible intensity that had the wee man shrinking back in terror. Kenny could not believe the instant change in the man. One second he was reveling in Gus' discomfort, now something completely different was going on.

Potter was now looking across the bar at the two women. Without taking his eyes off them, he put out his hand and said to Gus, " Give me a card."

The tone of his voice alerted Kenny that the evening was now about to take a turn for the worse.

239

"Eh, the rest o thems in the briefcase, like," said Gus.

"Just get me a card, wee man."

"Eh, Potter. Let's think about this. If we started a rammy every time he got a KB it would be worse than the Arabs and Israelis," said Kenny.

Gus had finally retrieved another card from his briefcase and passed it to Potter. With his other hand he reached into his jacket. "Oh for fuck's sake," thought Kenny. "He's going to bring out a gun." As it happened the only thing Potter withdrew was a rather stylish gold pen.

"Don't worry, boys. Back in a couple of minutes," said Potter, as he set off towards the two women.

"What's he gonnae do, Kenny?" asked Gus. "Ah didnae think this evening could get any worse. Now ah'm no sae sure, like."

"I honestly don't know"

Potter had sat down at the table and appeared to be talking to the women in a low voice, as they were both leaning forward to hear him speak. After a couple of minutes they both smiled and as Potter offered them the pen, they both reached out to take it at the same time. The younger of the two won out and scribbled something down on the card proffered by Potter, who then took the pen back and offered it to the other woman. Before she could write he turned the card over, making a comment which caused her to blush.

When she had finished writing, Potter took the card and pen off her. As he stood up he said something that caused both women to smile.

As he walked back across the bar, Potter returned the pen to his jacket pocket and palmed the business card. He took a quick drink from his pint and turned to look at Gus.

"Never ever embarrass me like that again, Gus."

"What the fuck? Embarrass you? Ah had to do the ultimate walk of shame away fae that table, like. No' you, Mr. Fucking Popular - who always leaves them smilin; walkin away wi' the stride o' pride!"

"What did you say to them?" asked Kenny.

"I told them Gus wasn't the full shilling, they should have been able to tell that by the way he was dressed. Also that he had taken my personal card to try and make an impression."

"Get tae fuck. No the full fuckin' shilling! Ah cannae believe this."

"I had to try and help him emerge with some kind of dignity."

"Emerge with some kind of dignity! Emerge wi' some kind o' fuckin' dignity! You've made me out to be a special needs case and ah'm coming out o' this wi' dignity? Do me a fuckin' favour." Gus took up his pint and took a large mouthful of lager. His anger was so great he tried to speak before successfully swallowing the drink, thus bringing on a gagging reflex as the lager sluiced down his throat. As he drooled lager down the side of his mouth, Potter spoke to him.

"Well the way you look today, it wasn't a hard sell. They thought Halloween was two months ago and now you're drooling. What a sight."

At that moment the jukebox changed and as the dulcet tones of Noel Gallagher floated across the bar, Kenny started laughing.

"For fuck's sake, Kenny. What's got you goin' now?" asked Gus.

"They're playing your song, Gus," said Kenny, tears forming in his eyes.

"Oh aye, what song's that, like?"

"Oasis, "Don't Look Back In Anger!"

"Oh, ha fuckin' ha. Ma public humiliation is just a cheap joke for you pal."

Kenny wiped his eyes with the back of his hand and looked back at the table with the two women. They were looking intently at Potter, who was smiling back at them.

"So, what were they writing Potter?" asked Kenny.

Potter reached towards Gus' left ear. As Gus flinched, Potter produced the business card with the two phone numbers as if from thin air.

"See that?" he asked as he moved card in front of Gus' face in a circular motion and showing both sides of it.

"What? What is it?" asked Gus as he screwed his face up trying to keep the card in his line of vision.

"They're my Lumber Numbers. Plural."

"Aw, fuck off, man. Those burds gave their numbers to somebody whose old enough to be their fuckin' dad. That's sick and twisted. Ah'm glad ah got a KB off them now. They're clearly a couple o' psychos, like. Ah would be kept in a chest in a cellar wi' that pair. Just taken out to be their sex toy on a regular basis before being locked up again."

"I thought that was one of your ultimate fantasies," said Kenny.

"That's no the point, like."

"Well, I don't think you need worry about seeing them again," said Potter.

"Why's that?"

"Watch." Potter turned his back on the table where the women sat. He ripped the card in two and placed the pieces on his tongue like a communion wafer, closed his mouth and started chewing. After a few seconds he picked up his Guinness and took a big mouthful. He swallowed and stuck out his tongue at the two of them.

"Amen to that, Frank" said Gus.

CHAPTER 25

"Well ah have tae admit it. Ah wasnae too impressed with the idea o' this game being replayed but now ah'm here.....Ya Fucken Dancer!"

Gus McSween was standing outside the arrivals hall of Nice airport as he spoke these words. From the grey skies of Luton, Gus and Kenny had arrived in the Cote d'Azur on a gloriously sunny day. The blue sky stretched out above them without a cloud to lessen the view. Directly opposite the arrivals hall, a stretch of palm trees swayed in a gentle breeze, the gently moving palms appearing to beckon Gus towards them.

"Believe the hype, eh?" said Dominic.

"Right, where's the taxi rank?" said Gus looking up and down the tarmac in front of him.

"There's the sign," said Kenny who moved off in the general direction indicated by the sign.

Dominic lagged behind, his concern over the cost of a taxi appearing to handicap his walking pace.

"Is there no' a bus we can get? How much will a taxi be? This is the south of France remember!"

Gus stopped in his tracks and turned back to face his trailing travelling companion.

"Dominic, look here son. We're in Nice, the playground of the rich and famous. Let's try and act wi' a wee bit o' style, like. We don't know where the hotel is, we don't know what bus we should take, like, let's just cut out that fanny merchant of a middleman and do the right thing. OK?"

Gus placed a reassuring arm round Dominic's shoulder. "We'll be alright, Dom. Don't worry about the expense as these places are always talked up to be more expensive than they really are."

"You really think so, Gus? I've heard some real horror stories."

"Ah know, ah know. But don't worry about it. Me an Kenny will keep you right,

243

OK?"

"Cheers, I appreciate it" said Dominic visibly brightening. Gus waited a moment before continuing in a low voice so Kenny wouldn't hear him.

"The thing is ah didnae get a chance tae get tae the bank before ah left so have you got any Francs for the taxi?"

"Oh for fuck's sake." Dominic shrugged off Gus' arm.

"Nothing changes with you does it? No Francs but you're wanting us to get taxis and me to pay for your share. The same sob story every fucking time. Still look on the bright side."

"Oh aye, what is the bright side if he's no' got any money?" asked Kenny who felt similarly aggrieved.

"Me and you bought the rounds at Luton Airport , Kenny. So Gus is on the bell. I think I might have a pint of lager with a champagne chaser. Five pounds a pint I think it is as well." Dominic punched the air with both fists like a victorious boxer until his sports bag slipped off his shoulder and dragged his right arm down. Having sorted out the bag issue, Dominic and Kenny walked off arm in arm.

"Hey, hey, wait a fuckin' minute. That's no' on. No fuckin' way, like. Five pounds a pint, yer arse!" cried Gus as he tried to catch up on his friends.

Kenny had an abnormal dislike of sitting in the front seat as that meant he often had to chat to the taxi driver. He'd had enough of those conversations from the driver's point of view so was quite happy to let Gus attempt to find out from the driver where the best places to drink were.

"This on metero?" asked Gus who turned to Dominic and Kenny with a big thumbs up front from the front seat.

"Yes, you can see the charge" said the driver in perfect English, pointing at the taxi meter.

"Barro, much cheapness, el cheapo vino and beero" said Gus, clearly immune to the driver's ability to speak English.

"Have we slipped into a different time and space continuum?" asked Dominic.

The last time I looked we were in France not Spain."

"Look here Dom, ah'm making all the effort here. Why don't you just leave it to me? Ah'll find out the best boozers from this boy. Pas de problem."

"Excuse me," said Dominic. "Can you recommend anywhere to eat and drink in Nice?" asked Kenny who could see where this was going.

The driver looked at Kenny in the rear view mirror.

"You are spoilt for choice. The best food, the best wine, the most beautiful women. We have them all here in the Cote d'Azur." replied the driver.

"Aye but what about the bevvio?" asked Gus.

"Are you fucken deaf or something," said Kenny. "Speak to the guy in English and he will answer you. Stop adding o to the end of every word. It is embarassingo." Kenny nudged Dominic.

Gus turned round from the front seat.

"Ah'm trying to speak to the boy in his native tongue and you just presume he can speak English like everywhere else."

"I am presuming nothing. He can speak better English than you."

The driver held up his right hand to silence them.

"Guys if you want to drink, try Wayne's Bar. English bar, ok crowd. Eat anywhere, it is all good."

Gus looked at Kenny with a triumphant smile on his face.

"See, ah knew I was getting through to him, Kenny. Oh ye of little faith Bradley, oh ye of little faith."

The taxi dropped them off at the Best Western Nice in just under ten minutes.

"Magic," said Kenny. "More faded grandeur" Their hotel was a grand villa that looked about one hundred years old. The garden was well tended and there was no litter but something about the hotel suggested its best days were behind it.

"Is this what they call shabby chic?" asked Gus once he had borrowed Francs off Dominic to pay his share of the taxi back to Dominic.

"Am I the fucking banker again?" Dominic wailed.

"Look we need somebody responsible to hold the kitty. You are responsibility personified in my humble opinion. Isn't that right, Kenny? Do you want me to hold the kitty?"

"No," Dominic mumbled.

"Well, there you go," said Gus who gently patted Dominic on the face a couple of times.

"Bradley, what the fuck are you doing now?" asked Gus bemused at Kenny's antics.

Kenny had put his sports bag on the ground and was searching through the side pockets.

"I'm looking for the voucher for the room."

"Voucher for the room?" asked Gus who looked at Dominic for support. "What the fuck are you on about, a voucher? This isnae an Esso service station an you're savin up for a set o' glasses."

"It's the voucher confirming the booking of the room for us. Alison printed it off the internet for me. I need to give it to the boy on the desk as proof of our reservation."

"Aw right. Ah thought you'd just phoned up. What's wi' this internet thing? How do you use that?"

Gus and Dominic looked at each other, their mutual ignorance giving them a combined feeling of serious inadequacy.

"Best Western have this website apparently and you can book any hotel in the world through it. Alison went on, found this one in Nice, which is the cheapest in their range and paid it on the credit card. Which reminds me you owe me, or rather Alison, one hundred quid each for the hotel. She even signed me up for their loyalty scheme. I've got a card - the works!"

Kenny produced his Best Western loyalty card from his wallet to flash to them.

"Wait a minute, thinking about it I might just need to show them the card. The booking details may well be on it already. Tres bon, mes amis."

The details were not on the card, but their reservation was on the system. The remarkably young looking receptionist dealt with them very quickly and they were soon setting their bags down in a large triple room.

"I've worked out what it is wi' this place that doesnae do it for me," said Gus.

"What's that then?" Dominic replied.

"Pale green! It's the colour. Old pale green paint, light green curtains that have been up for ages, pale and emerald green striped wallpaper. Are you sure this place isnae the headquarters of the Nice Celtic Supporters Club Kenny?"

Kenny was just finishing his unpacking as Gus asked the question.

"Aye, I see where you are coming from Gus. I keep on thinking of Tom Jones, the Green, Green Wallpaper of Home. Come on let's go and check out the niceties of Nice, boom boom!"

*****

At that moment, some twelve miles away in Monte Carlo, Atholl McClackit unfolded the Saturday edition of the Financial Times. He was seated outside his favourite café enjoying a double espresso and a cigarillo. His day had started well as he had awoken at 5am, drenched in sweat convinced he was still in Partmui prison. He considered this progress since it meant he was no longer having drug related nightmares following his treatment at the hands of Harold MacMillan in Tallinn. He had commenced an exercise regime to help fill in time until he had worked out what to do next with his life but also to try and cleanse his body, sweat out the impurities of prison and what had happened to him in the last few months. A sense of failure still swept over him from time to time but those were the low moments, periods that were few and far between.

He had just picked up the travel section when he glanced down the road and broke out in a cold sweat. Three men were walking towards him, each wearing a kilt and a Scotland top.

Calm down he told himself, calm down, this must be a flashback of some kind. As they approached him, one of them stopped.

"Excuse me pal" he said "I take it you speak English."

Atholl was dumbstruck.

"Parlez vous Anglais?" the guy pointed to the paper, clear proof that Atholl could at least read English.

"Eh, yes, yes I do. Forgive me, I was just taken aback by the sight of three Scots walking up the street in Monaco. How can I help you?"

Atholl put the paper down on the table.

"We're trying to find the station but we're a bit lost." said the one who had asked about speaking English.

"A bit lost? Try totally fucken lost," said a second fan. "Ah told ye to keep the harbour on the right but you wouldn't fucken hear it."

"Look, can we no leave this till later?" said the third.

"Aye, leave it till later when he's sobered up."

"Am totally fucken sober. Who could get gassed on these prices?"

"A two-can dan like you!"

Atholl cleared his throat.

"If you walk up to the top of the street and take a right, the station is about two hundred yards on the right."

"Ok, cheers pal," said the first fan.

"Before you go, can I ask why you are here?" enquired Atholl.

"Aye, Scotland are playing Estonia here on Tuesday night. We're the advance party of the Tartan Army," explained the second one, trying to appear like he knew what was going on.

"Ah right. I had no idea," said Atholl picking up his cigarillo. "You wouldn't happen to know a chap called Kenny Bradley by any chance? Big Scotland fan, travels with another fan called Gus McSween."

"Ah know McSween," said the third guy, a huge smile breaking out on his face. "Once met, never forgotten that wee prick. He's the guy that told everybody he's had sex in every car he'd owned till Kenny pointed out he couldn't drive so he

248

was talking out of his arse."

"No, the poison dwarf! Excellente. Do you know him? Come to think of it, have I not seen you on a couple of trips?" asked the second fan who was sobering up by the minute.

"No, I've not been on any trips. I have heard of those guys through a friend so thought I would enquire. They sound like a couple of characters."

"Well they should be here. Going to the game yourself pal?" asked the first.

"No, I didn't even know it was taking place but thanks for letting me know. Is there anything else I can help you with?" asked Atholl looking to bring the conversation to a close.

"No, cheers for the info. See you around," said the first fan who was now appearing keen to get away.

The second fan was about to ask a question but was pulled away by the first.

"Come on, let's beat it to the station. You can lead the way, Pathfinder Harper!"

CHAPTER 26

It was a dry, warm Sunday in Nice. Kenny, Gus and Dominic had met a few other fans they knew and were sitting in a cafe off Place Grimaldi. The crowd was a mixed bag. Some guys had kilts on as they would have for the duration. Others, like Kenny and Gus had on jeans and Scotland t-shirts. What had caught everyone out was the weather which continued on the rapturous sunshine from the Saturday. It had been a bit of a heavy one the night before and that, coupled with the price of drink in the café, had led to a quiet nursing of drinks as the previous evenings events were recounted. Some people were even drinking water. Gus, never one to be backward in coming forward with his version of a previous night's events, was sounding off.

"Ah gave that lassie all ma best lines last night, like. Each one fell on deaf ears," he grumped.

Dominic had had enough of his sob story.

"Fell on deaf ears? She was a foot taller than you. Reached up to deaf ears more like! Then couldn't take the altitude. I'm sure she said to her pal she was fed up listening to you. It was nothing to do with what you were saying. She was getting a sore neck bending down and trying to look interested."

"Get tae fuck. She never left my side the whole night," Gus replied, looking around the group for support.

"Aye, because you had her pinned against the wall. She only managed to escape because you couldn't hold it in any longer and had to make a mad dash for the Gents."

"Shut it, you! I would turn to drink for consolation but wi' these prices ah'm only going to get more depressed. Are we going to have a kitty, as paying up once has got to be better than paying up each time, like. Dom, can you put in for me, please. Ah still cannae get tae a bank wi' it bein' a Sunday."

Dominic reached into his pocket for his wallet. As he leant back in his seat, trying to extract it, he looked at Gus. "This is the last time, right? You're up to a thousand francs already and we've been here less than 24 hours.

Kenny was surveying the area around the cafe as he kittied up. It seemed reasonably busy for a Sunday. All of the shops were shut apart from a small corner shop and a boulangerie. The baker's was doing steady trade with locals buying traditional French sticks which were poking out of the top of the shopping bags like a couple of periscopes. He was looking at the baker's door when a tall Frenchman exited wearing a pair of navy blue overalls with rough writing on the chest area which appeared to have been painted on.

He could just about make out the writing on the front but could not believe what his eyes were telling him.

"Can somebody take a look at this guy coming towards us? Has he really got "pussy hunter" written on the front of his overalls?"

They all looked at the guy as he approached them.

"Oh for fuck's sake," said one of the others. "Never mind the pussy hunter, he's wearing a beret."

The man in the overalls walked past them into the cafe, carrying his plastic bag with a couple of tins and a French stick. On the back of the overalls Kenny saw an image but again had to ask the group for verification.

"He's got pussy hunter on the front and on the back, he's got a large red cock. Did I see that right?"

Dominic looked at Kenny. The main part of the back of the overalls from the waist up was taken up with a well-painted picture of a rather angry looking, flamingly erect red penis. The bell end was perfectly drawn and perhaps it was the sunlight, but there did seem to be some shading around the base.

"Just as well it had been circumcised otherwise he would have been wearing a hood."

"That's incredible. It's the first time I've ever seen anybody dressed worse than McSween."

Gus had a big grin on his face.

"What's that boy doing with an image o' ma cock on his back?"

"Aye, magnified three million times" nipped Dominic.

"Shut it you," Gus growled. "What a fuckin' sight. Oops, shhh, here he comes."

The guy in the overalls had left the cafe with a glass of red wine in his hand. He looked at the Scotland fans and came and sat at a table close to Kenny.

Kenny groaned inwardly. Why did every foreign nutter pick on him? Guys in kilts attract nutters like shite attracts flies. But yet they don't go and speak to the main characters in this play. No, he's sitting quietly in the shadows when a guy with a giant fucking phallus painted on the back of his overalls comes over and sits next to him. This could be a long half hour coming up. He had worked out over the years thirty minutes was the average time that it took the jakeys and the nutters to get the picture he wasn't interested in talking to them. If they wanted to mooch fags or bevvy they could try elsewhere as they were getting fuck all off him.

The guy in the overalls sat down and arranged his bag under the chair. He took a sip of wine and then produced a packet of Marlboro red top from a pocket in the overalls.

He turned to Kenny and asked, "You have eh light?"

"Sorry pal - don't smoke." He turned to the table. "Anybody here got a lighter for this guy?"

One of the others threw the lighter to Kenny who passed it to the Frenchman. He lit his cigarette and passed the lighter back to Kenny.

"Merci. You are Ecossais? Scots?" he asked.

"Aye. We are," replied Kenny. "Are you French?" If I'm going down I'm taking someone with me," he thought.

"Yes. You cannot tell?" came the reply.

"Just checking, you never know. I was expecting maybe a stripey jumper and a beret, not a pair of overalls with a cock painted on the back."

The Frenchman laughed and extended his hand "Ah am Yves. Ah am artist."

Kenny shook his hand, saying "I am Kenny, I am taxi driver. This is Gus, He is piss artist."

"Piss artist? He drink ze piss?"

"No, he normally takes the piss. Gus say hello to Yves."

Gus leant across Kenny to shake the hand of Yves.

"Enchante, like. Nice is tres expensive. Are there are any barros near hero for cheapo vino, like? Je t'aime!"

Dominic burst out laughing as did several others in the group. Yves looked around them and then back to Gus. He was not smiling.

Gus realised what had been meant in jest had got somewhat lost in translation.

"OK, Yves. Just ma wee joke, like."

"You joke about love? Ah never joke about ze love for women. Ah am ze pussee unter!"

"Yes, well we're the Tartan Army and it looks like we're off," said Kenny who had finished his half of Kronenburg and was standing up. He was making faces and nodding his head in a direction away from the cafe to ensure the others got his drift about dumping Yves. Gus who for once had taken a hint gave the thumbs up sign to Kenny and also finished his drink and went to move off with Kenny.

A French voice behind them called "A moment, Ecossais. Ah come with you."

All of a sudden Kenny thought that as if a raging hangover, high prices for drink and an unexpected, but very welcome, beating sun were not enough, this day was going to be even longer than anticipated.

There were about eight in the original group sitting at the table. Kenny now found himself walking down the street with a French guy who had obscene images painted on his clothes. Fortunately Yves was now talking to Dominic. Gus chortled.

"What now?" asked Kenny.

"Well, ah've just noticed we're on Rue de la Liberte and is he no taking libertys wi' those overalls, man. D'ye get it like? Rue de la Liberte - taking libertys. Get it?

253

Eh? D'ye get it?"

"Gus, you know talking to foreigners doesn't really do anything for me. So can we dump this guy at the first opportunity? Sadly he looks like he's going to be with us for some time."

Kenny was walking at a fair pace, trying to distance himself from the rest. If Dominic wanted to do the care worker bit, fair play to him. But this was not Kenny's idea of a pleasant Sunday afternoon in Nice. It was bad enough getting stared at by people due to the guys in kilts, but clearly they had in tow a bit of a local character. Some of the locals were nudging each other when they saw Yves and pointing at him.

He turned to Gus who was struggling to keep up.

"You know how you think you're a bit of a fanny magnet? Well, it's no you, it's me. Every time we go somewhere, a complete fanny decides to hook up with me and there's no getting rid of the fucker."

"Slow down, Kenny. The boy will think we're trying to leg it." Gus was out of breath and toiling in the unseasonal heat.

"I am trying to leg it, you daft twat. Can you not walk any faster?"

"OK, OK. Ah've tried to appeal to your better nature but if that's no good enough, remember Dominic's got the whip and ah'm brassic."

Kenny stopped. 'Well, when you put it like that, perhaps we had better do the decent thing."

By this time they had come to an intersection. Kenny looked up at the street sign and saw Rue Chauvain. By this time the rest had caught up with him and Gus. Kenny turned to look at the group, specifically Yves."

"Alright, Yves. You're the local. Anywhere you would recommend? Où est la bar pour les Ecossais?

"Aye, cheapo, like" said Gus.

Yves put his hand to his chin and appeared deep in thought.

"We go right ere. Zer is a bar but ah cannot go in. C'est defondu for me. How you say, forbidden."

"Got a right one here," Gus murmured to Dominic.

"You ain't heard nothing yet. Wait till I tell you he's got hepatitis B."

"Whit?" Gus took a step away from Yves.

"Zer is anuzzer bar, one undred metres. Un moment, c'est defondu aussi. No, I am forbidden."

"Is there any boozers in this place you can go into big man" asked one of the group. They laughed but Yves failed to appreciate the joke.

"You are findin me funny?" he shouted. They fell silent.

"Eh, no. We are not finding you funny" said Kenny. Some other tourists across the road had stopped to look at them.

Dominic had produced a map from his bumbag.

"If we go down here we'll come to the old town and the docks marina thing after a walk through the gardens. What do you reckon?"

"Sounds like a plan?" asked Kenny as he looked for a group consensus.

"Aye go on, is le coq sportif comin wi us though?" asked Gus.

"Looks like it but if we ignore him, he might fuck off," said Kenny. He was about to head off in the direction indicated by Dominic when he felt a tug on his arm. It was Yves.

"Ah need to ask. Why are ze Scots ere?"

Kenny realised there was to be no easy way out of this one.

"There is a football match in Monte Carlo on Tuesday. Scotland are playing."

"You are playing France?"

"No, we are playing Estonia," came the reply.

"Why are you playin Estonia in Monte Carlo?" Yves was leaning close into his face. Kenny had always thought it was a bit of a cliché about the French and garlic breath but this guy lived up to the cultural stereotype. Admittedly the cock on the overalls was a new one on Kenny so there was some originality there. Had he heard Dominic say something about hepatitis B a minute ago?

"We played them in September last year but they didn't have the right floodlights and let's just leave it at that." Kenny knew Scots who couldn't get their head around the three-second game, so he was fucked if he was going too waste time explaining it to this French jaikey.

"Your English it is very good?" Kenny hoped this would divert the guy from asking about the game.

"Ah worked in New York as chef but ah am artist. You see?" He stood back and held his arms out wide do Kenny could see the writing on the front. He then revolved slowly and Kenny was able to take in once more the full glory of the member painted on the back of the overalls. Kenny could hear the laughter from the tourists across the street.

Yves turned and glared at them.

"Aye, I can see that. Why do you have "pussy hunter" written on the front?" asked Kenny who had decided to try to catch up with the others. They had seen Kenny stop and had taken the opportunity to put a bit of a spurt on. They had the kitty, Kenny had the Frenchman. Bastards!

"Because ah unt ze pussy!"

"What?" said Kenny who was looking up the street.

"Because ah unt ze pussy," repeated Yves in what Kenny took to be an exasperated tone.

"Yeah, but a lot of guys "unt ze pussy" but they don't feel a need to write it on the front of their shirts or draw pricks on their back," Kenny could see that others had stopped in a cafe about 50 metres ahead. "I knew I could count on Gus to wait for me," thought Kenny, probably because if he didn't have a stop his heart or another vital organ would likely give way.

"Ze women should know what they are getting. You ave been to New York ma friend?"

"Brilliant," thought Kenny. "Friends now. I'll put you on my Christmas card list"

"No, never been."

"Ah unt ze pussy in New York all ze time. Ah ave girlfriend but she leave me."

Should have popped a couple of tic tacs pal, that might have saved the relationship, thought Kenny.

"Oh aye, what went wrong, Yves?

" Ah got epatitis B."

"Oh for fuck's sake," said Kenny.

By this time they had reached the cafe and the group were sitting outside. They had taken over a couple of tables and some drinks had been ordered. Kenny hoped there was one for him as by this stage he was gagging for a lager.

"This is good" said Yves "I am not forbidden ere."

"It's early yet," said Gus

"Pardon, you say what?

"Eh, nothing, big man. Shout yoursel up a vino, like. Ah'm sure the whip can stretch that far, like. Here Kenny, got you a lager. Ah know you probably feel like a bigger one but that wee bottle's four quid like, so take it easy."

Kenny took a seat next to Gus. He had a long pull on the bottle then put it down. Gus turned to him.

"So Kenny, tell me all about Yves? All about Yves, d'ye get it, eh? All about Yves, like."

"Fuck off. You bastards were putting in a bit of speed there, weren't you? You were going to leave me with that pussy hunting, hepatitis B ridden, disgrace of a Frenchman."

"Ah thought he seemed alright, like," said Gus.

"You think he seems alright because you've not been talking to him. I tell you what - when he comes back he can have my seat and you can talk about "unting ze pussy" all day long. I know it's one of your specialist subjects."

Fortunately for Kenny when Yves returned with what looked like a suspiciously large glass of red wine, he chose to sit away from Kenny and Gus.

"Magic. Your ability to bore the arse off some poor twat now stretches to French jakies, Kenny. Are you sure you're no' the one wi' the disease, like? Borinbastarditis ah think is the precise term," laughed Gus.

Kenny was necking half his bottle of lager by this stage. He was past caring about the price.

"No complaints from me," said Kenny who turned to look at Yves just as he exploded.

"Shitknee, what ze fuck is shitknee?" cried Yves who had been talking to a newcomer to the scene who hailed from the very top of Scotland.

"It's the game I played at school and it's called "Shinty"." The guy looked a bit embarrassed and turned to the group. "I asked him if he played football and he said he did at school. He asked me if I played at school and I told him no, I played shinty. Anybody else want to speak to him? I've done my bit."

Everyone looked at Kenny for a lead.

"Yves, can you recommend anywhere to eat?" asked Kenny who was starting to feel a bit peckish. A continental breakfast could only carry you so far in a day.

"Aye, somewhere you're no' forbidden," murmured Gus.

"Pardon, you zed zumthin?" asked Yves.

"No, you're alright, Yves," Gus mumbled as he turned to Kenny. "Good to see hepatitis B doesnae affect your hearing like."

"Ah no a good place to eat. It is ze best seafood restaurant in Nice."

"Oh aye," said Gus. "Where is it? Ah know we're in France but ah've never really subscribed to the "march till you drop" philosophy, like."

Yves looked at Gus across the table.

"What are you talkin about? March or drop? Je ne comprends pas."

"What am I talking about? You're the Frenchy! Beau Geste, like. March or drop, ken? The desert fort. Guys that are dead shootin' the Arabs fae the ramparts. Beau fuckin' Geste."

Kenny thought if the walking doesn't kill Gus, this guy's ignorance of French literature just might.

"Ah am zinking of a place to eat" said Yves." Cafe Corso. Ah take you zer now."

"Lead on, McDuff," said Kenny as he got to his feet.

Half an hour later they finally arrived at the Cafe Corso overlooking the Quai Cassini. The looks on the faces of the waiting staff told them they were as popular as a fart in spacesuit. Having a local in tow appeared to do little or nothing for the credibility of the group.

As they sat down they were presented with menus, one look at which confirmed this place was well out of their league for eating and drinking in large amounts. Yves went to the toilets as they perused the menus.

"Holy fuck, Kenny. Why did you bring us here?" asked Dominic. "It's sixteen quid for their cheapest plonk."

"Don't blame me. I was only coming where matey boy suggested. I might have an understanding of what he's after. He touches us for a couple of drinks and now he thinks he can tap us for a seafood extravaganza. Christ, they don't even have overpriced bottles of beer. Right, sorry about this chaps but we get two bottles of wine between us, drink it at our leisure, get out of here then dump "all about Yves". Sound like a plan?"

There was a general nodding of heads around the table.

"Nice view, like," said Gus who had stood up to stare out the large windows that opened on to the port area.

"At these prices it should be," said Dominic.

Yves returned from the Gents just as the waiter was taking their order for the two bottles of house white. Whilst the waiter appeared relatively nonplussed over this, Yves was outraged.

"Ah ave brought you to ze best seafood restaurant in Nice an all you want is to drink?"

"Eh, aye," said Gus. "You never told us it was also ze most expensive seafood restaurant in Nice by the way. D'ye think ah'm made of money?"

Dominic cleared his throat as if to make a point.

"Aye, well like," mumbled Gus who had taken an interest, yet again, in the view. Kenny had given up on Yves and was talking to another in the group about the team for the game on Tuesday night and other plans for the trip. He felt a tap on his shoulder and turned to see Yves with a sad look on his face.

"Kenny, zis is embarrassment for me. Why you are not eatin?"

Kenny did not know whether to laugh or cry.

"Yves, you want to eat, don't let us stop you. Fill your boots."

Yves looked at Kenny, a frown on his face.

"Ah eat if you eat. Ah cannot eat by maself. Ah am leavin if you only drink. Zis is an insult to me and to France." At this Yves threw down his napkin and flounced out of the restaurant. Even the penis on the back of his overalls looked angry.

"Unbelievable," crowed Gus. "Only you could let a French Rab C Nesbitt get away on the moral high horse. Would you Adam and Eve it? Wait a minute, wait a minute, it's more like would you Adam and Yves it."

Kenny leaned back clutching his head in his hands but Gus was not to be deterred.

"Get it, eh, Adam and fuckin' Yves it!!! Ah'm on a fuckin' roll here the day, like. Three belters, one, two three. Comedy gold, like."

CHAPTER 27

Kenny had never been on a bus where there was so many audible "oohs" and "aahs" before. Then again he had never taken a bus ride along the coast road from Nice to Monte Carlo. Unfortunately, he had not realised the best side of the bus to sit on would be the right hand side but he was still getting a good view of the sea, the bays and some fantastic looking houses as they wound their way round the curves in the road.

The people on the bus were split down the middle in terms of dress. An odd contrast generated by the desire of some to ensure entrance to the casino, which in turn led to them looking exceedingly smart in kilts, Bonnie Prince Charlie jackets, kilt socks, ghillie brogues and black bow ties, topped off with a dress sporran. For the other half, it was the usual motley collection of Adidas samba trainers, ill-fitting jeans and old Scotland tops, the Euro 96 top a consistent choice among the discerning fan. Kenny had not wanted to go the casino as he thought it was a mug's game and had decided to save the Scotland gear for the day of the game. If he was in Monte Carlo he wanted to try and look a bit smarter than normal, so had on a smart shirt with chinos and a leather jacket.

"When you get in there, can you find out one thing for me Gus?" asked Kenny as another wave of "oohs" rippled round the bus.

"Aye, whit is it? Would ye look at that place, man. That's a fuckin palace – no' a hoose." Gus was bouncing up and down on his seat like a five year old on Christmas Day.

"Why is it called Monte Carlo but the team is called Monaco?" Kenny had stood up to try and get a bit of a better view. A yacht appeared to be drifting aimlessly out at sea, a lone white traveller on the vast carpet of pale blue sea.

"Aye, no problem. What the fuck are you going to do wi' yoursel if yer no comin to the casino wi Dom and me?" asked Gus, a bemused tone to his voice.

"I don't know. You know gambling does little or nothing for me. I might walk the Formula 1 route."

Dominic leant over from the seat behind and looked at Kenny. He was wearing a rather cheap looking suit and tie and Kenny hoped he would be smart enough to get into the casino.

"But you hate Formula 1, Kenny. You don't gamble and you hate Formula 1. The two things I know are true about you." He looked at Gus for back up and Gus was nodding in agreement whilst pulling at his winged collar of his dress shirt.

"Aye, I know. But I am going to do it to fuck off all those other taxi drivers who go on about it all the time but couldn't organise themselves to actually visit this place. I'll be winding them up like a cheap watch when I get back."

Gus was now standing up in the aisle to get a better view of the marina they were passing.

"Where's this place?" he turned and asked Kenny.

A voice from behind them spoke out.

"Well maybe if you sat down and stopped blocking my view I could tell. I'm trying to look at a sight of great natural beauty, no one o' natural ugliness," said Coulter, an old friend of Gus' who was sitting a few rows back.

"Coulter, you wouldnae know a scene o' natural beauty if it hit you on the head. You've never been out wi' any beauties either, natural or unnatural."

"Aye no' like you Gus. All the burds you go out wi' are all supernatural cos they're a figment of your imagination." The guys around Coulter started laughing.

"How much are you payin' these guys to laugh at your jokes, Coulter. Must be costing you a fortune to keep the Chuckle Brothers laughing, like." Gus was shaking his head with a smile on his face.

"Ah'm payin' them nothin', Gus. Like most people, they just start laughin' when they hear your name. Can you come over and lean forward, ah got a wee treat from the breakfast bar for that thing on your head. I hear hamsters like muesli - wait a minute - or is that gerbils?"

"Why don't you just feed the wee rat deep down inside you instead? Sorry, I forgot that's your personality."

"No need to get personal, Gus. Just havin' a wee joke. You've always got to get bitter and twisted."

"Bitter and twisted? Bitter and fucken twisted!" Gus exclaimed.

"Sit down, it is Beaulieu Sur Mer we've just passed, Coulter. Just looked it up on the map." said Kenny.

Gus sat down with a big smile on his face.

"Cheers, Kenny. A voice of reason in a wilderness of bullshit," came a voice from behind them.

"Coulter, you never get the last word wi' that bam," said Gus who was still trying to look out the far side of the coach to take in the view.

The next minute they were in a tunnel, the darkness coming as a shock after the stunning images of the Mediterranean and the coastline.

"Dom, you looking forward to this?" asked Gus as he turned to look at the seats behind him.

"Oh, aye. Really looking forward to it - though I've had to set myself a limit on how much I spend."

Gus snorted derisively. "Last of the high rollers wi' me then Kenny, eh?"

Dominic bridled in his seat and leant forward to tap Gus on the back of his head with the flat of his palm.

"When I say I've had to set myself a limit, the main reason I am limited is because I've lent you so much money so far on this trip. Don't give me any high roller grief when you've been doing your "Minnie the Moocher" bit."

"Whoa," said Kenny as they came out of the tunnel and were once more stunned with the brilliance of the sea. The quality of the light impressed Kenny more than anything. Even through the bus windows, the clarity was astonishing. He began to think places like this don't get a reputation for nothing and must have something going for them to be so popular.

"This is pretty amazing when you think about it Gus. Hemingway, Scott Fitzgerald, Picasso all lived along this coast. It's a truly special area if it can attract that sort of person."

"The demi-monde of the artistic community normally inhabits places of rare beauty, Kenny. Ah always think ah would have fitted in nicely in those circles. They need a common man to kid themselves they've still got a grasp o' normality. Ah could have done a power o' shaggin' wi' those intellectuals burds, like."

Dominic had leant forward again.

"Sorry, but I'm not interested in a grasp of normality. I want you to get a grasp of reality. When am I going to get my money back?"

Gus was leaning back in his seat stretching his arms above his head.

"See what ah've tae put wi', Kenny? Here's me trying to get mentally prepared for a once in a lifetime visit to the world famous Monte Carlo casino and ah've got him nippin ma heid about a trifling two thousand Francs." He lowered his arms and turned to Dominic.

"Dom, ah've done this before. As soon as ah'm up the two grand, you'll get your money back tout suite, mon cherie. Worry not, like."

By this stage the bus had arrived in the town centre of Monaco and had actually parked in the bus park next to the stadium where the game would be held the following night.

The organiser informed the travellers that the bus would be leaving at 6.30 pm and wouldn't be waiting as there were plenty of travel options back if people wanted to spend more time in the principality.

The group headed immediately for Casino Square attracting a variety of strange looks from French women wearing expensive looking fur coats, despite the fact the temperature was in the low 60s.

As Gus walked past one particularly attractive woman in her early 60's who was wearing an ankle length mink coat, he said, "Ah wonder if she's all fur coat and nae...."

"That'll do, Gus," said Kenny, who gave the woman a large smile as he went to cross the road.

He felt an arm grab him and pull him back just in time to avoid him being hit by a Rolls Royce which had swept into the square.

Gus still had hold of his arm as he turned round to thank him.

"Kenny, after what you went through in the last few games, for fuck's sake don't get killed crossing the road." Gus took his hand off Kenny's arm and brushed down Kenny's sleeve.

They were now standing outside the Hotel de Paris in the Square. To their right was the casino and just beyond that, the Cafe de Paris.

Dominic was looking at the Hotel de Paris restaurant menu displayed in a glass case just outside the entrance to the hotel.

"For fuck's sake! They've got a starter here that works out at forty-five quid a pop. Mind you it is caviar so I suppose that's quite reasonable. Jeezo, it just gets worse and worse. Thirty-five quid for roast chicken as a main. Am I missing something here?" He turned to look at the others but they had already headed off to the Cafe de Paris and outside tables had been taken to allow a good view of the motors and well dressed women who inhabited the square.

Gus shouted up the round and, as expected, it was five pounds a pint. Kenny had picked up a menu thinking a "croque monsieur" might go down quite well as a light lunch but decided against it when he saw it was a tenner.

"So, what's the game plan then, Gus? Don't really see you as the sort of man to be counting the cards like Dustin Hoffman in Rain Man. Mind you, in normal circumstances I would see certain similarities between the two of you."

"Oh aye, the high IQ hidden behind a mask of slowness?" said Dominic.

"No, the really shit taste in clothes" came back Kenny.

"Laugh all ye want, like. But when ah've made a few bob and taken care of young Dominic here, ah will be lookin to have a good time, ah can tell you."

As he spoke the last words, Gus was rubbing his hands together.

"Ah think I'll start with "chemin de fer", like. Ah seem tae remember Sean Connery playing that in Goldfinger."

265

"You've got the wrong film," said Kenny. "He never played it in Goldfinger, he caught the girl, Shirley Easton, reading Goldfinger's opponents cards. She ended up covered in gold paint, if memory serves."

"Eaton, ya dummy," piped in Dominic. "You're thinking of Sheena Easton, the girl in the film was called Shirley Eaton."

"Dominic, ah would normally bow tae Kenny's superior knowledge of Bond films, like, but I think you are right. Losin' your touch maestro." Gus said as he ruffled Kenny's hair.

Kenny moved away from Gus' hand to sort his hair out.

"So, you're not going to have a go at roulette? I thought that was a given?"

Gus sat back in his chair and put his hands behind his head. This action caused his shirt to rise up out of his kilt exposing a solid rim of fat over the top of his kilt belt.

"Oh, put it away, for fuck's sake. There's kids kicking about here," cried Kenny who was pretending to cover his eyes with his hands.

Gus immediately sat up tucking in his shirt. His face coloured.

"There's no need tae draw attention to the fact ah've got a wee bit o' a pot at the moment."

"Ha, ha! A wee bit of a pot at the moment!" cried Dominic. "You make it sound like it's something that's going to go away. That's never going to leave. It's got permanent residency just below your ribs for fuck's sake."

"More like squatter's rights," said Kenny. "Then again, let he who is without flab, cast the first scone."

Gus stood up, trying his best to hold in his gut.

"Well, if that's your last word on the matter Bradley, we'll be off. Don't wait up, it could be a long night." Gus nodded in the direction of the casino and he and Dominic moved off from the table, leaving Kenny on his own.

"Oh, for fuck's sake," said Kenny. "Are you going to spend the rest of the day looking like the incredible Hulk trying to hold it in? Good luck, Dominic, with him looking like that you'll need it on and off the table. Catch you later!"

CHAPTER 28

Well this wasn't quite what Kenny had expected. Everyone else from the bus had either gone into the casino or legged it from the square, searching for a cheaper boozer than the Cafe de Paris. He was flying solo and was at a bit of a loss. He had been staring at the Rolls Royces and Ferraris parked outside the Hotel de Paris, wondering how many miles they got to the gallon when he heard a familiar voice with a friendly tone.

"Kenneth Bradley, on his own? Is everything alright in the world?"

He turned round to see Frances Fairweather standing a few yards away. She had just come out of the hotel and spotted him gawping at the super cars. As ever, she was immaculately dressed, wearing a pale green shirt, navy blue slacks and a white raincoat. Her blonde hair reflected the February sun. The ensemble was not quite completed by an SFA holdall slung over her shoulder but as any Scotland fan would tell you, you can't have everything in this life.

"Frances, delightful to see you," said Kenny who had to suddenly drag his attention away from the cars.

He was in his usual state of confusion whenever he met Frances. Should he shake her hand or give her a wee peck on the cheek? To play it safe, he offered his hand, which she took then moved forward and gave him a kiss on the cheek.

"How the devil are you then, Kenny? Where's Gus? And Dominic?"

"Brace yourself, they've gone into the casino." He pointed towards the squat grey building where doormen wearing top hats and frock coats flanked the entrance. Fortunes were won and lost in there but knowing McSween, at most it would be next month's wages that went into the vaults, unless Dominic was stupid enough to lend him anymore money.

"Oh, dear. I shan't comment but if you are as lucky in love as Gus can you really be expected to be that lucky in a casino?" Frances had cocked her head to one side. As ever, she had cut to the heart of the matter and was just waiting for his confirmation on her statement.

Kenny hesitated.

"I would not say being lucky in love is quite an accurate description of his activities, Frances. I very much doubt the term "good fortune" applies to any of the women he has loved."

"Ah, fair point, Kenny. So what are you up to now?"

"I am considering my options, weighing up the possibilities but basically just planning to wander aimlessly until I meet someone I know. As you are the first person I have met, would you care to join me?"

Kenny surprised himself by making this offer, as he was pretty confident it would be refused. He saw it as an opportunity to make a grand gesture then be in a position to bugger off to the pub. There had to be one, even in bloody Monte Carlo.

Frances looked at her watch.

"Well as it happens I have an hour to spare before I need to be back at the hotel to meet someone about the match tickets. I would love to join you, Kenny. I must say you are looking very smart. Alison is clearly keeping you right."

Kenny coloured.

"Oh right, eh, well where do you want to go?" Kenny was tugging his right ear as he pondered the implications of this. An hour on his own with Frances Fairweather! She would have his life story out him in thirty minutes. Best keep it cool and shut the fuck up. One word answers to questions - that would be the strategy. Verbally tight at the back and solid in the oral midfield.

"Shall we head up to the top of the square and take it from there?" suggested Frances.

"No problem," came the reply.

They walked away from the Hotel de Paris, Kenny maintaining his distance from Frances. The clipped gardens of Casino Square were across the road on their right hand side, forming the sloping centre-piece of the square. A constant stream of high-end cars passed up and down, ferrying people to rendezvous in either the hotel or the casino.

The immaculate state of the cars and the lawns in the square plus the dazzling fountains all led Kenny to feel he was having an out of body experience. Frances asking him a question brought him back down to earth.

"Sorry, just a bit of culture shock there. What were you saying?"

"I was asking how Alison was keeping?" She was now staring at him intently.

"Oh, fine, fine. Working away with her dad."

"Her dad? I never realized she was in the same line." Her tone had hardened.

"Aw, eh, no, she has a totally separate business interest from him. Souvenirs, gifts, see you Jimmy hats etc. No, completely unattached to him."

Christ, he hadn't seen that one coming.

They had reached the top of the square and paused, trying to work out which way to go.

"If we head up to the left, I think we can get to the botanical gardens," said Frances. "There's meant to be a beautiful view out over the sea from a vantage point, I believe."

Kenny now realised the pub would have to wait, but was it that much of a hardship walking around Monte Carlo with an attractive woman who actually seemed interested in talking to him?

"So, I believe your mother is now engaged to Harold McMillan," continued Francis.

Kenny's shoulders slumped. He had given up on the pub but now needed a drink more than ever.

"Eh, aye, that's true. The jungle drums been beating at Park Gardens then?"

Kenny was wondering who had passed on that little gem. There was only one contender.

"Yes, I had Gus on the phone last week thanking me for sending his ticket out for the game and asking me what I was doing on Friday night. We had a good wee chat after I told him I was already booked up on Friday with Frankenstein's brother. He's one of those men that once he starts talking, you really find it hard to get him to stop." She smiled at Kenny.

Kenny's shoulders slumped once more. He was fucked.

They were now walking past some shops. Kenny searched their windows in vain, searching for something that might drag the conversation away from his personal life. "Wow, look at that. Alligator shoes, 20000 Francs. Good grief, that's nearly two grand!"

They had stopped outside an exclusive menswear shop. The window display featured black leather jackets, black suits, black jumpers and black shoes.

"Any colour you want as long as it's black," said Kenny who was looking for something he could afford. He quickly worked out that if a tie was a hundred quid, there was precious little chance of him getting a full rig-out in there.

"Are you looking for something for your mother's wedding?" asked Frances who was leaning in to take in what was on offer.

"No, I don't think she'll be getting married anytime soon." "Not if I can help it", he felt like adding - but he was back on his game plan. Give nothing away.

They continued walking. The streets were very quiet considering the time of day. Kenny had expected a bit more life, maybe even bumping in to a couple of other fans to take the pressure off him. Somebody to come along and score a breakaway goal. He was keeping it tight. He just needed an out ball.

"And what does Alison think about her dad marrying your mum?" Frances was pulling the strings from a deep lying position no mistake.

"I don't think she's best pleased to be honest. We've got a lot going on in our own life so this added stress didn't really come at the right time."

Well done, he thought, a mislaid pass back to the keeper and it's an own goal.

"Not best pleased?" Frances had stopped to look up the entrance to the botanical gardens. She had her hand up shading her eyes and when she turned to Kenny, he could not make out her expression.

271

"Well, you know what it's like. No woman is ever good enough to look after a mother's wee boy, so I think she always feels that pressure from my mum. I don't see it myself but then again, I am not in the same situation as her."

Kenny tried to pull the same trick and put his hand up to shade his eyes. Unfortunately for him, the sun had just gone behind a cloud and he had to try to convert this gesture into running his fingers through his hair, only succeeding in poking himself in the eye.

"Ooh yah, bast.....!" he exclaimed, hurriedly shutting himself up in front of Frances.

"Are you OK?"

"Yes, just a bit, ah, thrown by the, eh, angle of the sun." He tried to regain control of himself. He rubbed his eye with the palm of his right hand, only adding to the pain.

Frances had turned to look him directly in his good eye.

"So, if you don't mind me asking, what's going on in your own life?"

Did this woman's curiosity never end?

"It's a long story," said Kenny, the pain in his eye subsiding ever so slightly as he stopped rubbing.

"And you don't want to tell me? Not like you Kenny." Frances had shaken her head after this last statement and was walking into the gardens.

As Kenny followed he realised it might be good to talk to her. He couldn't talk to Gus as he never listened and, if he did, he never appreciated the seriousness of the conversation or how Kenny might be hurt by some of his comments. He had no friends amongst his fellow taxi-drivers as they knew his connection to Harold, and so kept their distance. He was fed up talking to Alison about it as that was the dominating topic of conversation in their lives.

Kenny caught up with Frances just inside the park.

"If you want to know what's going on in my life, it's not that long a story now I think about it. We'll gloss over the events in Tallinn as it's for the best you don't know what went on there. In the last few months, as you probably know from your informant McSween, I've met my biological dad, heard my mum had got engaged to my father-in-law and been thinking about trying to start a family."

"And your real father is Frank Potter?"

"Oh come on!" exclaimed Kenny. "This is too much. You know more about me than I do myself. Gus told you all this?"

"No, let's get a seat and take in this magical view." The Med had opened out below them. There was a spare park bench that gave them a panoramic view of the sea. A couple of yachts flitted in and out of the wind. Somebody has got it good there, thought Kenny.

He saw an ice cream stall and knew he could buy some time away for the interrogation. Frances Fairweather had a good knowledge of his life but he knew one thing about her that was her weakest link, a liking for ice cream.

"Fancy a Fruits of the Forest Solero?" said Kenny pointing at the stall.

"Oh yes, but can you see if they have a chocolate Magnum first?" Frances clapped her hands together an excited look on her face.

"Aye, no problem," came the reply from Kenny.

As he bought the ice creams Kenny wondered why she had brought Potter into the conversation. He started to get an uneasy feeling. The same sort of feeling he had when Alison asked him how much a trip to a game was costing or Harold said he needed a hand with some DIY. Admittedly the latter was normally a sick joke on Harold's part but he definitely had that feeling again.

He bought the ice cream by pointing at the pictures on the van's windows and holding up his fingers. He was trying to think of what to say next as he walked back to their seat.

He handed Frances her Magnum and sat down.

"So, Frank Potter. What's the story with him?" he asked, worrying over the reply.

Frances was taking her time unpeeling the wrapper of her Magnum. She extracted the ice cream and deposited the wrapper in a bin next to the bench.

She bit into the Magnum and savoured the first mouthful, her free hand coming up to pick a bit of loose chocolate from the ice cream and pop it in her mouth before it fell on her raincoat.

"Well, when Gus mentioned his name, I thought "that's a bit of a coincidence" as a Frank Potter has just joined the Travel Club."

Kenny was in the process of running his tongue up the length of his Solero to extract maximum Fruits of the Forest flavor. He knew it looked like he was committing felatio on the ice-lolly but didn't care as he loved the taste. He let out an involuntary yelp.

As he turned to look at Frances, a drop of purple juice landed on his chinos.

"Joined the Travel Club? Really?" he asked in a muted tone.

"Yes, really." said Frances, who took another bite of her Magnum.

"Well, it's quite a common name if you think about it," said Kenny. He thought the ice creams might have leveled the scores between them, but this was a forty-yard screamer into the top corner. Potter had joined the Travel Club? He'd kept that quiet. Fuck, was that a stain from the lolly on his chinos?

"Yes, I take your point," continued Frances. "I doubt it would be much interest for you either, that he's ordered a ticket for this game in Monaco. Isn't this the most wonderful view?"

Kenny had been rubbing at the stain but was only making it worse. He looked up. "Now, wait a minute. Potter's here?"

"I don't know if he's here or not, but a Frank Potter residing in the Merchant City area of Glasgow has definitely bought a ticket for tomorrow night's game."

Kenny sighed.

Francis continued, "I can only presume he is here if he's bought a ticket."

She was concentrating on the Magnum but looked sharply at Kenny as she continued.

"I thought if he's your real father, you might have wanted to come with him to Monaco. No?"

"No. The truth is he's been angling for an invite but I couldn't bring myself to ask him. I try to understand the situation he is in but it's all a bit too quick for me. Have you seen the third Indiana Jones film? Indy has this problem with his dad who turns out to be a mental sha, eh lover, and there is this sort of rivalry between them. Well there's no rivalry but I just feel I am on the losing end all the time. It's like he's a nicer version of Harold." Kenny stopped abruptly as he did not want to get into his relationship with Harold in front of Frances. That was a step too far.

Frances was concentrating on her ice cream.

"I take your point Kenny but from what Gus has told me, Mr. Potter's life has changed incredibly over the last few months. A bit like your own on finding out who your father is. Maybe you have more in common than you think. Maybe you should try and come to terms with your new relationship and seek some common ground."

"Oh come on, are you trying to encourage the healing benefits of the Scotland team in bringing harmony to dysfunctional families? I've heard it all now." Kenny finished his Solero and dropped the stick in the bin next to the bench. He stood up.

"Let me walk you back to the hotel. I think I am going to need some time on my own to come to terms with all that you've just told me. I don't want to think of him travelling on his own but I'm not ready to travel with him if you understand what I am trying to say."

Frances stood up and took Kenny by the arm.

"It's your life Kenny but try to think of others when you can. Sometimes these things just need a bit of time."

CHAPTER 29

Atholl opened the door to his flat and there she was, his ex-wife and tormentor in chief, Fiona. She had been gently moving from one foot to the other but stopped when their eyes met.

"Good morning, Atholl."

It took a good ten seconds for Atholl to recover his poise. He thought at one point it was another drug-induced flashback, but even this was too weird to be drug related.

He heard a voice, which he eventually realised was his, say "So how can I help you? Heard about the Laird dying and presumed you could cash in? Sorry love but the divorce settlement was final and now, well, you hardly look like you have the wherewithal to take me to court."

Atholl looked his ex-wife up and down. She looked a mess. Filthy jeans, canvas shoes that were stained with oil, a grubby white t-shirt with "Going Loco in Acapulco" in faded red letters and a sort of nautical jacket that looked ill-prepared for the onslaught of a European winter. Even one in the South of France. She did, however, radiate an effervescent beauty. Her face with it's high cheekbones and her ice blue eyes, a complete contrast to the charity shop cast-offs she was dressed in. Every inch of her oozed class and it broke his heart to think she had once been his.

"Could I come in please, Atholl. I need to talk to you."

Atholl shrugged his shoulders and opened the door wide to let her pass. As she walked down the corridor, past the Miro prints and the small bookcase filled with books he knew he would never read, he felt vague stirrings.

As she entered the lounge, she turned to face him. Her face had a penitent expression and she clasped her hands in front of her.

"May I sit down?"

"Just a mo'," he replied before nipping into the kitchen and re-appearing with a large towel which he draped over an armchair covered in an ivory fabric.

"The flat is rented and I would not wish to lose my deposit due to you staining the furniture."

"Ever the pragmatist, Atholl," said Fiona, in a resigned tone, as she positioned herself on the towel, ensuring none of her frame touched the fabric of the chair. Atholl took up a position on the leather settee, his arms spread across the back, one leg crossed over the other, attempting to give an impression of confidence. But that's all it was, an impression. He could not remember the last time he had been so surprised to see someone - but then Tallinn came to mind and he quickly brushed that thought from his mind.

With a grand sweeping gesture from his right arm he said, "The floor is yours, madam. But I thought you were in Wengen?"

Fiona sat up ever so slightly in the armchair. She looked poised and in control which did little or nothing for Atholl's state of mind.

"Atholl, I would appreciate it if you would allow me to say what I have to say without interruption. You must think I am very desperate to turn up here unannounced and you would be correct. Of late, I've thought a great deal about us. About what we had when we were together, and I have come to realise I failed to appreciate the good thing that we had. I believe we both failed in that respect. Things were never that bad between us were they? I admit to making some, eh, errors of judgment shall we say, but you were no angel yourself. I loved you then Atholl, and I love you now. I was in Wengen until just before Christmas then was offered the opportunity to help crew a yacht across the Atlantic by an acquaintance. "

A silence filled the room. This was not what Atholl had expected and he realised he had to buy some time.

"But why now?" he asked. He brushed an imaginary speck of dust off the top of his knee and looked out the balcony window on to the Med. His first expectation of Fiona had been a request for money. A profession of deep enduring love was not exactly in his top ten opening statements for her. He had loved her but never

277

completely trusted her. The emotion of distrust was currently out-ranking any feeling of love.

"Without sounding too much like a blues singer, I woke up this morning and I have never felt so disgusted with myself in my life. I've been here for two days with the Canadian ski team."

""With" the Canada ski team?" interrupted Atholl.

"Yes, just *with* the Canadian ski team. I am well past fucking a whole ski team Atholl, for God's sake!" She had grasped her knees and was gently rocking back and forth.

"Well, there was that time with the Harlequins second XV - but I digress." Atholl was trying to establish some control of the conversation but had clearly misjudged his interruption.

"If I may continue?" asked Fiona, a more controlled tone to her voice, as she shifted in her seat, the towel beginning to irritate her.

"Of course."

"I arrived here on a yacht which explains my somewhat tired, shall we say, appearance. The skipper's brother is in the ski team and I have been hanging out with them the last couple of days. I have been drugs-free for the last six months. When I went to the Caribbean the skipper insisted I have a test every week. I haven't had a drink since we left the Bahamas. Things went a bit awry yesterday when we met some Scotland football fans and went on a mega bender in the back streets. Long story short, when I woke up this morning I was in bed with the ugliest version of the male species I have ever had the misfortune to meet, never mind sleep with. I think he might even have had a ginger hair transplant."

Atholl's ears pricked up at this and he leant forward on the couch.

"A Scotsman with a ginger hair transplant? Oh dear Fiona, that's a bit off. Happen to remember the chap's name?"

"Russ, or maybe Gus. Yes, Gus. That was the dreadful creature's name. But what's that got to do with anything?"

She was becoming shrill again so Atholl decided to let that one go. Gus McSween had been sleeping with his ex-wife. This day just got better and better.

"I just wondered how out of it you were on a scale of 1 to 10. Clearly if you can remember his name it wasn't a 10. I know you've a few 11s in your time and even the odd 15." He was smiling at the thought of his wife and Gus on the job.

Fiona had gone very quiet.

"Come on," said Atholl. "There's out and there's out. So please continue, "woke up disgusted, felt like a complete tramp, etc, etc""

"Thank you, Atholl. Your bitter sarcasm is just what I came for. If that's all you have to say, I'll go." At this Fiona sprung from the chair and started walking quickly back down the corridor to the front door.

Atholl caught up with her just as she was about to open the door.

"Don't go. Please don't go. I was being an ass but think about this from my point of view. My ex-wife, who I have neither seen nor heard of for at least a decade, suddenly turns up and tells me she's always loved me, then tells me the act that made her realise her feelings for me was that she woke up next to a ginger, Scottish gremlin."

At this point Fiona broke down. She slumped against Atholl, heaving great sobs of tears. He could feel his collar get wet as she wept. He had never seen her this emotional and depressed. He put his arms around her and patted her on the back.

"There, there. Come back to the lounge and we'll get you a brandy. There, there." Fiona put her arms around his shoulders and they half walked half stumbled, like a drunken three-legged race team, into the lounge.

Atholl laid her on the couch.

"Hadn't you better get the towel," Fiona whispered, her face turned to the back of the couch.

"Sod the deposit, let's make sure you are OK."

CHAPTER 30

Dominic and Kenny stood at the barrier looking over the plaza next to the ground. Below them a couple of hundred Scots fans were indulging in the type of behaviour that he didn't imagine was a regular occurrence in the principality. Drinking straight from the bottle was the most obvious sin. Possibly topped by enjoying yourself in public.

Kenny kept on looking down at the crowd as spoke to Dominic.

"So there was no sign of the wee shite then?"

"No. Nothing. Five o'clock and there's still no sign of him. Something's not quite right, Kenny."

Dominic was looking around the area they found themselves in whilst Kenny stared downwards at the crowd.

He turned to Dominic.

"So, remind me, where was the last place you saw him?"

Dominic looked exasperated.

"I've told you five times. We were walking past the marina after we'd left the casino. He was in another world after winning the three thousand francs at the casino. He gave me my money back then when we met this Canadian ski team, he insisted on buying them a drink as he's got an uncle in Toronto. They were right up themselves and were taking him for a mug. I tried to get him to leave but eventually gave up and left him to his own devices. You could tell he was getting totally blootered. They had some blonde in tow with them that he took a shine to so you know the script."

A weak Mediterranean sun had now come out but Kenny was not feeling any warmth. Visions of Atholl McClackit coming towards him were going through his mind, his paranoia fed by the absence of McSween.

"I really can't believe anything has happened to him" he said though he knew his tone was unconvincing. "Want to go down and have another look?"

Dominic looked less than happy but shrugged his shoulders and went "Ok".

As Dominic left, his place was taken by another Scotland fan.

"Some place this, eh?"

"Aye, some place indeed," said Kenny who was not really in the mood for chat.

"Is it true there's a car park under the pitch?"

"Aye, funnily enough parking's at a premium in this place. Given they are only getting an average home gate of 4000, I suppose they need all the income they can get."

The guy looked suspiciously at Kenny.

"You are taking the piss?"

"Of course."

"Fair enough, I might throw a few centimes in the bucket collection on the way out then." The guy smiled at Kenny and wandered back to a bench where his mates were sitting with a very large carry out.

Kenny suddenly felt a presence by his side. He turned to see Gus McSween still wearing the same clothes as the day before when he'd entered the casino. His bow tie was gone but he was still wearing the Prince Charlie jacket, the waistcoat, the kilt, socks and ghillie brogues though his flashes were missing. He was also wearing the look of a man on the verge of a nervous breakdown.

"What the fuck happened to you then?" he asked looking Gus up and down. "You don't look quite all there."

"Don't ask. Talk about a night of nights. It a very long story. I would appreciate it if you respected my wishes and say no more on the topic."

"Ok. Do you want a drink, I was thinking of heading into the supermarket for a carry out."

"Sounds like a plan."

As they moved off Kenny noticed that Gus was limping and there appeared to be some bruising round his neck.

"Are you ok? You don't want to sit down and rest?"

"No, all ah want is a couple of quiet beers and to try and get my head round last night."

"Ok, let me know when you want to talk about it."

When they walked into the supermarket they realised logistics had become a bit of a problem. The supermarket was trying to get a pallet of beers in but could not due to the number of fans blocking the tills. One of the guys who had been working on the till was trying to manoeuvre the pallet meaning the fans were not getting served.

"Aw fuck" said Gus "Ah'm on the verge of a fucken collapse here like and this isnae helping Kenny!"

Kenny was appalled to see tears welling up in the wee man's eyes as he looked at the chaotic scene at the entrance to the supermarket.

"Look go outside and sit down. I'll get a case of lager when they sort it out. Give me ten minutes."

"Can you get some Vaseline as well please?" asked Gus in a muted tone.

"Are you sure you don't want a small brush and some Dettol instead?"

"Its no for ma cock ya daft prick. Ah'm chafed tae fuck wearing this kilt."

Gus turned round and limped across to a bench.

As Kenny tried to work out what was the best option a cheer rose up as an attractive young girl appeared to open up a second till.

As the crowding eased, Kenny was able to simply walk up and take a case of beer from the pallet. He was standing in the queue behind a guy he had never met but looked vaguely familiar. This fan carried a case of lager with a bottle of Smirnoff vodka balanced on top.

"Are you getting the celebrations in a bit early with the voddy?" Kenny enquired.

"No, my mate's just had a bit of a voddy frenzy and he's already tanned one bottle. We've just met some guys and they've nicknamed him Captain Vodka. He's drinkin it like water."

Kenny was in the queue being served by a young guy. The young girl was one of a type he'd rarely encountered, foreign, attractive and with a sense of humour. As one or another Scotland fans went "voulez vous couchez avec moi ce soir" she gave them the thumbs up "We close at 8, I see you zen" Guys were in raptures till they realised it was an 8pm kick off.

Kenny was eventually served and lugged the case of beer outside to where Gus sat on the bench. Gus ravenously ripped the paper case open and pulled out a bottle.

"Where's the opener?" he cried.

"I haven't got one" said Kenny

"Oh no, ah cannae take this anymore. It's too much like. Just fucken too much." Gus started crying.

"Ah've done some weird things in the shagging world Kenny but last night took me to the brink. She's broken me, mentally and physically. Fucken broken me, like. Ah'll never shag again. She was on the Charlie an then ah don't know what planet she was on. Ah've got love bites going up my inner thigh on each leg. D'ye want to see them?"

"No, I'll pass." said Kenny who turned to look at the wee man.

"You weren't on coke were you? You know that really fucked you up the one time you tried it."

"No it was just her. She was off her face. Ah can't believe ah fell fur it."

Gus' shoulders started heaving as his crying turned to weeping.

"Look calm down for fuck's sake. People are beginning to stare."

Around them a few guys had started nudging each other and pointing at Gus. To be fair he did look a state. A couple of Scots were pointing and sniggering until Kenny gave them a look.

The guy from the queue in the supermarket walked over towards them.

"Is everything ok wi your pal, Kenny. He looks in a bit of a state."

"He just needs a bottle opener. Do you have one?"

"Oh aye, we've all been there." He dug in his sporran and produced a saltire bottle opener.

"Keep it for as long as you like. My mate's got one. Good luck with him." The guy clapped Kenny on the shoulder. As he watched him walk off he wondered how the guy knew his name. Bastarding Atholl he thought. The guy with the opener had probably seen him around loads. Kenny definitely recognised him so why be suspicious of someone being helpful and simply knowing your name. He was seeing demons when there was nothing to see.

"Can I have the opener please?" a small voice asked from his side.

"Christ, you must be feeling broken if you are asking nicely for something. I'll give you the opener but you need to tell me what happened."

"Ah got in too deep Kenny," Gus pulled a bottle from the box. He opened it and necked half the contents without taking the bottle from his lips.

"Ah, that's better," he murmured looking approvingly at the bottle of Kronenburg 1664.

"You didn't end up at a pool party?" Kenny realised it was a weak joke but he was at a loss how to proceed.

"If only," said Gus with a rueful shake of the head.

"She was a dom Kenny. A fucken dom!"

"A what? Don't tell me it was a bloke for fuck's sake. No wonder you're feeling broken."

Gus shook his head and looked up at Kenny. He pointed at Kenny with the bottle. "She was a dominatrix ya daft bastard, no a bloke. At one point I had to sit and read a paper for ten minutes before I could kiss her. Ah was tied to the bed wi ma kilt over ma head an her knickers in ma mouth when the maid found me this mornin. Ah'm no quite sure what happened as ah passed out at one point with her choking me that much. Ah've got a terrible taste in my mouth from her knickers. It was brutal Kenny. Brutal. She had this strange power over me."

Gus took a swig of lager.

"She always travels with five silk scarves. Two for the wrists, two for the ankles and one for the neck. Am never wearing silk again in ma life after what ah experienced."

"You're not going to throw out all your underwear are you?"

"Whit? Ah could have fucken pegged it last night and you're makin' cracks about ma pants? No more than ah might have expected. Sympathy is a rare commodity in the tartan army at the best of times so why should a near death experience make any difference for fuck's sake."

"Were you hypnotised or something?" Kenny was having problems coming to terms with what he was hearing. The sight before him proved everything that Gus had said about being brutalised. As Gus finished the bottle and burped, Kenny thought things might be getting back to normal.

"Give's another bottle Kenny. Ah'm fucken parched, like. Ah can still taste those knickers."

Kenny passed him a bottle.

"By the way, ah'll tell ye how out of it ah was last night." Gus shook his head as he thought back.

"Ah thought ah saw Potter. I was in this bar wi the burd, whatshername, and the Canadians. Ah could have sworn ah saw him walk past the pub when ah glanced out the window. Probably some French boy that looked like him, like. Boy was ah wasted."

Kenny scratched the back of his head and scanned the crowd the below with even more attention than before.

"You might be right."

"Whit? No way Potter'll be here. It was a vision or whatever you call it."

Gus took a long gulp on the bottle.

Kenny looked at him.

"I went for a walk with Frances Fairweather yesterday."

"Oh aye?" Gus had a knowing look on his face.

"Aye, really romantic. I went for a walk and bought her an ice cream. Next week I am asking her to the school dance. Get real. She told me you had grassed me up about Potter being my dad. She also told me that someone called Frank Potter had just joined the travel club and had bought a ticket for this game."

Gus took another long gulp on the bottle of 1664.

"Oh fuck!"

"I thought he was angling for an invite but it's too soon!" Kenny said slapping his hand down on the balustrade. "He's just come into my life. There's got to be boundaries somewhere, man."

"Fair point Kenny. But thinking about it, he was laying it on a bit strong a couple of times. Maybe he's just wanting to get a bit closer to his boy."

"That's true, he could come on the trip and babysit you. Keep you away from pervy blondes looking to humiliate you. I could actually get back to having a life on these trips."

"Aye, well in your babysitting role pass me another bottle unless you want to suckle me. Am fucken well dry, who would have thought S&M made you so thirsty."

As Kenny handed Gus the bottle he looked up to see Dominic coming along the walkway with an Estonian fan.

Gus looked up and groaned

"Aw for fuck's sake, how does he do it? That boy is so fucken naive, the locals just take him for everything."

Dominic had a large smile on his face as he approached Kenny.

"Great news, Kenny. Brilliant news come to think about it. This is the result of results." Suddenly Dominic looked a bit guilty as he glanced at the Estonian.

"Well for us maybe."

Kenny looked at the Estonian fan who had a large Estonian flag draped round his considerable shoulders. Judging by the size of the guy Dominic had met he might have been in the special forces.

"This is Alexi. Met him down in the plaza after some wee twat from Stranraer had spilt a drink all over Alexi's shoes. Managed to calm the big man down."

"Oh aye, well done Mother Teresa" said Gus. "What's the good news coming out of this experience? He knows that burd Bibecka or whatever her name was that dumped ye after you'd paid for her trip to Scotland at New Year?"

Dominic looked crestfallen.

"No, forget about her. Alexi works in the prison at Tallinn. He says Andy Muir is dead."

"What?" Kenny was staring at Alexi with new eyes.

"Little bastard Andy dead" said Alexi who was looking intently at Kenny. "You know him?"

"Yes, I knew him" said Kenny. "I only met him the once and that was in the sauna at the Hotel Sport where he tried to kill me."

Alexi was staring around trying to take in the sights of Monaco. He had a large video camera with him and was attempting to get the lens cap off. He suddenly stopped and a tear rolled down his cheek.

He was still staring at the lens cap as he spoke softly.

"Andy kill my best friend. He start fire in prison. He die. Best friend Viktor die. Kitchen destroyed."

Kenny was having trouble taking this in. Could it really be true he was free of the wee shite Atholl? He could stop worrying about what was going to happen a few years down the line when Atholl was released. Oh yes, fuck the game tonight, this was the result he had been hoping for all along. Atholl killed in prison, hopefully after being raped by Mr Big in the showers but yes! Oh yes, yes and double yes!

"How are you here though big man?" asked Gus who had opened another bottle and was offering it to Alexi.

"I win competition in Scots bar in Tallinn. I would be here with my best friend now but he is dead. I come with sister's husband. He chase pussy all time. We go back to Estonia, maybe I kill him."

287

He took a long pull of the bottle.

Kenny raised an eyebrow at Gus.

"Sounds like an Estonian version of you Gus," said Dominic who had clearly not forgotten the earlier crack about the girl at New Year. "You couldn't kill Gus now and do us all a favour?"

Alexi shook his head then took another long pull on the bottle before handing the empty bottle to a bemused Gus.

"Sorry to go back to this Alexi but I need to know how they knew it was Andy's body?"

"Teeth file, I not know words" said Alexi with a puzzled look.

Dominic looked at Kenny.

"I think he means dental records. If the body was too badly burnt that might have been all that would be left to identify him."

"I can't take this in to be honest" said Kenny.

Gus burped.

"Kenny, I thought me getting freed from the bed was the best news of the day but this goes some way to topping it, like. What a result. That guy was pure bad news. Ah reckon ah could have taken him, like, mano a mano but I guess we'll never know."

Gus handed Alexi and another beer and opened one for himself.

"That was a classic Gus McSween sentence. Started off well then descended into ten tons of bullshit. Mano a mano. Where do you get these terms from? TV? Films?"

"Ah'm just sayin ah reckon ah could have had him."

Dominic burst out laughing.

"He would have battered fuck out of you" said Dominic who reached down to get a beer.

"Remind me about your trip to Blackpool last year. Did a ten year old girl not club you with a stick of rock to keep you away from her mother? She chased you off the pier if the story I heard was correct."

"Listen. Listen. Ah was just doing it to get away from the mother. Ah was trying to chat up the auntie who was bang up for it, by the way, so the mother got jealous and set the daughter on me. Ah was trying to get the sympathy vote from the auntie but by the time ah got back she's fucked off wi the coach driver. That's some job for the side benefits of shagging by the way, coach driving. Ah wonder how you get a licence?"

"In your case it might be a start by learning to drive," said Kenny.

"Fair point well made, young man."

Gus took a drink from the bottle.

"So Alexi, predictions for tonight? Are yous actually goin tae turn up" Gus nudged Kenny

" We turn up, yes. But Scotland 4 Estonia 0. Big win for Scotland."

"Can't disagree wi you on that. Easy peasy, lemon squeezy. We get the three points we should have had for your mob's no-show in Tallinn."

" Game crazy" said Alexi. "But what happen to friend make football nothing. Friendship is life, life is friendship. No friends, no life."

"Well said, big man" said Gus. "If only ah could find some decent pals."

"Oh for fuck's sake" said Dominic and Kenny as one.

"So why do you blame Atholl, eh Andy, for killing your friend Viktor?" asked Kenny.

"Investigation after fire. Viktor have cut throat. Investigation kept quiet. Andee Muir dead. Viktor dead. No point in, how you say, stirring things up. They no want to investigate but I know. I will always know. Andee kill Viktor to try and escape then fire kill him."

Kenny and Dominic looked at each other, not knowing what to say.

Viktor picked up his camcorder and stared at the lens.

"I go now. Thanks for beer."

Gus raised his bottle in his direction.

"Good luck big man. And if your brother in law needs any help wi the pussy, tell him to get in touch."

"Feeling better then?" asked Kenny.

"Getting there."

CHAPTER 31

Kenny and Gus left the Stade de Gerland in numb disbelief. A 0-0 draw with Estonia rated alongside the worst ever Scotland result they had physically witnessed.

"Could somebody please tell me why the fuck we were shouting Estii, Estii at the end of that game?" said Gus. "Last time ah looked we were all Scots together."

"Not the best end to a night of utter shite. What the fuck was Ferguson playing at? Did he give us the fingers at the end?" Kenny was kicking an empty McDonalds' box as he walked.

"Aye, that boy's brains are in his baws. Ah can't think of one positive we can take fae that apart from the fact we didnae get beat. They really raised their game the Estonian bastards."

"Aye well I suppose they had a point to prove after the 3-second game."

"Too true, Kenny. Too true."

Gus and Kenny were wandering in no particular direction and had become separated from the larger body of the fans. It was a mild night for February, but precious few Scots needed warmth. The embarrassment and anger generated by what they had just witnessed had stoked the boilers to generate maximum heat. After a few more minutes they discovered they were only 100 metres or so from the train station.

"Did you tell that boy we'd definitely get the bus back?" asked Gus. "Ah was thinking it might just be easier to get the train. Ah'm fucked if ah want to fanny about here drinking five pound pints of lager when it could be cheaper in Nice."

They crossed the road to the station where a couple of Scots stood around, looking as miserable as sin. Kenny looked up.

"Aye, fair enough. We'd have to walk back down nearer the ground anyway. Here's the buffet. What do you want?"

"A time-machine to take me back to yesterday when I met Stephanie Powers. Ah would ask her to take me away from all this to her luxury pad in Beverly Hills where she could hold me as her sex slave, keeping all the bad news of the world, especially Scotland results, away from me. What a fucking night!"

Kenny entered the bar and discovered Alexi the Estonian fan he'd met before the game attempting to turn his Estonian flag into a kilt.

"Kenny!!! What a night! We beat you 0-0. Estii! Estii! We are so happy. I go back to Nice and we party hard. No?"

Kenny had not the heart to tell Alexi a see-through Estonian flag revealing a rather gruesome pair of Baltic y-fronts did not make the best of kilts, but settled for this as the one small victory over Estonia there would be that night.

"No, sorry Alexi. I can guarantee I will not be partying hard tonight. Have a word with Gus here, he parties hard, win lose or draw."

Gus had been speaking to some other fans and came over at that comment.

"Win or lose, always booze. You know that's my motto Kenny."

"Gus remember Alexi, he's the Estonian prison guard we met before the game."

"Awright Alexi? You must be a happy camper tonight son?"

"Very happy after you no-show in Tallinn."

"*We* never showed in Tallinn? What the fuck are you talking about? You lot were the no-show, pal."

"Estii, Estonia, show at time of kick off. No Scotland players on pitch."

Gus looked at Kenny with raised eyebrows then back to Alexi "Look, have it your way, pal. Ah'm so fucked off ah cannae be bothered to argue wi' ye. Who wants a drink? Kenny, did you get the time of the next train as there's no way ah want to hang around here any longer than need be, like."

Kenny realised he had no idea of the train times but was sure there would be one along soon enough, as it appeared to be a mainline stop on the Cote d'Azur line.

"I go to Gents, Kenny," said Alexi who headed off in the direction of the facilities. He left his video camera on the counter and for the first time Kenny had a chance to look at it. Never mind Panasonic, it looked like it had been made by Meccano. He was just trying to work out how heavy it was, when he heard a voice that chilled him to the bone.

"Nice bit of kit, Kenny. Didn't have you down as the Bill Forsyth of the 1990s," said Atholl, a whimsical smile on his face. Just behind Atholl, Kenny could see a rather washed out blonde who looked somewhat anxious. For fuck's sake where was Gus?

"Hi Atholl, didn't expect to see you here," he squeaked. For the first time in his life he could feel cold sweat running down his back. He had thought the night could not get any worse after the final whistle but, in retrospect, that may well have been the high point of the evening.

"Calm down Kenny, I only want to talk. All that happened between us before is in the past. Let's look forward. I have some explaining to do."

At that the Gents opened and Alexi emerged. He looked for his video camera first but then he saw Atholl standing next to Kenny.

Athioll looked back and a look of horror appeared on his face as he suddenly recognized the Estonian prison guard.

With an almost animal growl, Alexi rushed forward and grabbed Atholl by the throat, throwing him to the ground. He then leapt on Atholl, both hands firmly round the throat of the somewhat stunned heir to the clan McClackit. Kenny could not believe what he seeing, the washed out blonde shrieked and then out of nowhere Potter appeared and hit the Estonian in the small of the back with what appeared to be a cosh.

As Alexi arced back with a yelp of pain, Potter hit him in the back of the neck and he slumped forward over Atholl. The bar owner was leaning over the bar shouting "Allez vite ! Allez vite!" at Potter who needed no second telling. He pushed Alexi off Atholl with one arm and pulled Atholl up with the other.

"Come on, we're out of here."

As they dashed through the door of the bar, Potter pulled Atholl aside.

"Cafe d'Azur on the front at Nice. 12 tomorrow lunchtime!" he ordered.

Kenny had followed them outside.

Potter took Kenny by the arm as he turned away from Atholl. They quickly walked off in the opposite direction towards the station.

Kenny had thought all this nonsense was behind him but as soon as he met Atholl McClackit it had all kicked off again.

"What the fuck is all that about?" asked Kenny.

"No idea but there was no way that Estonian prick was going to take out the Laird's boy," said Potter who still had a firm grasp on Kenny's arm and was marching him up to the station. Kenny shrugged himself free and looked back for Gus. Ten yards behind him the wee man was trailing along, looking somewhat abashed.

"Well, well, what a surprise. First bit of trouble and you powdered. Where the fuck were you?"

"Eh, ah didnae see the trouble as ah had already done a runner once that blonde came into the bar. She's the one fae last night."

By this point they had entered the station and were on the platform.

"What? Who the fuck is she?" said Kenny

Gus looked down at his feet. "Eh, ah think it might be his ex-wife but we didnae spend too much time on pillow talk, like ah was saying earlier."

Gus leant his head towards Potter as if to say "Lets not go there". He then looked along the track to avoid looking at Kenny.

"Oh look, here's the train to Nice."

A large double decker inter-city train was pulling into the Monaco station. They had no tickets so just decided to chance it on the fifteen-minute journey.

As they took their seats, Kenny turned to Potter.

"I thought all this mystery and intrigue pish had come to an end when we left Tallinn. But it never stops. What the fuck are you doing here and how did you know where we were?"

Potter looked at both of them sitting opposite him. "Did either of you see a buffet as I could definitely do with a drink? Gus? Kenny?"

CHAPTER 32

Potter walked along the Promenade Anglais, taking in the view. The rise along the shore stretched out in front of him, the port laying just around the bend and down the hill.

He'd last been here in the early 1960's visiting an old buddy from the French Foreign Legion. What was his name? Jean Claude Lemarque? That was it. Great guy but a stupid bastard getting himself killed working as a mercenary in the Biafran Civil War. And to think he'd phoned me up just before he left offering him a commission in the rebel army. As soon as Potter heard they had made Jean Claude a Major, he knew they were doomed. Jean Claude was a good enough Sergeant but a Major? Dear God, it was a mission with suicide written all over it in capital letters.

Potter looked across the road noting the Hotel Westminster. The café should be about another fifty yards, below road level, on the beach. He hoped Kenny and Atholl would make it as he needed both of them to be there. Hopefully Gus would not be there. Potter had a lot of time for Gus but he had no idea when to shut the fuck up and Potter needed a bit of peace and quiet this morning of all mornings.

The Med shimmered on his right. Every cliché ever written about it being reinforced by just standing there taking in the whole thing. OK, it was warm for February but it wasn't just the heat. It was the whole package. He had loved this place in the 60s and, as ever with these sorts of places, he was at a complete loss as to why he had never been back sooner.

A young girl in her early 20s, wearing a halter neck top and a pair of very tight crop shorts came gliding up to Potter on her inline blades. She flashed him a smile but Potter did little to encourage her interest. He was on a mission.

Thinking about a complete loss brought him back to the here and now. He had contemplated a stiffener to see him through the next hour or so but thought better of it. He was going to try and view this as an Op. Get in, break the bad news and get out with minimum collateral damage, not least to himself. That was all well and good but he'd been thinking on the hoof and there was no real planning around this one. At least he knew the lay of the land but what Atholl would do he didn't know. He was the wild card that could put a dampener on everything when all Potter wanted was everyone to be as happy as they could be in the circumstances.

He approached the steps down to the café on the beach but kept on walking past them for another twenty yards before turning to see who was down there. He reckoned Atholl would be sitting facing the steps, watching out for who was ever coming down them. Potter looked back and could see a table with a couple sitting at it. The man was facing the steps but the woman was facing his direction. She had a number of bags by her chair and it took Potter a moment to recognise her. Good God, it's Fiona! Where the fuck had she come from? He vaguely remembered Atholl being with a blonde in the bar last night but nothing had prepared him for this. He thought back to their last encounter but dismissed it. Focus man, focus.

Somewhat incredibly she was waving at Potter, clearly having spotted him at the railings. Atholl turned round and waved as well. So much for a discreet recce of the enemy's position. As Potter walked back towards the steps down to the beach he looked up at the sky. An endless pale blue. And for the first time since he'd left, he wished he had stayed in the Highlands.

In the distance he could see the depressing sight of Kenny Bradley. Potter thought he would go on down on his own so that he appeared to be independent, not wanting to be seen to be in league with either Kenny or Atholl. He took his time on the steps, allowing Kenny to catch up and see that he was also in the process of just arriving.

As Potter approached the table, Atholl stood up and stretched out his right hand.

The café itself was tucked in under the promenade but Atholl was sitting outside on the pebble beach. There were two other tables but they were deserted. Potter looked out at the Med and suddenly wished he could dive in.

 "Potter, good to see you," said Atholl. He was wearing a blazer with a pale blue button-down Oxford shirt and chinos. Potter found it hard to think of a man more in the place he deserved to be. The fucker.

With his left hand Atholl gestured towards Fiona who had remained seated but had half-turned so she could extend her hand to Potter.

"You remember Fiona, my wife?" His pleading eyes put an expression on Atholl's face crying out to Potter to play nice, but he was having none of it.

Potter's face turned to stone and he made no effort to move towards shaking her hand after Atholl.

"Good to see you, Sir. I thought she was your ex-wife?"

"Ah, yes. You are correct of course but at the moment, we are trying to make another go of it," said Atholl who appeared caught off-guard by Potter's attitude. He had placed a re-assuring hand over her's but it was immediately shaken off. Fiona dropped her hand back into her lap, her cheeks a bright pink. Potter looked down at the range of designer bags by her chair. Max Mara, Au Printemps, Galleries Lafayette and last but not least, Chanel. To Potter it looked like she was trying to make another go of nearly bankrupting the boy. Her failed ventures, the antique shop in the Chilterns, the interior designer consultancy in Kensington were stuff of legend. How much had he flushed down the pan trying to keep her happy? What she had done to Potter was small beer in comparison.

Atholl pulled out a chair for Potter and as he pushed the seat back in, he looked up to see Kenny coming down the steps.

"And here comes Kenny. Excellent." he said, looking up at the steps.

Potter turned and looked along the paved area to the side of the beach. In a complete contrast to Atholl, Kenny looked as comfortable in the Promenade Anglais as George Best would in Riyadh. He appeared to be trying to hide from the sun inside his clothes and if he had been wearing a hood on his leather jacket, Potter didn't doubt it would be favourite to have been pulled up. His jeans looked decrepit and the Scotland top underneath the jacket was from Mexico 1986 if Potter knew his strips. Christ, they were still making Adidas Sambas as well! On the bright side there was no sign of Gus.

"Eh, alright, Potter?" said Kenny as he shuffled up to the table. Potter nodded.

"Kenny, excellent to see you again," said Atholl extending his right arm to shake Kenny's hand, a somewhat bashful look on his face.

Kenny took Atholl's hand very gingerly and murmured "Alright."

"And this lovely creature is my wife Fiona."

"Ex-wife," murmured Potter which earned him a dirty glance from both Atholl and Fiona. The ex Mrs McClackit having been embarrassed by Potter's snub of a moment ago, decided not to take any chances on this one and moved a few fingers of her right hand through the air by way of a greeting.

Kenny who had been moving towards a full handshake but was now caught mid-offer managed to waggle his fingers in reply. He drew out his own chair and sat down.

Potter thought he should be doing something to make sure it was clear he was in charge. But just before he could speak, Atholl butted in.

"Firstly, I would like to say a very big thank you to Potter for possibly saving my life last night."

"Possibly?" exclaimed Kenny. "That guy was going to do you!"

Atholl was looking not a little disconcerted by Kenny's outburst.

"Kenny, let's just draw a veil over last night. Best forget events on and off the field of play," said Potter

"I hardly think that is an accurate portrayal of events, Kenny. He had the drop on me and once I had realised just what was going on, my experience and training would have kicked in."

Atholl was trying to save some face but only managed to provoke an outburst from Potter.

"Well, when is your experience and training going to kick in with this one?" asked Potter as he jabbed his thumb in the direction of Fiona. "Did the Laird teach you nothing about women?"

"Right, that's it!" exclaimed Fiona. "I don't need to sit here and take this nonsense from a jumped up NCO like you, Potter. Are you really going to let him talk to me like that, Atholl? I am your wife!"

"Ex-wife," murmured Potter.

"God, you men. You get yourselves into all these problems over some silly bloody clan chieftainship and you expect us women to sit here and shut up like the good little Stepford Wives you want us to be." At this she started picking up her bags. "Well, I'm off, Atholl. I will see you back at the flat. If anything we talked about yesterday holds true after this meeting, I will see you there at 3pm. I will give you half an hour and if you are not back I know you were only saying what you thought I wanted to hear. Please don't let that be true."

At this she tried to storm off across the pebble beach but only succeeded in pulling off one of her shoes. She hobbled to the pavement and took off her one remaining shoe before coming back in her stocking soles to retrieve the lost shoe. She glared at Potter as she stood up.

"Happy now?" she asked.

"Delirious" came the reply as Fiona gingerly stepped back to the paved area before putting on her shoes and storming off.

Atholl stared at Potter.

"Eh, is there any chance of a Cappuccino?" asked Kenny.

Atholl turned to Kenny and looked at him blankly.

"What?" he asked.

"A cappuccino, a coffee. The hotel's hot water system was bust so I only had an orange juice and a croissant. I could murder, eh, really fancy a coffee."

"Aye, no problem Kenny," said Potter who waved over the waiter.

"Two cappuccinos and what do you want Atholl?"

"Probably a three-day session with Relate, but failing that a double espresso," came the reply. "Thanks," he added almost as an afterthought. He was looking out to sea as he spoke and Potter realized he was thinking to what lay ahead of him if he didn't turn up at 3pm, or maybe worse, did turn up at the arranged time.

Potter felt relieved to have seen the back of Fiona and sensed he had gained a bit of a strategic victory. All that remained now was to capture the village, slaughter all the inhabitants and blow up the orphanage.

"Right, so I expect you are both wondering why I am here in Monaco and why I called this meeting today. To get something out of the way first - Kenny, you should have invited me with you and Gus but I'll let it pass this time. Just don't do it again." His right index finger was pointing straight at Kenny's heart.

"Aye OK Potter. No problem," Kenny had suddenly found his feet very interesting.

"Right. Glad to get that out of the way. And here's the boy with the coffees. First class."

As the waiter set the coffees down in front of them, Atholl started to speak but Potter held up his hand demanding silence.

"Couple of moments, Sir. Let the staff clear the area first, please"

"Certainly," murmured Atholl. Kenny was trying to get the biscuit accompanying the coffee out of the plastic bag but with no joy. Potter picked his up and in one swift movement opened the bag and handed the biscuit to Kenny.

"Please, take it."

"Oh magic, thanks. Can never get these bloody bags open. Nice one, Potter." Kenny took the biscuit and started spooning up the froth of the cappuccino before sucking it off the biscuit.

" So, here we all are," said Potter.

"Yes, indeed," said Atholl. "But to what end?"

"Well, firstly I believe you owe Kenny an apology for trying to kill him in three separate locations around Europe and an apology for killing two of his friends." Potter took a sip of his coffee and sat back in his chair giving Atholl a piercing look.

On the promenade an ambulance roared past, it's wailing siren demanding space on the busy road.

Atholl sighed.

"What can I say? I was acting in the best interests of the clan McClackit. A clan that you once served loyally, Potter." He looked at Potter, unbowed by the stare Potter held on him.

"Eh, there's really no need for that," said Kenny. "I never could stand Tadger Currie so he was no loss. It was only really one friend he killed and he was on his last legs anyway." Kenny gave a shrug of the shoulders at the end of his statement, as much to say, these things happen.

"And the three attempts on your life all for nothing," muttered Potter.

"Oh aye, I'd kind of forgotten about those" said Kenny in an embarrassed tone, his eyes suddenly regaining their interest in his feet.

"All for nothing?" asked Atholl, who was looking from one to the other as if expecting them to pull some kind of stunt.

"Yes," said Potter. "All for nothing. I have some news for you on that score. I am Kenny's biological father, not the Laird."

"Is this true, Kenny?" asked Atholl with a quiver in his voice.

"Yes. From what my mum says, Potter's my dad. We've done the DNA tests, the works. He's my dad and we, you and I, are not related. Sorry." Kenny shrugged then stared out across the Med desperate to avoid Atholl's eyes.

Potter watched Atholl stare out across the pebble beach. Not only had he failed on three missions, all his efforts had been for nothing. He'd been banged up in an Estonian prison and then had escaped only to find himself back in a prison of his own making with the ex-wife as the chief gaoler. Time to blow up the orphanage.

"That's not quite true, Kenny." said Potter. He raised the coffee to his lips to let his last words sink in.

"Not quite true?" said Atholl who was holding on to the table with his right hand. Not so much holding on really, as trying to compress the plastic between his thumb and forefinger.

"No, not quite true. Atholl, I am also your father." Potter was staring out at the sea as he uttered these words.

Atholl's mouth dropped open.

At this Kenny piped up.

"I've got a question for Atholl, Potter."

"Go ahead ask it," replied Potter still staring out to the Med.

"Are you wanting your biscuit?

CHAPTER 33

Gus, Kenny, Potter and Cammy were sitting round a table in Tennents Bar in the West End of Glasgow reviewing the trip to the Cote D'Azur. The bar was busy on the Thursday night, the usual combination of students, punters and media types trying to act working class creating a hubbub of noise. Unfortunately for Kenny Bradley, he was the focus of attention on the table.

Gus finished his lager.

"So, let me get this right, like. You ignored that bombshell dropped by young Frank here and asked Atholl for his biscuit?"

"Aye, what had changed? I knew Potter was my dad and Atholl was still my half brother. Those were fucking tasty biscuits by the way, a sort of a continental ginger snap."

Kenny sat back and folded his arms across his chest.

Cammy shook his head.

"Where was the poison dwarf when this was all kicking off in the station boozer?"

Kenny turned to look at Gus who was now idly fidgeting with a bar mat whilst looking out the pub window, ignoring Cammy's question.

Kenny nudged him.

"Gus, answer the man or do you want me to tell him?"

"Aye OK. Ah fuckin' shat it. You don't know what that blonde had done to me the night before, like. Ah was more scared o' her than that wee prick Atholl. If that hotel chambermaid had nae stumbled intae the room ah would still be tied to that fuckin' bed. Silk scarves or no, there were bruise marks on ma wrists. Bruises ah tell ye."

"God knows what state your cock must have been in," said Cammy. "Sorry. If I am worrying about the state of the wee man's cock, I need to have another drink. Everybody on lager except you, Potter?"

This question was met with a series of nods before attention returned to Gus.

"So there you are tied to a bed and because of that when I am looking for a bit of support you are fucking AWOL," said Kenny.

"She totally brutalised me!" screeched Gus. A few heads in the bar turned in their direction.

Gus lowered his head.

"She totally brutalised me!" he whispered.

"Aye right. So what's that boy Atholl going to do now?" asked Cammy as he stood up to get the round in.

"He's planning to buy somewhere in the Dordogne and then wait until his dad's estate is sorted then decide what to do with the rest of his life. Doubt I'll hear from him again. No big deal."

"The Dordogne in France?" asked Gus

"No, the Dordogne just outside Cumnock! Of course the Dordogne in France. How many fucking Dordogne's have you heard of, for fuck's sake?"

"Just asking, like. Is it your bad week or something? You are one moody fucker these days Kenny. Is it findin out you've got a half brother whose idea of brotherly love was trying to strangle ye in a Tallinn sauna that's got ye in such a mood?"

"Will you see him again Potter?" Asked Kenny who was nervously twitching his right leg.

"I might. If he is still with that wife of his I very much doubt it."

Gus perked up at this comment.

"Oh aye Frank. Kenny tells me you were a bit hard on his ex."

Kenny shot Gus a look.

"I'd have paid good money to see that, given what she did to me, like."

"Aye well, you're not the only one at this table to have suffered through her ministrations, shall we say, in the bedroom. But we'll speak no more on that score!"

Potter stared hard at Gus as he ended the sentence.

Gus twitched his head both ways.

"Hang on, did ah miss somethin? Was there any female in Castle McClackit you didnae shag?" He jabbed his thumb at Kenny.

"His mum, Atholl's mum, Atholl's wife, never mind the Monarch of the Glen, you are the Shagger of the Glen, pal!"

Potter tensed and Kenny could see something was just about to go pop.

"Have you heard about Dominic?" said Kenny trying to change the mood of the conversation.

Gus looked round "Oh, for fuck's sake, he's no in love again?"

"No, no yet. He's spunked a grand on a personal computer and got connected to the internet. He's been going to classes at his local library."

"A grand for a portable telly?" snorted Gus. "The boy's lost the plot." He took a long gulp of the pint of lager Cammy had just set down in front of him.

"You can laugh your cock off but he claims he's got three dates lined up for next week after using the internet to meet women," said Kenny who turned to Cammy for back up.

Cammy nodded and smiled as Gus sat up straight.

"Dominic has three dates? The only person wi worse luck wi women than him is Inspector Morse. Holy fuck. Three dates? Dae ye think he would let me have a shot at it, like?"

"Ah donno, Gus" Cammy was scratching his head and looking round the table.

"What do yous reckon? You have to write a profile of yourself and also what you are looking for in a woman."

"A pulse. And even that's negotiable." said Potter.

"Shut it you," growled Gus. "Go on Cammy, ah can do all that no problem. Might have to be a wee bit economical with the truth here and there, like, but it doesnae sound like mission impossible."

"Fair enough, Gus. But the tricky point is then the fact you have to put in a recent, and I stress the word recent, photo."

"Aw fuck!"

"Define recent" said Kenny "Pre hair transplant?"

"Maybe you could try and get one of those photos from Riga developed?" said Cammy, a broad smile spreading on his face. "They might have got your best side when you kissed Rab's cock."

"What the fuck!" shouted Gus. "Kenny ah fucken told ye, fucken told ye, never to mention that to anybody ever again. It was a pure fucken accident man."

He turned to Cammy.

"Who was yer source? Come on, who grassed me up? It was Bradley here, admit it!" He turned to Kenny.

"Some friend you are, like."

Gus had crumbled and appeared on the verge of tears.

"Ah never meant to kiss his cock, honest," he mumbled.

Cammy clapped his hands and laughed.

"Chins up wee man. You told me yourself the other night ya daft bastard when you were off your face in Clatty Pats. You'd seen one of the other guys across the club and when I asked you how you knew him you told me the, eh, circumstances of your coming together. With the emphasis on coming from what you said. You appeared to find it quite funny that you'd kissed a guy's cock that night but clearly it is different when you're not completely off your face on voddy and coke!"

"Ya bastard! Ye never thought to bring this up before now, like!"

Gus had spoken with a mixture of relief and bitterness in his voice.

"I'll accept you apology anytime," said Kenny, "No rush, you take your time in dismounting the high horse situated on the moral high ground. I don't know, couldn't wait to point the fucking finger could you?"

Potter drained his glass.

"Well I'm for the off. I will leave you three amigos to work out what's going to happen for the rest of the night but I've had enough of kissed cocks and Fiona McClackit to last me a life time."

As he stood up, Kenny nodded to Gus, then nodded at Potter. He had to repeat the gesture before Gus twigged to what he was meant to do.

Gus caught up with Potter as he reached the door.

"Eh Frank, ah was wonderin what you were doin at the start of June?"

"Why's that Gus?" Potter was looking back towards Kenny who appeared deep in conversation with Cammy.

"It's Harold's stag party and we're takin him to Minsk."

"We as in Kenny and you? Minsk as in Belarussian Minsk?"

Gus hesitated.

"Eh aye, me and Kenny. We're takin him to Minsk for the qualifier. Do you know it?"

"Eh, you could say so." Potter was zipping up his leather jacket as he spoke.

"Visited it a couple of times back in the day. Unofficially, of course."

Gus looked at Potter, wondering if it was a wind-up.

"What? Like spying?" he asked.

"Eh no, not really. It's a bit hard to explain. I have never really got that joke "I'd tell you but I'd have to kill you" as it does apply to some things, but not this."

"What do you mean?" Gus was gripped. This was the most exciting conversation he'd had in a long time. Admittedly most of his conversations were with Kenny centring round football and Gus' lovelife, or lack of.

"The Laird had a few hairbrained schemes from time to time and this was one of them. Muggins here was left to pick up the pieces."

"Oh aye, James Bond. I see you as a shaken not stirred kinda guy."

Potter laughed a gentle laugh.

"No, nothing that sexy Gus. Observation stuff mainly. You know Lee Harvey Oswald used to live there?"

"No way! Lee Harvey Oswald?"

"Aye, scrawny arrogant bastard. I spent a week following him once."

"Why?"

"I don't know, to be honest. The Laird had got pissed up in some gentleman's club in St James and volunteered my services."

Gus wondered out loud. "Ah thought it was a closed city. No foreigners allowed sort of thing?"

"Ways and means, Gus. Ways and means." Potter reached for the handle of the pub door.

"So, what happened in the end?" asked Gus.

"Nothing. I know it's a complete anti-climax but, like a lot of the Laird's plans, it ended up going nowhere. Or at least that's all I am saying."

"But there must have been some kind o' thrill surely?" Gus was the most enervated Potter had seen him.

"Gus, listen to me. You see these cheap magic tricks I do which you and Kenny seem to think is some kind of natural talent? It's not. I learnt these wee tricks in the amount of time I sat on my arse doing nothing. It was so boring for 99% of the time you had to find something to take your mind off what you'd done or were about to do, for the other 1%."

Gus let that last comment sink in.

"OK, we'll forget about the 1%. Now, Minsk. In or out?"

Potter looked Gus straight in the eye.

"Seriously?" he asked.

"Eh, aye. ah've squared it with Kenny. You're welcome to come with me and him, but we're goin for a few days. The organised trip is just the weekend."

"I don't get this" said Potter. He closed the door he had pulled open.

"Why on earth are you going to Minsk for a few days? There's fuck all there."

"So ah believe, but me and Kenny have a cheap deal, like. Some punter left a copy o' the Independent in his taxi. He was readin through it and saw an ad. Lufthansa are doing 2 for 1 from Heathrow. Giving it away, like. The alternative is the Scotball weekender - though it is Scotball, so fucken good luck. Harold's going wi them."

"OK, I'm definitely interested as this might be our best chance of qualifying for a World Cup for God knows how long. Let me think about it. I have to say I am not really that keen to spend any more time there than I have to."

"That's a bit negative on the World Cup front, Frank. Ah had expected a bit more positivity from you than that, like. We've only missed one of the last six." Gus felt a bit aggrieved. He didn't really understand why someone like Potter would run the team down.

"The world is changing, Gus. Once these eastern European countries get themselves organised, the game's up. Ukraine has a population of 60 million and a great football heritage. They've split up Yugoslavia, so there are four more teams at the qualifiers instead of one. You confident we'll be getting results against the likes of Croatia and Serbia down the line? Even somewhere like Belarus will be on the up eventually. All these countries see sport in the same way as the Soviet Union. It enhances their status as a nation. It broadcasts to the world - we're a country in our own right! If they get on to a European or a world stage, the politicians are made up. Sorry, I'm ranting a bit here. I'd better go"

On leaving Gus and Kenny in the bar, Potter decided to have one for the ditch on the way back to his flat. He'd enjoyed the banter earlier in the night but still felt there was something missing between him and Kenny. He was slightly fuzzy-headed as the result of the earlier pints, wondering if should have gone straight home to bed. The next pub appeared appeared quieter, but warmer than the last one. Clearly having extended a post-work couple of drinks into a bit of a session, a couple of guys in suits stood at the far end of the bar. He knew no-one in this pub and realised this was another example of him still getting used to city life. The noise, people bumping up against one another and just the general presence of life that had been absent in his last few years in the Highlands was all taking some acclimatisation.

His physical discomfort matched his emotional turmoil. He found it hard to admit, but he was getting on better with Gus than Kenny. It was Gus who was helping him come to terms with life back in the real world, but it was Kenny he really wanted as a friend as much as a son. He traced the word dad in a wet patch on the bar, trying to take in the full meaning of the word.

He underlined it twice with his index finger then, in a moment of exasperation, used three fingers to obliterate it.

He returned to staring at the optics, trying to come to work out what to do to get into Kenny's good books. A moment later, an attractive forty-something brunette appeared next to him and ordered a gin and tonic. She wore a perfume that he could identify as "Dolce Vita" and nearly commented, but decided he wasn't really in the mood. The perfume only brought back memories of a relationship that had gone skew whiff so maybe that was an omen.

The woman gave him a sly glance as she turned and moved towards a seat at a table behind him. Potter tracked her in the mirror above the bar trying to get the measure of her figure beneath the black tailored coat. As she sat down she looked up in the mirror and their eyes met for a moment before Potter turned back to his pint.

He suddenly wondered if it would have made any difference if it had been a daughter rather than a son who came into his life at this point in time. Would he have, what was the word, "bonded" with her in a way he could not achieve with Kenny? Thinking about it, he would probably have ended up chinning her boyfriend. If she'd been anything like Denise she would have probably then have chinned Potter.

But no, there was no daughter, only a son. He glanced up in the mirror and the mystery brunette was on her mobile phone, looking somewhat distracted. She had the phone in her right hand but was toying with a beer mat with her left. The square of cardboard was snapped in two like a cream cracker as she killed the call. Potter immediately looked away pondering the fact that she might have been stood up. It was a more attractive thought than improving father/son relations. He'd contemplated discussing the issue with Gus but then common

310

sense had prevailed. He was sure that given time, he and Kenny would develop a better relationship. Informing Gus of any relationship concerns would only reveal a chink in Potter's armour and the piss taking would be brutal.

As he sipped his pint he glanced in the mirror again. The brunette was tapping a message into her phone with an intensity he had rarely seen by anyone using a phone. In fact, he reckoned she was the first person he had ever seen sending a text in a public place. As she finished the text she tossed the phone in her bag and picked up her drink. As she was about to take a sip, she looked up and their eyes met again and this time they both stared for a few seconds before she took a large mouthful and Potter looked away.

On the pub television, the weather forecast had come on at the end of the ten o'clock news. Rain was forecast which did little to help Potter's mood. Then again, his head had cleared up a bit and maybe a new day would give him a new plan to help him and Kenny come to terms with the fact that meeting your dad for the first time late in life was a good thing

As Potter finished his pint the woman in the mirror came up to him, pointed to the Glasgow Herald lying next to him on the bar and asked, "Do you mind if I borrow your paper?"

"Not at all," he replied. "But I should warn you there's good news and bad news."

She looked him in the eye.

"Oh aye, and what's the bad news?"

"Everything that's in that paper," said Potter.

She looked puzzled.

"So, if it's all bad news, what's the good news?"

"I'm going to buy you a drink. Large gin and tonic was it?"

ACKNOWLEDGEMENTS

I would to express my immense gratitude to John Daly for all his support and encouragement in finishing this book.

Anne Robertson's contribution has also been invaluable in completing the final stages of the book.

I would also like to thank Gavin Anderson for his comments on the early stages of the book and Craig McDowall for his help in clarifying some of the stories that were lost in time and continental lager.

Alexandra Davidson provided the artwork for the cover and I shudder to think what it would have looked like without her help.

The assistance and encouragement of Wayne and Aaron at Circle of Misse have also been invaluable. They provide the perfect environment to encourage writers. If you can't write there, you can't write anywhere. Check them out at www.circleofmisse.com

All proceeds from this book will be going to the Tartan Army Sunshine Appeal, the aim of which is to make a donation to identified children's charities in every country in which the Scottish National Football Team plays matches

Their website is www.tasunshineappeal.co.uk

Made in the USA
Charleston, SC
02 December 2015